LOUIS I. KAHN

LOUIS I. KAHN

**BUILDING ART,
BUILDING SCIENCE**

THOMAS LESLIE

GEORGE BRAZILLER, INC.
NEW YORK

First published in the United States of America in 2005 by George Braziller, Inc.

For information, please address the publisher:
George Braziller, Inc.
171 Madison Avenue
New York, NY 10016
www.georgebraziller.com

Library of Congress Cataloging-in-Publication Data:
Leslie, Thomas.
Louis I. Kahn : building art, building science / Thomas Leslie.—1st ed.
    p.   cm.
Includes bibliographical references.
ISBN 0-8076-1540-4 (hardcover)—ISBN 0-8076-1543-9 (pbk.)
1. Kahn, Louis I., 1901–1974—Criticism and interpretation. 2. Architecture—United
States—20th century. I. Title: Building art, building science. II. Kahn, Louis I., 1901–1974.
III. Title.
NA737.K32L47   2005
727'.092—dc22   2005005783

Designed by Jesse Meyers Willenbring

Printed and bound in the United States of America

First edition

To my family

Papers do not prevail against monuments.

—Paul Philippe Cret

CONTENTS

ACKNOWLEDGMENTS

My inspiration for this project came while I was an architect with Norman Foster and Partners, during a long series of discussions that took place after office hours with David Nelson, Nigel Dancey, and Chris West about the nature of the firm's work and our architectural heroes, Kahn in particular. David Nelson continued his support of this project after I began teaching at Iowa State University. Kenneth Frampton, under whom I had the good fortune to study at Columbia, also supported this project at key moments, and I am grateful for the *lieber meister*'s encouragement and influence, which I hope will be apparent to the reader.

If the initial idea for this project came from my colleagues at Foster's, I owe its execution to the generous assistance, advice, and encouragement of Julia Moore Converse, William Whitaker, Laura Stroffonino, and Nancy Thorne of the Architectural Archives at the University of Pennsylvania. At the Kimbell Art Museum, Patricia Cummings Loud generously assisted in my search for new material on the project's design and construction, and very graciously read and commented on a preliminary draft of the Kimbell chapter. Suzanne Boorsch and Lisa Hodermarsky at the Yale University Art Gallery provided guidance and access to newly found drawings, while José Branco allowed me to tour and photograph the building while it was being renovated. Katy Harris at Foster and Partners provided images for chapter six, as did staff at Richard Rogers Partnership and the Renzo Piano Building Workshop. Archivists and staff at the San Diego Public Library, the Fort Worth Public Library, the Manuscripts and Archives Department at Yale University's Stirling Library, the Architectural Archives of the University of Texas, and the Library of the University of Texas at Arlington provided access to newspaper records, drawings, and ephemera that helped to illustrate the power of Kahn's buildings in those locales.

Several of Kahn's colleagues lent their time to discuss their experiences. In particular, I am grateful to Jack MacAllister, who spent a day with me at the Salk Institute for Biological Studies in 2001 and provided an invaluable opportunity to examine the building in depth and to test and develop my initial thoughts. Nicholas Gianopulos and Thomas J. Leidigh shared their experiences of working with Kahn while they were engineers with Keast & Hood, and Anne Griswold Tyng kindly explained the development of the Yale Art Gallery's structure. Robert Lizarraga at the Salk Institute provided access to numerous unexplored corners of its mechanical and laboratory spaces. I was able to speak with Marshall Meyers only briefly before his death in 2001, but I am grateful to Anne Meyers for the opportunity to have had that conversation, and for her encouragement and willingness to share some of Mr. Meyers's notes on the Kimbell's history.

Support for the chapter on the Kimbell Art Museum was provided by the Graham Foundation for Advanced Studies in the Fine Arts. Iowa State University provided an initial research grant from its Science, Technology, and Society program, and the writing of three chapters was funded by Iowa State's Center for Excellence in the Arts and Humanities. The cost of images, reproduction rights, and three-dimensional CAD modeling were supported by the Iowa State University Publication Endowment Fund. Iowa State's Department of Architecture also generously supported this research through travel grants, and I am grateful for the willingness of Cal Lewis, Mark Engelbrecht, and Kate Schwensenn of the Department of Architecture and the College of Design to support such research by junior faculty.

Colleagues at Iowa State and elsewhere provided valuable advice, read preliminary papers or chapters, and generally shared in the excitement of this project. Jason Alread, Deborah Ascher Barnstone, Julia Badenhope, Bruce Bassler, Richard Becherer, Chris Beorkrem, Karen Bermann, David Block, Jim Bolluyt, Clare Cardinal-Pett, Robert Findlay, Matthew Fisher, Marwan Ghandour, Michael Golec, Carlota Gutierrez, Debra Hearn, Jean

x

Holt, Jamie Horwitz, Jean Jonas, Igor Marjanovic, Charlie Masterson, John Maves, Mikesch Muecke, Dan Naegele, Arvid Osterberg, Gregory Palermo, Lynn Paxson, John Rice, Clare Robinson, Carl Rogers, Paul Shao, Mitchell Squire, Mark Stankard, and Mary Joyce Veverka have all, whether they realize it or not, contributed to this book in ways both measurable and immeasurable. Joe Kupfer has aided and inspired my understanding of Kahn's work in relation to experience. Chris Beorkrem, Kevin Scott, and Jeff Stafford contributed their talents to building the digital models, and students Sara Esser, Joe Friedman, Zach Helmers, and Christina Monk carried out studies that deepened my understanding of key buildings. Kevin Dong, Mark Shapiro, Max Underwood, and James Wright also contributed valued insights and information, and two shoe boxes of index cards are a testament to the ongoing, profound, and greatly appreciated influences of Chris Butler, Mary McLeod, Lydia Soo, and Adele Suslick.

I am very pleased to have written the second book on Kahn published by George Braziller. In addition to being inspired by the first, published in 1962, I am grateful for the opportunity to work with a publisher so devoted to quality. Meaghan Madges, A. Krista Sykes, and Mary Taveras provided strong advice, encouragement, and brilliant editorial commentary, and this is a much better book for their involvement.

Finally, the logistics of travel and writing have been possible only with Kathy's forbearance and the willingness of our children and our parents to put up with summer research trips and my daily immersion in stacks of books and paper. For those reasons and for so many others, this book is dedicated to them, my family, with gratitude and love.

i

BEGINNINGS

No American architect has been more influential in the past quarter century than Louis I. Kahn (1901–1974). Set against the formalist decadence and pastiche of late modernism, Kahn's rigorously conceived yet humane and inspiring buildings have represented alternative approaches for a wide range of architects and theorists seeking richness, depth, and clarity within the fabric of building itself. This inspiration has taken several paths. While Kahn's final works were being completed in the mid-1970s, a young generation saw him as a father figure in the development of postmodernism for his ability to synthesize the formal planning of his Beaux-Arts training with modernism's flat planes and abstractions. More recently, however, others have seen his philosophical appeals to such metaphysical values as light, silence, and order as an impassioned call to a new spirituality in architecture and have picked up the emotional appeal of Kahn's buildings as a way of recovering a sense of timelessness and monumentality. Kahn's interest in the revelation of material qualities and processes has likewise inspired a movement toward the frank but carefully considered deployment of simple materials such as brick, glass, and wood in ways that allow them to speak, unadorned, to our senses and intellects.

Louis I. Kahn, 1961

2

Each of these interpretations has some validity. Throughout his writing and his built work these themes emerge again and again, flowing into one another, staking out their own claims on our interpretation of his dense, rich buildings. Kahn was demonstrably an influence on postmodernists such as Robert Venturi and Michael Graves. He was unquestionably the father figure to spiritualists such as Tadao Ando, and more recently his reverence for materials can be found in the work of Williams + Tsien and Rafael Moneo, to name but two. Yet these influences, all well documented, do not account for another, often suppressed, strain in Kahn's work. In addition to the aforementioned principles—architecture as a language, as an appeal to our spirituality, and as the thoughtful consideration of materials—the technologies of building construction and function were of profound interest to Kahn, an aspect that has been recognized but never fully explored. His buildings, while often of such primitive components as brick, frequently used more sophisticated materials, including posttensioned concrete or brake-shaped stainless steel. His favorite collaborating engineer, August Komendant, was one of the most advanced structural minds of his day, a leader in the development of engineered concrete. The construction of Kahn's buildings often involved highly experimental processes, many of which, after their success in his hands, have become standard procedure on jobsites during the past quarter century.

Beyond the technical expertise of his buildings, however, there is evidence throughout his built and written work that Kahn saw the assembly and performance of architecture as fundamental elements in a building's composition and aesthetic. For Kahn, it was not enough to simply solve a functional or constructional problem, or even to solve it efficiently. It was more important to understand these aspects as a design came together and to knit them into an integrated, expressive architectural conception. The aesthetic of a building, Kahn believed, could properly spring only from a thorough knowledge of what the building was intended to do and how it was to be made. While other compositional strategies would enter into his work, all of Kahn's buildings are fundamentally based on this idea: that form and space should arise from a full consideration of a building's needs and the resources available to it. It is, therefore, not only the linguistic and phenomenological schools of architectural thought that can claim Kahn as an influence. Architects and designers who have explored the communicative, didactic, or simply expressive potentials of building engineering and technology have also been among Kahn's intellectual heirs.

Kahn and his teams rose to the difficult tasks of sorting out his clients' often complex charges into well-ordered constructions. While Kahn was expansive about the results of this hard work with engineers, clients, and contractors, speaking famously about space, light, and order in poetic terms, the buildings he created beg further inquiry into their constructive and functional languages. Kahn was a charismatic, sincere architectural philosopher, but his words, however inspiring, fall far short of the intense experiences that his spaces and buildings inspire. It is often claimed that the beauty of Kahn's built works is either otherworldly or poetic. However, it is my intent to show that the profundity of these buildings lies instead within the realm of the everyday, that far from being transcendental, the design and construction of Kahn's best works are entirely rooted in the prosaic realities of practice and technique. It was Kahn's great skill to build works of crystalline logic and tangible order out of base materials, fundamental principles, and often untidy aspirations.

4

This study thus seeks to explain, rather than to interpret, Kahn's buildings, finding in the stories of their conception and construction Kahn's built philosophy, a parallel to his better known, but perhaps unknowable, spoken and written thoughts. While scholars have noted Kahn's interest in structure and construction, a full exploration of these influences on his designs represents a new approach. In fact, much of Kahn's written and drawn legacy provides ample evidence that the physics of building and the functional performance of buildings were fundamental to both his process and his architectural beliefs. Building science—the engineering, functional design, and daily performance of architecture—was neatly woven together in Kahn's work with building art—the craft of construction, fabrication, and assembly. The results were buildings that unquestionably have diverse and diffuse associations. But in all cases, his buildings were extraordinarily well conceived and rigorously executed, and their emotional and aesthetic impact derives from the care with which Kahn thought about these performative and constructional aspects. Telling these stories—of the drawing table, the client meeting, the factory floor, and the jobsite—reveals a new layer of meaning in Kahn's work, one that relies less on references to historical precedents or connections to a metaphysical realm than on the day-to-day details of practice, design, and building. Kahn worked with the same brick, the same concrete, the same steel and glass that all other architects of his time did, but what he conceived from these common substances surpassed, in effect, the work of his entire generation. This, to my mind, is Kahn's most powerful legacy: a set of works that built up the common desires, resources, and means by which all architecture is created into orchestrations so logically conceived and so rigorously executed that our intellect is saturated by their experience and our poetic sense is provoked. This claim does not preclude other readings, nor should it lessen the awe in which we hold his achievements. Instead, I hope to show that how these buildings came about played a key role in shaping what they became and that the extraordinary hold of Kahn's work on our senses arises from a lifetime's worth of knowledge, experimentation, and dedicated effort.

5

Kahn's Process:
Empiricism and Rationalism

Kahn's work and his rich struggle to find architectural poetry within the prosaic confines of building technology were the results of a two-way process common to most accomplished architects but particularly intense in his own career. His training in the Beaux-Arts atmosphere of Paul Philippe Cret's program at the University of Pennsylvania took a rationalist approach, in which an a priori vision guided the development of a design. The *esquisse*, a rapid sketching out of a design's underlying idea, had to percolate through every aspect of the studio project in the Beaux-Arts method. One can find the legacy of this in Kahn's obsessive detailing; his tendency toward mathematical, geometrical forms; and in his insistence that every element of a finished building have its place in the overall structure's order and pattern. Yet Kahn's early career was of necessity based on a different process, an empirical approach that was forged from the strict budgets and schedules Kahn faced in the publicly funded housing projects that were his métier prior to 1950. In these circumstances, Kahn's designs represented solutions built up from the financial, constructive, and functional necessities of onerous requirements and limitations; their forms resulted from the forging of a single vision that meticulously balanced resources and needs.

In his later career, Kahn integrated these rationalist and empiricist methods. Architects, of course, engage these realms constantly. On the one hand, we have certain beliefs about form, style, and proportion that we invariably impose on any design, whether they arise consciously or not. While these may have come from experience and are thus not truly "rationalist" in the philosophical sense, they are often imposed, a priori, in that they have come to the project in the architect's mind. They are, therefore, part of a common, rationalist goal. On the other hand, all buildings have, as well, purely empirical aspects, those that arise solely from the experience of design and construction. Again, this is strictly true of architecture only in a limited sense; knowledge of construction techniques, for example, may actually be brought to bear intuitively on the design process. Here, "empirical" describes the building up of a design from the experience of its situation and the means available. Design is very often a struggle to reconcile rationalist conceptions with empirical realities, that is, to achieve the ideal within the milieu of the real. When architecture fails, it is often because there is a lapse of balance between these two realms. An overly rationalist approach will fail to integrate adequately the means of construction with the ideal concept, leaving us with a striking image but with a building either unsound or disappointing in its physicality. Perhaps more commonly, an overly empirical approach will fail to touch our mind in any way, simply solving problems as they arise and lacking any sense of greater meaning or import. The former may make for a great photograph, and the latter may turn a profit, but neither gives us the sense that the architect has grasped the full complexity of a discipline that requires engaging the mind while simultaneously housing the body.

The rich, thoughtful balances and weavings of Kahn's later work stemmed from an intellectual process that was rigorously rational *and* empirical, one that took seriously architecture's challenge to adhere to both the ideal and the real. Kahn's bivalent process insisted on building up a project's concept by understanding its requirements and later teasing out a resolution of this general idea into supportive details, components, and systems. Kahn's designs arose through the

7

gradual ordering of information based on programmatic, site, material, structural, and environmental
necessities. At some point in each of his major projects, a solution emerged that offered some measure
of integration, solving several issues in one easily
grasped layout, section, form, or pattern. While this
kernel of a given project's solution was still subject
to scrutiny—and abandonment if it did not continue
to prove itself—it set the stage for a top-down, rational process by which each design decision was tested
against its ability to express the previously established,
overall order. Beyond even this, however, Kahn insisted
upon allowing his buildings to speak for themselves,
to express the patterns and marks of their construction, and to communicate the designed logic of their
functions. Kahn's buildings speak to us because their
conceptions and executions are so logical, so thoughtfully ordered, and so carefully expressed.

The subject of "order" was one of Kahn's earliest
stated philosophical concerns. Among Kahn's more
widely quoted architectural koans, "Order Is" (1955)
gives us a window into his two-way process:

> Order is
> Design is form-making in order
> Form emerges out of construction
> Growth is a construction
> In *order* is creative force
> In *design* is the means—where
> with what on when with how much
> The nature of space reflects what
> it wants to be[1]

Here, Kahn posits architecture as an ontological scaffold, whose constructed nature bridges the
mundane, circumstantial world of everyday building
(the groundwork for the bottom-up, empirical, and

8

inductive process) and the transcendence of architectural experience (the basis for the top-down, rationalist, deductive process of the Beaux-Arts methodology). This is perhaps more clearly elucidated in his often-quoted view that architecture links the "measurable and the immeasurable," beginning and ending in the latter, yet moving through the former during design and construction.[2] Order is somehow preexisting—it *is*, regardless of the designer's actions, waiting to be discovered. Design is an action, in this description the very quest for the ever-elusive Order, both on paper and in building. Form is the manifestation of this search, emerging out of construction and thus empirically derived, yet "made in order," that is, with an overarching rationalist sensibility, a working out of an idea through materials and details.

Performing a bit of linguistic algebra, we can derive from these lines that, for Kahn, Design is the making of something—form—which emerges out of construction but aspires toward Order—that is, Design builds up global meaning out of circumstance. Architecture for Kahn was thus the expression of timeless ideals through contingent realities. It was the designer's task to approach as nearly as possible the realms of Order through work that springs from the untidy realities of the everyday. "Gold," he wrote in 1944, "is a beautiful material. It belongs to the sculptor."[3] Architects, on the other hand, are left with the humble stuff of construction—concrete, brick, metal. In Kahn's view it was architecture's particular charge to create beauty not out of finery and surface, but out of coarse materials marshaled into carefully woven constructions. The patterns and assemblies of these constructions would, if properly considered, reveal the depth of ordering required by the program at hand, as well as the actions of fabricators and builders.

9

Other writing by Kahn reveals more coherently his belief in a hybrid system of architectural conception that links the transcendental with the mundane and inductive conceptualization with deductive "working out." Speaking at Yale University in 1953, Kahn emphasized his twofold approach:

> I believe the concept should be equal
> to that of planting a seed, in which
> the concept, that is, the result you
> are going to get[,] should be quite
> clear. As you progress and develop, the
> form will be modified, and you should
> welcome this, because the concept will
> be so strong that you cannot destroy
> it. How you accomplish all this comes
> with the knowledge of how a thing is
> done, knowing the process you must
> go through. The whole thing is a
> building process. It's very different, in
> my opinion, from conceiving the end
> product and then finding a means of
> doing it. There is a regular training
> that is necessary to do this because
> with this training comes assurity.
> I believe you must know about the
> mechanical equipment and also about
> your affinity for structural members.[4]

This process was thus simultaneously rational, seeking the sudden distillation of principles into an ordering concept into which any leftovers, so to speak, must be subsumed, and empirical, springing from direct experience and knowledge of how things are done. While the organic, all-encompassing Order was thus the goal, Kahn was uniquely attuned to the need to build it up from such basic assumptions as structure and mechanical services, an admission of the contingent into the realm and constitution of the universal.

More explicitly, Kahn explained his ambivalent feelings toward his rationalist Beaux-Arts education at a conference at Princeton University in 1953:

> I studied at the University of
> Pennsylvania and, although I can
> still feel the spiritual aspects of that
> training, I have spent all my time
> since graduation unlearning what
> I learned.... I believe that we are
> speaking about order when we are
> speaking about design. I think design
> is circumstantial. I think order is what
> we discover the aspects of, so as to get
> a plan—a plan of a city or building,
> or even of a poster.... I think we are
> constantly confusing design and Order.
> Order includes all the designs of
> construction—mechanical and
> spiritual; and design is merely the
> process of fitting them into conditions
> and coming up with a certain
> experience which strengthens and
> even enriches the order.[5]

For Kahn, it was therefore important that architecture not only reflect an overall architectural Order—timeless, immutable, and all pervasive. It was also crucial that all aspects of an architectural endeavor be considered in relation to one another to find the proper order of the task and time at hand—immediate, contingent, and applicable only to a specific instance. This sensibility was most critical, in Kahn's view, where systems or components met, where joints occurred. Here, the need to express "how it was done"

11

became for him the "basis of ornament," the opportunity to reveal the particular designed and constructed orders of a building. This revelation was, again, as important to Kahn as the efficiency of the solutions themselves. If conceived and expressed properly, these lower-scale orders would build our experience up to a greater sense of Order that would challenge and reward our perceptions. Kahn therefore repeatedly emphasized the need for architects to understand the inner workings of structural, mechanical, and constructional systems so they could best locate and express these systems within an ideal hierarchy of spaces. It was vital, Kahn taught, to arrange and compose these mundane, contingent elements so that we could, in our experience of the building, work our way up the ontological ladder to find something transcendental in the basic stuff of building. The proper order for a given set of functional requirements and constructive means could, in Kahn's thought, reveal hints of that greater Order that structures nature and human endeavors.

This idea found its most robust manifestation in Kahn's integration of structure and services. Kahn famously referred to these hybrid elements as "hollow stones," inviting a comparison with the solid constructions of antiquity. More illustratively, he called such spaces "harbors," voids carved or injected into large-scale structural elements that carry—and usually conceal—mechanical services. Intriguingly, this is exactly the terminology Kahn used to describe his accommodation of the automobile in his Midtown Philadelphia plan of 1953. Large-scale structural and architectural elements intentionally enclosed the rather unsightly realities of circulation, both accommodating and corralling these and preventing them from overwhelming spaces whose rank was higher. Order, for Kahn, was thus a result of understanding, mastering, and manipulating elements and their concurrent spaces; finding hierarchies in usage; and delineating buildings to reflect and express these. Order was to be teased out of the objective requirements at hand and manifested through structural and architectural components, their relationships to one another, and to the overall architectural situation. The grain of a project for Kahn necessarily reflected a hierarchy of harboring spaces and forms, all finding their appropriate level within the all-pervasive architectural Order whose traces had been discovered within the everyday requirements of function, performance, and assembly.

At the same time, once this architectural Order emerged from the design process, Kahn's methodology shifted. The basic comportment of a design from this point forward would remain largely unchanged, and Kahn's attention would focus on the expression of the *esquisse* through the language of a building's material and detail. Elements of the design that had not participated in the emergence of the overall Order were now considered in relation to that expressed logic and were designed and detailed in ways that visually, tactilely, and conceptually strengthened the broader reading of the project. The working out of these lower-level design problems within a larger conceptual framework occupied much of the office's time. This process was often subject to experimentation (sometimes on the construction site), refinement, and, occasionally, revision of the *esquisse* based on unforeseen but important contributions from these secondary systems and elements.

Kahn's process was thus both inductive and deductive. His clients noted that he approached each problem with a tabula rasa, keen to discover the contingencies of each project early on and to develop a design that would respond to the unique qualities of each site, each program, each aspiration. In choosing the projects for this study, it was important that there be typological similarities—two buildings for art, two for science—so that the divergent results based on similar programs could reveal Kahn's unwillingness to simply plug old solutions into new situations.[6] Kahn's designs show instead an evolutionary process, building on lessons learned in earlier projects but tending to see the raison d'être of each building within its own unique circumstances.

Clients also reported, however, that one of their major frustrations in working with Kahn was the enormous number of changes he proposed during development and even construction. This, too, was indicative of Kahn's ongoing search for the proper expression of the building's order—and occasionally the alteration of that very order as new contingencies arose and refocused his efforts. Throughout the design and building processes, Kahn and his associates were keen to continue the search for each project's ideal combination of logic and order as they learned from contractors and experiments on site. Indeed, some of Kahn's most successful endeavors involved ongoing investigation throughout several projects, building on earlier failures and achievements and constantly refining one detail or another to hone an idea that had occurred, in some cases, a decade or more earlier. Particularly in Kahn's concrete detailing and in his development of a unique stainless-steel curtain wall system in several projects, one can trace Kahn's growing confidence in the material under study and in his ability to project that knowledge back into the process. These elements, common in some measure to each of the buildings discussed, show Kahn's sense of the jobsite as a laboratory.

14

This book, then, explores and demonstrates Kahn's holistic approach. Early in his designs, Kahn invested each project with a probing search for its proper order, the ideal *esquisse*, based on a building up of minute statements, requirements, techniques, and contextual forces. This typically took the form of extensive, iterative studies, most of which failed, but which, nevertheless, built up an intuitive sense of how the project should develop. Once this order emerged as a clear compelling *esquisse*, or fully considered scheme, it defined his approach to subsequent details and systems. This building up and percolating down was defined by Kahn as moving between the realms of the "measurable" and the "immeasurable," suggesting a constant play between high-minded aspirations and the daily grind of such minutiae as door schedules, job administration, and budget meetings. While Kahn occasionally complained about these seemingly petty elements, in particular the constant constraints of his clients' budgets, he also threw himself and his colleagues into the exercises and investigations necessary to integrate these details into the higher aspirations of each job. The obvious enthusiasm that Kahn showed for tackling this seemingly minor but potentially ruinous chaff meant that every project was a dynamic process, with discovery lurking in areas where a lesser architect would have simply been content to specify a standard detail or component. Such constant refinement, such attention to the potential of every detail to recast the whole, separated Kahn's work from his contemporaries and set him apart as the influential model that he has become for a subsequent generation of technically minded designers.

15

Kahn's Background

Louis I. Kahn's background and education were critical to his early development as a practitioner, which
in turn was vital to the development of his late career.
He was born in Estonia in 1901, and his family moved
when he was three to Philadelphia.[7] Kahn's parents,
like many other immigrants, were poor. His father, a
glass painter, was disabled soon after their arrival,
and the family was supported by his mother, who
worked for various textile companies, a Philadelphia
industry then in terminal decline. As a young student, Kahn took advantage of the city's public school
system. He enrolled in supplementary classes at the
Public Industrial Art School, where he did well in
drawing courses. Eventually he earned a place in
Philadelphia's prestigious Central High School,
where he was introduced to architecture through history courses. Parallel to his formal education, Kahn
took public art classes on weekends and informal
piano lessons, at which he excelled.

Kahn's childhood was an example of Philadelphia's
commitment to public education and of the aspiration among immigrant families that their children
assimilate and become successful beyond the means
and status of their origins. The public school system in particular offered working-class families such
as Kahn's upward mobility; in school, discipline and
ability were recognized and rewarded based on merit,
not class. While a parallel system of private schools
in Philadelphia catered to wealthy families, Kahn's
roots in the liberal arts–based public schools helped
him rise into the professional class and left him with
a very personal understanding of the importance of a
socially benevolent government. Likewise, his background in the immigrant culture of early twentieth-
century America gave him an appreciation for the

community's role in daily urban life. His experience as a first-generation immigrant would, as well, link him to two of the most important collaborators in his later career—engineer August Komendant and Jonas Salk, Kahn's "greatest client."

Eschewing offers of music and painting scholarships, Kahn instead chose to study architecture at the University of Pennsylvania, an acknowledged leader in architectural education led by the Beaux-Arts trained architect Paul Philippe Cret. Cret's interpretation of the French system relied heavily on the rationalist methods and values put forth by Julien Guadet. While the alternative, construction-based teachings of Eugène-Emmanuel Viollet-le-Duc formed part of Cret's pedagogy, design at the University of Pennsylvania proceeded from the general to the specific, with construction and materials deployed in the service of composition.[8] For Cret, and thus for the University of Pennsylvania, Beaux-Arts was less a style than a method and a spur toward a "clearness," a "science of harmonious results," which would result in buildings that accurately portrayed their function, construction, and conception. Cret espoused six principles contained within Guadet's "Elements and Theory of Architecture": a faithfulness to the program, its arrangement based on the site's circumstances, constructability, an emphasis on architectural "truth" or the eschewing of excess effect, expressed structure or "strength," and an integration of utility and beauty. Cret believed that this ambitious program was critical to collegiate study in particular. "Practical requirements," he wrote in 1908, "will soon enough cut the wings of [the student's] dreams, but something will remain. It is necessary at one period of every [architect's] life that they shall believe that the object of architecture is to produce beautiful things."[9] The rationalist approach of Guadet's treatise relied on

17

the *esquisse* as a pedagogical and developmental tool in the Beaux-Arts system. Such an approach demanded discipline, but more importantly it required students to quickly distill the nature and character of a given program accurately and then to develop subsidiary spaces and details in relation to and in support of the initial sketch.

Kahn's recollection of the Beaux-Arts method is critical to understanding the evolution of his constructed theory. Speaking with historian William Jordy in the 1960s, Kahn summarized his training not in compositional terms, but in terms of process, logic, and experience:

> For beginning design problems Beaux-Arts training typically presented the student with a written program without comment from the instructor. He [the student] would study the problem, be given a period of a few hours in a cubicle (*en loge*) during which he would make a quick sketch of his solution without consultation. This sketch was filed as the basis for the elaboration of the problem which followed.... It was something that every student trained himself for, in order not to be grossly at variance with the nature of a library, or the nature of a legislative chamber; we looked up these places to see what they were like in preparation for the *esquisse*. Once the sketch was made we had to adhere to it during the time of study. So the sketch depended on our intuitive powers....[10]

Kahn, however, ended up being quite critical of the reliance on precedent in his own work, going on to note that the Beaux-Arts's main strength, the *esquisse*, was weakened in typical education by the need to see how a building type had been executed previously. For Kahn, an empirical strain lurked in the otherwise rationalist requirements of being *en loge*:

> I'm at my best when I talk about the nature of things—the nature of a library. It's not derived so much from knowledge because the examples are very ragged.... You start as though a library had never been built.... So I think the *esquisse* was valuable in giving a sense of what, out-of-the-blue, a library should be, as though we had never seen a library.[11]

Much has been written about the Beaux-Arts's compositional legacy in Kahn's work—the importance of *poche*, an emphasis on axial relationships, symmetry, or balanced asymmetry and proportion. However, this description by Kahn of the working method implied by Cret proves telling in the examination of his design process and its relation to building science.[12] Kahn essentially described two spheres of information that the designer can rely on as a scheme is begun. One can, of course, look to precedent or to a program document, but one can also try to derive the program's fundamental needs and work from there. Elsewhere, Kahn spoke of wanting to begin from "Volume Zero," in which no other projects of the type, indeed no other architecture, existed, and a design problem could proceed solely from first principles.[13] This, of course, is a slightly absurd notion, as typology and precedent played an obvious role in Kahn's work. Yet the process of divining the *esquisse* of a project based strictly on

its function, its program, and its performance without recourse to precedents marked Kahn's approach
as fundamentally modern and inductive. Over time,
he would expand the importance of the *esquisse*'s
derivation, taking up to two years of design work to
arrive, finally, at a sketch that incorporated ideally
balanced and woven solutions to the whole range of
problems presented by the program. These went far
beyond the Beaux-Arts's planometric exercises, however, and incorporated the often-ignored requirements
of structure, servicing, construction, and daily function as essential elements in the conception of even
the simplest schemes.

Kahn's early career as a young architect in
Philadelphia following his graduation in 1924 was
solid, but it foreshadowed little of his later career.
His first job was with Philadelphia's city architect,
John Molitor, assisting on designs for the city's sesquicentennial celebration in 1926, an event that was
plagued by budget problems and a shifting site.[14] Kahn
was credited as "architectural designer" on ten major
structures, under Molitor and two "architectural assis-
tants," and while scholars have disagreed about his
actual contribution, it is clear that Kahn was actively
involved in the rapid design and construction of the
event's major buildings.[15] The exposition was undistinguished stylistically, choosing an unremarkable
middle ground between the 1893 Chicago Exposition's
aesthetic unity and the architectural adventurism of
the 1915 Panama-Pacific Exposition held in San
Francisco. The need for quick design and construction, however, led Molitor and his staff to use lightweight steel structures, with solid plaster infills and
relatively little ornament, a pragmatic if uninspired
adaptation of Cret's growing interest in a stripped-
down classicism. Kahn undoubtedly learned a great
deal about the industrial methods used to erect the

20

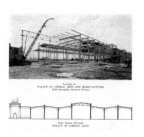

Palace of Liberal Arts,
Philadelphia Sesquicentennial,
1926. John Moliter,
City Architect.
Construction view (top) and
typical section (bottom)

temporary exhibition structures, but it is tempting to view his lifelong distaste for both light steel framing and concealing exterior skins in light of this experiment that gained only mixed aesthetic success.

Following his involvement with the Sesquicentennial, Kahn spent a year traveling in Europe and then worked briefly for Cret while that office was engaged in work for the upcoming 1933 Chicago Exhibition. Kahn's tenure with Cret was brief; he resigned as the Depression took hold and work dried up.[16] Better documented is Kahn's subsequent work with the Philadelphia firm of Zantzinger, Borie, and Medary, former associates of Cret. Here Kahn worked on federal projects as part of the government's attempt to boost employment; however, even this did not prevent him from being without work for much of the early 1930s.

George Howe and the Architectural Research Group (ARG)

The depression was unkind to Kahn, as it was to most young architects. Married in 1930, by 1932 he was unemployed, with work having dried up for both Cret and Zantzinger, Borie, and Medary. Kahn and his wife, Esther, moved in with her parents, and his lack of gainful employment led Kahn to seek out alternative paths. He fell in with a group of philosophically minded Philadelphia architects led by George Howe, then president of the T-Square Club. Howe was Philadelphia's most prominent architect, having designed the landmark PSFS tower (1929–32) on the east side of downtown with his partner, New York–based William Lescaze. Howe was to become the first of Kahn's champions, recognizing in the young, unemployed architect qualities that would eventually lead

21

the two to a brief professional partnership and a productive academic alliance.

Howe's architectural philosophy bears a remarkable resemblance to Kahn's positions as stated later in his career. While Howe's career had been built on residential commissions that began with designs close to the shingle style and ended in an americanized International Style, it was PSFS that gained him stature beyond the northeastern United States. Perhaps as a way to stave off criticism of the controversial tower, but certainly as an impassioned defense of his cautious dressing of the tower's engineering in streamlined, modern façades, Howe deemed himself an "organic," as opposed to "ornamental," architect. This was a thinly veiled distinction between the Beaux-Arts and the modernist approaches, and Howe further parsed the organic, or modern, as having three streams: the "mechanical, the functional, and the stylistic."[17] The first two were easily defined. The American designer and industrialist Buckminster Fuller, whose Dymaxion projects had been published in 1929, represented the first: architecture as a series of connected and integrated mechanisms and components. The second stream, functional, was an obvious description of the European functionalists, whose efforts to reform the housing market in Germany and France, in particular, had been widely published, if not actually successful on the scale imagined. Howe, on the other hand, placed himself in the "stylistic" category, with a lengthy defense of its mix of science and art:

> The business of the architect in
> cooperating with the engineer is to
> produce beauty over and above utility.
> They differ from the ornamentalist
> only in claiming that beauty is

more than skin deep, and that
superficial decoration unrelated to
organic structure is as passing and
unimportant as fashions
in cosmetics or the length of skirts.
They strip their buildings bare
to expose an athletic and well-
conditioned body.... On the other
hand, they mould these
bare forms with disciplined care,
and unlike the mechanists and the
functionalists, hold beauty always in
view as their objective.

It is evident that this organic
architecture, however emphasized, is
in fact a projection of the engineer's
ideal. It is the engineer who has
converted the amoebic cellular
building into an elaborate skeletal
structure with a complicated organic
system of circulation, breathing,
hearing, nerves, and so forth, and it
is consciously and gratefully on the
foundation of engineering progress
that the organic school of architects
proposes to raise its structure.[18]

Howe's definition of "organic" was unique, and Kahn
would later use this troublesome word in a similar
vein. For both Howe and Kahn, it meant a holistic
conception of structure, assembly, and function that
would provide the basis for a building's aesthetic—
not necessarily unadorned, although Kahn would push
this point further than Howe. Notable, too, was the
importance ascribed by Howe to mechanical systems
and the beauty inherent in an "athletic structure."
These "projections of the engineer's ideal" would play

23

fundamental roles in Kahn's work. While structure was already an allegedly key element in the rhetoric of International Style modernism, Kahn would adopt it as a primary formgiver. The inclusion of mechanical systems in Howe and Kahn's theoretical discussions, however, marked an absolute departure from the stylistic norms of the day.

Howe's T-Square Club produced a journal that was widely read in and beyond Philadelphia, in particular as it began to take on the mantle of European modernism. Howe famously engaged Frank Lloyd Wright in a long-running debate in the journal in 1932; with Howe's encouragement, Kahn contributed a short piece entitled "The Value and Aim in Sketching" in 1931.[19] This article was in substance unremarkable (although decrying "pose and artifice" in drawing), but it presented Kahn with his first published forum, whose importance he recognized and soon sought to repeat.

Part of Kahn's appeal to Howe was his burgeoning leadership of a small group of unemployed architects that met under the name Architectural Research Group, or ARG. The group was inspired to tackle the problem of housing, which became acute as the Depression worsened. A variable group of about two dozen architects, ARG entered housing competitions, drew up proposals for local agencies, received sponsorships from firms, and generally debated the state of contemporary architecture. Kahn formed a strong friendship with ARG member David Wisdom, who, like Kahn, had grown up in Philadelphia (albeit in the suburbs) and had received his degree at the University of Pennsylvania. Five years younger than Kahn, Wisdom worked with Kahn throughout his career, becoming a trusted second and leading much of the research into materials

24

and construction techniques that would characterize the office in its mature period.

Much of ARG's work was influenced by contemporary developments in Philadelphia, in particular the construction of the modernist Mackley Houses by Oscar Stonorov and Alfred Kastner, which achieved widespread recognition for their humane approach to public housing. Educated in Florence and Zurich, Stonorov had worked with Corbusier and André Lurcat, while Kastner's European background was complimented by work in New York, in particular for Hood and Foulihoux. The pair had the distinction of placing second in the Palace of the Soviets competition in 1930; however, despite its success, the partnership had dissolved by 1935, with Stonorov staying in Philadelphia and Kastner relocating to Washington to pursue further housing work for the government.

The Architectural Research Group disbanded in 1934 after which Kahn carried out independent projects for a friend's paint store outside the city and a synagogue in northern Philadelphia.[20] In 1935 he was recruited by Kastner to work on a project for factory housing in New Jersey, which was built in 1936–37. In 1938, Howe recruited Kahn back to Philadelphia, where the two worked on local housing projects that were ultimately rejected by a reactionary city council and mayor who were politically opposed to the idea of social housing. Stung by this wasted effort, Kahn spent the next three years advocating a more liberal housing policy in Philadelphia, organizing colleagues—some from the ARG—into a socially active political body. Allied in their view that decent dwellings could be constructed out of meager budgets and official indifference, Howe proposed a formal partnership to Kahn in 1941 to pursue wartime housing commissions.

25

Howe, Stonorov, and Kahn

Two of the projects executed under federal auspices during World War II gained Howe and Kahn international attention. In 1942, they completed work on a 450-unit war housing complex in Middletown, Pennsylvania. While undistinguished architecturally, the project provided apartments at a unit cost of under $2,800 (about $33,000 in current figures). Howe's hand is apparent in the units' roof lines—low pitches that compromised between a weather-resistant gable roof and the stylistically popular flat roof of the International Style. However, the project's real importance was its low cost, which gained it a short feature piece in *Architectural Forum*.[21]

Oscar Stonorov joined the partnership in 1942 after Howe was called to Washington as a consultant and supervising architect for the Public Buildings Administration. Carver Court in Coatesville, Pennsylvania, designed by Howe, Kahn, and Stonorov and completed in 1944, provided permanent housing for one hundred workers and families—all African-American—who were employed or dependent upon a nearby steel mill. While the government's stated goals were almost obscenely low, the project's execution demonstrated an attention to detail and an integration of function with aesthetics that transcended the war housing program's mean standards. Writing of its conception, Howe, Stonorov, and Kahn noted that the government's "cheap" standard housing plans often included basements, necessitating expensive excavation while "eras[ing] . . . all trace of the natural beauty of the site."[22] Carver Court contained some on-grade housing, but its primary innovation was a standard three-bedroom unit raised one story above the ground on concrete shear walls in a rudimentary interpretation of Corbusier's *pilotis* (exposed ground-level col-

26

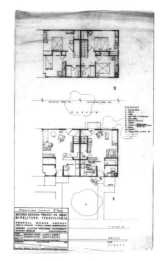

Defense housing project, furniture layout, Middletown, Pennsylvania. George Howe and Louis I. Kahn, 1942

Carver Court, Coatesville, Pennsylvania. Oscar Stonorov, Louis I. Kahn, and George Howe, 1944

umns). This provided natural space for small utility and storage rooms and a carport, which could serve as a sheltered play area in inclement weather. Construction was simpler because of the smaller, shallower foundations, and grading was eased by allowing drainage from the site to pass under the houses— a key provision on a sloped site such as the one at Coatesville. While the overall impression of the building designs at Carver Court is a recognizable hybrid of Howe's streamlined shingle style with Stonorov's International Style massing, there is also a very clear articulation in these units between the ground level service areas and the brighter, lighter living areas above. Likewise, the execution of the basic principle was disciplined by a rigid budget, with innovations in solar shading and daylighting achieved through simple but carefully worked-out wood and glass details, featured again in *Architectural Forum*.[23] The group's approach was summed up by *Forum*'s editors as scientific and resolutely empirical: "Oscar Stonorov and Louis I. Kahn," they wrote, "ride only one hobby, their white charger Reform out of Dismal Condition by Data Sheet.... They gather reams of Significant Information which magically turns into gardens, community recreation rooms, workshops and nursery schools."[24]

Given the dire nature of war-housing work, the modest achievements of Howe, Stonorov, and Kahn were almost miraculous. They received further commissions for housing in Washington, D.C., Philadelphia, and Detroit—although this last project was an infamous victim of labor battles—each of which distilled complex planning and architectural ideals into inexpensive, functional, yet articulate dwellings. Innovations in daylighting and construction continued the experiments of Carver Court, with ceiling monitors, intentionally unfinished materials, and a careful delineation of public and private space marking each design. Stonorov is generally credited with the political savvy necessary to negotiate the complex bureaucracy and financing of these projects. Kahn, on the other hand, seems to have taken over the majority of the design work in the small firm, particularly after George Howe departed for Washington in 1942. Kahn thus spent over a decade and a half engaged in difficult, tightly budgeted projects, whose realization relied on disciplined efficiency, and whose successful completion was seen as an ethical and social obligation. We can see in these simple projects a hint of Kahn's mature thought in his creation of legible designs from constructional and functional requirements and in Kahn's willingness to see cost as an editor rather than an adversary, a key to the grander projects of his later career.

Parallel to their war-housing work, Kahn and Stonorov's participation in *Architectural Forum*'s "New Buildings for 194X" program brought them considerable recognition. *Forum*, starved for material during wartime, commissioned two dozen leading architects to design major civic and residential projects using Syracuse, New York, as a site, taking into account the changes in demographics, economics, and technology likely to follow the cessation of hostilities. Ludwig Mies van der Rohe's "Museum for a Small City" and Charles Eames's "City Hall" were both major contributions to this project, as were lesser-known commissions by Pietro Belluschi, Carl Koch, John Johansen, and Perkins, Wheeler, and Will.[25] Kahn and Stonorov's design for an urban hotel, however, was given the lead position in the journal. While fairly conventional in plan and layout, Stonorov and Kahn's assessment and transformation of the program were noted by the editors. Unwilling to see the hotel only as a commercial enterprise, they suggested integrating "requirements

Hotel for 194X. Louis I. Kahn and Oscar Stonorov, 1943

Hotel for 194X, prefabricated bathroom. Louis I. Kahn and Oscar Stonorov, 1943

28

of sound investment" with the possibility of "community functions."[26] To that end, the scheme strictly divided civic and guest functions, formally articulating the project's dual logic. "The modern architect," they wrote, "not only seeks to solve functional problems by more rational use of forms and materials, but also trains himself to sense the psychological implications inherent in the tasks he is called to solve." Here, in rather pedestrian language, is Kahn's nascent architectural philosophy—the achievement of an acsthetically satisfying result based on the proper assessment and deployment of material resources to programmatic ends, beyond the mere spatial quantities indicated in a client's brief.

The publicity from *Forum* earned Kahn a stage for his developing theory of architecture based on objective standards that would balance resources with needs in an expressive synthesis. In 1944, he was invited to participate in a published symposium that sought to forge new paths for architecture and urban planning in the imminent postwar era. Kahn was faced with his first major public stage, and he responded with an essay that contained his earliest cogent formulation of a technically derived architectural theory. The stated topic, "Monumentality," could have easily been devoted to a reconciliation of Kahn's Beaux-Arts training and the International Style influence of Stonorov. Instead, Kahn chose to address issues of fabrication, materials, construction, and economics, along with a socially inspired plea for a communitarian sensibility in urban planning and design. This latter theme sounds very much like Stonorov, but the technical themes of the essay would resonate throughout the projects of Kahn's mature career. The character of monumentality, Kahn argued, derived not from its composition or its bulk, but rather from "a striving for structural perfection."[27] Cathedrals, pyramids, palaces, and other institutions gained their presence from a (relatively) true expression of timeless physical absolutes through available materials and techniques. While these could serve as examples up to the present day, Kahn argued that the era's scientific progress demanded new insights. "Stimulated and guided by knowledge we shall go far to develop the forms indigenous to our new materials and methods," he wrote, acknowledging the debt of the past but recognizing the need to respond to new conditions of materials and techniques. Echoing the Beaux-Arts's great dissident, Viollet-le-Duc, Kahn proposed four eras of integration between architecture and engineering, science and art. In the architecture of ancient Greece and Rome, the cathedrals of the Middle Ages, and the structural design of the nineteenth century, Kahn found "common characteristics of greatness upon which the buildings of our future must, in one sense or another, rely." These characteristics involved the clear, refined expression of the structures' performance and assembly, weaving together how they worked with how they were made.

To Kahn, the promise of these examples was under threat in 1944 from what he termed "handbook engineering," or the reliance on conservative safety factors and standardization in structural design. In particular, the economics and well-studied behavior of the simple I-beam had led to its use in situations where its shape was not statically correct, for example, in a cantilever. In this instance, a structurally expressive cantilever should taper from its root to its tip, its form reflecting the lesser shear and moment loads toward the free end. However, common practice for small cantilevers would simply leave the beam as it was when it arrived from the shop, a common depth throughout, eliminating the need for costly modifications to a standard, mass-produced shape. Kahn felt that this was an opportunity missed to communicate simply a static truth, albeit at some expense. Likewise, in a statement that presaged much of his later work, Kahn spoke of the fundamental link between structural performance and architectural form: "To attain greater strength with economy, a finer expression in the structural solution of the principle of concentrating the area of cross section away from the center of gravity is the tubular form since the greater the moment of inertia the greater the strength."[28]

Kahn struggled here. He understood the elemental principle of structural form, that where a section's material is deployed in its cross section is often as important as the section's size itself. An ideal structural shape concentrates its material at its edges, where it can more efficiently develop an internal, resisting moment to counteract the external bending force applied by a load. However, a tubular shape is comparatively weak for a pure beam, since it doubles up material closest to the shape's center, actually lowering the section's crucial moment of inertia. An I-beam, conversely, deploys most of its material at its top and bottom edges, limiting the weight of structurally inefficient material around its center and putting the most material in the portions of the shape that do the most work in a beam. For a column, however, a tube shape is far better. While its primary load is axial, that is, parallel to the shape's long axis, a column's cross-sectional shape must resist buckling, which, unlike a beam's load, can occur in any direction. A column must therefore deploy its material equally on all possible bending axes, as it is only as strong against buckling as its weakest axis.

Pure static performance, however, was only part of the equation. The economics of steel fabrication, with which Kahn would become intimately familiar in

Typical I-beam shape (left) and tubular steel shape (right) showing stress distribution under beam loading

31

his later work, demanded shapes that could be easily made by rolling. Because they are closed, steel tubes could not be easily rolled at the time; instead, they were usually seamed out of flat plate. I-beams, on the other hand, could be easily rolled, and this fabricational advantage trumped structural purity in "handbook" steel construction. This would not be the last time that Kahn would only partially understand the statics of a building or structural element. But it is a notable moment in his development. He realized that economy, structural performance, construction, and aesthetics could be intricately linked in an overall conception of building—one that could attain the monumental qualities that he found lacking in contemporary design.

"Monumentality" included several tectonic experiments to demonstrate the new possibilities of structurally derived forms. Most remarkably, Kahn proposed reconstructing Beauvais Cathedral in tubular steel— again, a trope borrowed from Viollet-le-Duc, who had proposed rebuilding medieval structures in cast iron. With welded tube steel, Kahn argued, the cathedral could be reconceived so that columns and beams would become fused, and the spaces between structural members would open up to allow glass roofs and walls. "Beauvais Cathedral," Kahn concluded, "needed the steel we have." Considering Kahn's lifelong preference for concrete, this is a surprising argument. But here, Kahn was discussing structures that were, as he would say, insectlike, that is, lightweight and open, gothic instead of romanesque. Further sketches for a cultural and educational center show spidery, "unclothed" steel tubular members of changing diameter—a fabricational impossibility—bridging outdoor and indoor galleries and transparent roof lights. The heavy weight of concrete must have seemed, for so progressive a program, inappropriate. Yet Kahn's rediscovery

Illustration from Louis I. Kahn's "Monumentality," 1944

32

of antiquity a few years later would inspire him to change course toward structures of greater mass and gravitas, rejecting steel as a structural material and instead assigning it to lower orders of performance, in particular cladding and framing.

In his conclusion to "Monumentality," Kahn proposed a concise manifesto of his empirical approach, summarizing the aspirations of his early career:

> Standardization, prefabrication, controlled experiments and tests, and specialization are not monsters to be avoided by the delicate sensitivities of the artist. They are merely the modern means of controlling vast potentialities of materials for living, by chemistry, physics, engineering, production, and assembly, which lead to the necessary knowledge the artist must have to expel fear in their use, broaden his creative instinct, give him new courage, and thereby lead him to the adventures of unexplored places. His work will then be part of his age and will afford delight and service for his contemporaries.

> I do not wish to imply that monumentality can be attained scientifically or that the work of the architect reaches its greatest service to humanity by his peculiar genius to guide a concept to monumentality. I merely defend, because I admire, the architect who possesses the will to grow with the many angles of

33

our development. For such a man
finds himself far ahead of his fellow
workers.[29]

1947: A Pivotal Year

Among Stonorov and Kahn's larger postwar building commissions, an unbuilt project for the privately
funded Philadelphia Psychiatric Hospital gained
national attention for both its bold massing (clearly
derived from Alvar Aalto's Paimio Sanitorium) and its
innovations in planning, which were led by hospital
consultant Isadore Rosenfield.[30] The office was kept
afloat by commissions for private residences after the
war; however, Kahn and Stonorov also designed union
offices, medical establishments, and children's play-
grounds during this time, reflecting their commitment
to socially redeeming (though invariably low-budget)
work. Simultaneously, they took on work for commercial and retail clients, notably the Coward Shoe Store
in Philadelphia, whose "surprisingly direct design"
produced a simple, elegantly detailed interior, highlighted by a minimal glass and aluminum curtain
wall that created subtle but convincing signage out
of the latest construction techniques.[31] Their most
searching conceptual study, a Parasol House designed
as a publicity experiment for Knoll (a large furniture
company), included a structural system composed of
square "umbrellas" perched atop slender steel columns at their center and braced against one another
at their edges. Notably, these roof panels were hollow; their inner and outer skins were separated by an
aircraftlike web of vertical posts. While the project
never went beyond the conceptual stage, this hollow
roof idea was an important step for Kahn, as it provided a natural space for air ducts and pipes. The filigree of vertical posts within its structure would have

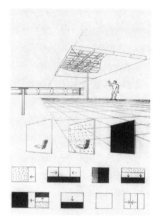

Sketch of the Parasol House
showing a lightweight
Vierendeel-framed roof.
Louis I. Kahn and Oscar
Stonorov, 1947

34

allowed each panel to work as a superefficient slab, its two skins acting much as the two flanges in a beam while posts did the work of a beam's web. Although Kahn apparently did not realize it at the time, the Parasol used the principles of a Vierendeel truss, in which rigidly connected vertical members separate the two flanges of a beam. While a regular truss prevents its top and bottom flanges, or chords, from shearing apart with triangulated, axially loaded members, a Vierendeel truss or beam fixes vertical members with robust moment connections. This allows more useful rectangular openings in the beam at the expense of slightly larger members and connections.[32] This truss type would later play a key role in two of Kahn's most influential works.

Kahn's forty-sixth year would prove to be an important turning point in his career. While he and Stonorov had gained recognition for their "intelligent conservatism," their ability to produce humanely scaled and detailed buildings on infinitesimal budgets, and for their forward-looking thinking on the roles of function and construction in architecture and urbanism, the firm had produced largely mainstream work. By this point, though, tensions between Stonorov and Kahn had surfaced, with each occasionally doing jobs independently of the other, leading to a complete break in 1947.[33] The apparent cause was Stonorov's use of the partnership's urban scheme for the Chinese Wall area of Philadelphia's downtown in an exhibition and publication without giving credit to Kahn.[34] However, this was only one of numerous differences between the two.

Anne Griswold Tyng, who began working with Stonorov and Kahn in late 1945, brought to the office a radical philosophy of mathematics, geometry, and architecture that exacerbated the partnership's professional tension. Born in 1920 to missionary parents, Tyng's childhood interest in building led her to earn degrees in fine arts and architecture from Radcliffe and Harvard.[35] She was introduced to the firm through a colleague from Harvard and quickly became involved in all aspects of the office's work. She also soon fell into an affair with Kahn, to Stonorov's consternation, and following the split, she and David Wisdom remained with Kahn in one form or another for the remainder of Kahn's career. Whereas Kahn's collaborations with Howe and Stonorov had been professionally productive, socially progressive, and aesthetically compelling, it was Tyng who explosively refocused Kahn's interest in the creative expression of building technologies. Inspired in part by the increasingly popular work of Buckminster Fuller and by her own brief tenure in the office of New York–based architect and engineer Konrad Wachsmann, Tyng's interest in mathematical rigor proved to be entirely at odds with Stonorov's compositional tendencies.

Another challenge to the partnership came with Kahn's part-time teaching commitment at Yale. Under a new dean, Charles H. Sawyer, Yale had expanded its program of visiting critics, using important figures in contemporary architecture to teach two afternoons per week. In fall 1947 Yale's first choice for a visiting critic, Brazilian Oscar Niemeyer, was held up by immigration authorities for political reasons. Kahn was an expedient replacement, known to Sawyer through his planning and design work but hardly equal in stature to other visiting critics—Wallace Harrison, Eero Saarinen, and Edward Durrell Stone—who had recently passed through Yale's doors. The prospect of adding Kahn to this esteemed list was, for students, a disappointment; later, William Huff would recall that students expressed "outrage" over such a selection, asking the administration, "What has Kahn ever built?"[36] Yet Kahn's gifts as a teacher—perhaps honed through his leadership of the Architectural Research Group, as David Brownlee has suggested—quickly became apparent.[37] His gently inspiring manner and obvious charisma soon made him a favorite among students, and he was asked to return on a semipermanent basis, eventually coordinating visiting critics and, by 1951, earning the title Chief Critic in Architectural Design. He also played a key role, in 1949, in bringing in his mentor, George Howe, as chair of the Department of Architecture.[38] Kahn, prone to bold pronouncements prior to the demands of practice, blossomed in academia, showing signs of his developing philosophy of architecture. Encouraged by the University's intellectual space and by a growing cast of acolytes half his age, Kahn expanded his engagement with architecture beyond his professional work with Stonorov.

This desire to transcend the pragmatism out of which Kahn had built a career became quickly apparent in several works that he, Tyng, and David Wisdom executed in the years immediately following the split with Stonorov. While often seen as the last gasps of his provincial career, three projects of this period demonstrate a move away from principles of pure spatial planning and default modernist composition. Indeed, the Libbey-Owens-Ford Solar House, the Weiss House, and two new wings for the Philadelphia Psychiatric Hospital all reveal a restless move in the direction of tectonic experimentation, with a newly rejuvenated expression of basic technical principles forming the conceptual basis for each project. Whether inspired by Tyng, his teaching at Yale, or simply by the confidence that came with his separation from Stonorov, the foward-thinking elements of these three buildings presaged the dramatic work to come.

37

1947–50: Hints of a New Synthesis

The Libbey-Owens-Ford (LOF) Solar Home, whose attribution was also a precipitating cause of Kahn and Stonorov's breakup, was an entry in a nation-wide design competition intended to publicize the use of the LOF's new Thermopane glass. While south-facing glass is useful in the winter to pick up free heat from solar radiation, single-pane glass is notoriously inefficient, as its thermal conductivity allows heat to reradiate from buildings at night. Early attempts at creating insulating glass used two sheets of plate glass with an air space formed by rubber seals between them; however, leaks that developed in the seals as glass expanded and contracted led to insoluble condensation problems. In 1934, a research team at LOF found a suitable seal made of metal alloy that maintained a bond even under thermal expansion, and production was geared entirely toward the war effort in the early 1940s.[39] In search of a market for the new material, the company sponsored a competition for house designs in each state that would use the new Thermopane product as an integrated part of a logical, scientifically based solar strategy. Kahn, Tyng, and Stonorov were undoubtedly helped by the presence of George Howe on the nominating panel, and they were asked to represent Pennsylvania in the contest. LOF laid out the strategy it wanted to see from participants, who were to use overhangs, proper orientation, and the inclusion of Thermopane to achieve a house that would respond to each location's climatic peculiarities.[40]

Most of the houses in the competition and subsequent publication were variations on typical suburban plans. Kahn's submission was one of several that

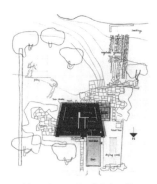

Libbey-Owens-Ford Solar Home, competition entry. Louis I. Kahn, Oscar Stonorov, Anne Tyng, and David Wisdom, 1947

adopted a form and aesthetic based on solar response, although it was carried out with a lingering sense of the americanized International Style absorbed from Howe. Here, of course, the use of large windows, single-pitched roofs, and overhanging planes could be convincingly deployed to meet solar needs—more sun in the winter, more shade in the summer. Kahn's design was trapezoidal in plan with a continuous masonry wall facing north and a mix of glass and vertically grained siding on the east, west, and south sides. This slightly counterintuitive shape was explained as providing good daylighting to all areas of the house, with deep overhangs at each story and vertical fins along the side windows. In unpublished drawings, the scheme was further elaborated with four different methods of daylight control: solid and louvered overhangs on the south side and sliding panels and folding screens on the east and west. Such an interest in modifying, controlling, and manipulating daylight would become a key theme in later work.

The Libbey-Owens-Ford experiment informed Kahn's finest pre-1950 house, the Weiss House in East Norristown, Pennsylvania (1947–50). Here, the solar house's tentative innovations were consolidated into a rigorous plan, with a division between public and private spaces, a hierarchy between main and service functions and a south-facing glass wall with vertically sliding screens that allowed front light or clerestory light, depending on the time of day. The house's form is recognizably Corbusian, with a V-shaped roof supported by heavy stone walls; it also has stylistic affinities to the raised dwellings at Carver Court. But Kahn and Tyng were increasingly willing to let the materials and structural elements of their designs accept the representational duties of Stonorov's compositional forms, and the Weiss House was a bold step toward the expressive, comprehensive approach that would mark

Weiss House,
East Norristown, Pennsylvania.
Louis I. Kahn, Anne Tyng, and
David Wisdom, 1947–50

39

Kahn's work of the 1950s and beyond. The façade of
the Weiss House is a straightforward presentation of
the glass and structural module, with a solid overhanging roof that covers the stone end walls, which
in turn contain a wood window framing system and a
porous *brise-soleil* halfway up the elevation. A clear
hierarchy of structure and cladding here mirrors the
developing logic of service and public spaces and is
expressed in a consistent language of shadow-joint
details, in which one material is purposefully held
back from another to emphasize the constructive or
functional separation between the two.[41]

Two final projects, which Kahn executed with David
Wisdom, set the stage for the extraordinary flowering of Kahn's career after 1950. Both projects were
done for the Philadelphia Psychiatric Hospital, which
had employed Kahn and Stonorov previously for an
extension that remained unbuilt. These two new wings
were to provide dormitory rooms and recreation and
therapy spaces for the Hospital. While construction
on both would extend to 1954, they represented a
definitive closure to Kahn's early career. The Pincus
Building is perhaps the better known of the two, with
a large sitting room delineated by exposed steel trusses
and a sliding window system similar to that used at
the Weiss House. Here, the distinction between structure and cladding was blurred, as the open web joists,
exposed on the interior, appear to rest on the glass
wall's framing. In fact, the structure continues out-
doors to rest on plain round columns. The interior of
this space is a dramatic synthesis of light and structure, expressed in a rigorous pattern that defines the
main space's grain and tenor.

The Radbill Building, on the other hand, is a cellular structure containing patient rooms and offices. Its
concrete frame is expressed graphically on its three-

story façade, in vertical members set flush with a slate and glass façade. Overhead, a *brise-soleil* of pierced concrete slabs steps out from the façade at each level, increasing in depth as the amount of glass to be covered increases in the lower, more public areas, tying together the elevations with a strong horizontal expression. Kahn's solution to the pierced slab is notable, using cast-in-place wood boxes to achieve permanent in-place formwork that scatters minute dots of sunlight across the façade throughout the morning. Both the flush column and the perforated slab would reappear as important expressive elements in the Richards Laboratories and the Salk Institute.

Nominated by his mentor and newly appointed chair at Yale, George Howe, Kahn was made a fellow of the American Academy in Rome in 1950, and while Tyng and Wisdom continued work on the few projects in the office, Kahn traveled during the winter of 1950–51. He visited Egypt, Greece, and much of Italy and saw the work of Corbusier, including the Unité d'habitation in Marseilles while it was under construction. The fellowship, his first extended stay in Europe since his trip of 1928, demonstrated that he had achieved a level of recognition in the profession, but also that his aspirations lay beyond his relatively modest practice in Philadelphia.

Kahn left for Rome as an accomplished professional, with a handful of nationally recognized projects in his portfolio—innovative social housing, well-conceived and detailed single-family homes, and occasional forays into speculative city planning and institutional work. Kahn's background had also prepared him for a major reassessment of his own work and ambitions, as well as setting him up for larger projects during the last twenty-five years of his career. He had earned modest success, and his commissions had come to him

Kahn outside the Radbill Building of the Philadelphia Psychiatric Hospital. Louis I. Kahn, Anne Tyng, and David Wisdom, 1950–53

41

through reputation alone. The projects he worked on with Tyng and Wisdom in particular achieved success not through eye-catching design or flashy styling but rather through well-conceived, logical approaches to difficult problems of budget, construction, and performance. While Kahn was more than willing to offer pronouncements on his developing philosophy of architecture he took, at this point, a wholly practical approach to its application. "Monumentality" offered a strikingly pragmatic theory of architecture, focusing on the ends desired and the means available as the ultimate equations of design. Kahn's more metaphysical pronouncements would come later, after his larger constructions earned him a broader stage from which to speak. This rigorous, practical experience, for the twenty-five years from 1925 to 1950, gave Kahn a firm technical knowledge, a fluency in standard practice, and in what could economically be done beyond the norm. The tectonic innovations at the Weiss House or the Pincus Building, for example, demonstrated a deeply ingrained knowledge of solar shading, materials, and mechanics. While the forms of these structures remained somewhat derivative, the care with which their components and assemblies were conceived and conjoined showed Kahn's solid grounding in the jobsite's necessities and the day-to-day lives of buildings.

Kahn was, however, also ambitious beyond the achievements of his early career. If the recipe of "Monumentality" was based in the practicalities of steel and services, its aspirations retained the progressive, optimistic outlook of Kahn's days with the Architectural Research Group. Architecture as a shaper not only of space, but also of society remained a powerful notion for Kahn. His work to this point reflected a respect for institutions and governments as agents of social change, ingrained from his childhood, that was arguably absent from the contemporaneous work of Mies van der Rohe, for example. The dignity lent to the Philadelphia Psychiatric Hospital by Kahn's careful working out of its structure and skins recalled to some degree the very premise of the Beaux-Arts philosophy: the rendering of a program's civic character through architectural expression. Likewise, in his unbuilt work to this point, Kahn's visions for cities were relentlessly progressive; his monumental proposals for Philadelphia, the Jefferson Memorial in St. Louis, and the entire 194X project all offered an architectural confluence of social, cultural, and political goals.[42]

By 1950 Kahn had already integrated, on an admittedly modest scale, Viollet-le-Duc's empirical process, building up designs from their constructive and performative components, and Guadet's rationalist belief in the platonic "program's" primacy and its consistency throughout, despite the contingencies of site and construction. On the one hand, Kahn's Beaux-Arts training left him with a palpable sense of the importance of a project's overall vision, its immediate comprehensibility, and its architecturally imposed order. On the other, his actual built work had progressed from the ground up, from an economically driven assessment of minute functional requirements and the equally mundane construction techniques available to him given typically limited budgets. Carver Court, for example, featured a house type derived almost entirely from the functional move of pulling the dwelling spaces up above the ground, and this idea's execution used the most economical means and materials available. Yet any number of choices throughout the design produced a scheme that was at once clearly conceived and ordered, one that instantly spoke of its character, its conception, and its use. Similarly, the Weiss House is a power-

43

ful form with a rigorously imposed and expressed order. However, this order was derived from a clear understanding of the available dimensions for window glass, the proper size and sequence of living spaces, and the house's orientation with respect to the sun.

Kahn's process had thus developed into one that built up a project's *esquisse*, its essential form and character, through precisely the contingencies that Guadet sought to overcome. Once formed, this *esquisse* was then to corral and marshal all subsequent elements and systems into an ordered, easily recognized whole. Kahn's designs to this point had demonstrated the inherent possibilities in such an approach, but the truly grand examples of this process would emerge only gradually later, culminating in several of the century's finest, most completely conceived works of architecture. Kahn's first large-scale statement of this process, of the dependence of the "immeasurable" spirit of a building on its "measurable" circumstances and components, was waiting for his hand upon his return from Rome in spring 1951.

44

Endnotes

1. Louis I. Kahn, "Order Is," in *Louis I. Kahn: Writings, Lectures, Interviews,* ed. Alessandra Latour (New York: Rizzoli, 1991), 59.

2. Louis I. Kahn, "Form and Design, 1961," in *Writings, Lectures, Interviews*, ed. Latour, 117.

3. Louis I. Kahn, "Monumentality," in *Writings, Lectures, Interviews*, ed. Latour.

4. Louis I. Kahn, "On the Responsibility of the Architect," in *Writings, Lectures, Interviews*, ed. Latour, 53–54.

5. Louis I. Kahn, "Architecture and the University," in *Writings, Lectures, Interviews*, ed. Latour, 54–55. Proceedings of a conference at Princeton University, 11–12 December 1953.

6. Indeed, one of the few instances of this, in an early scheme for the Salk Institute project, would prove embarrassingly shortsighted. See chapter 4.

7. Anne Griswold Tyng, ed., *Louis Kahn to Anne Tyng: The Rome Letters, 1953–54* (New York: Rizzoli, 1997), 8–17. See also the interview with Esther I. Kahn in *Louis I. Kahn: l'uomo, il maestro*, ed. Alessandra Latour (Rome: Edizioni Kappa, 1986).

8. See Kenneth Frampton, "Louis I. Kahn and the French Connection," in Kenneth Frampton, *Labor, Work and Architecture: Collected Essays on Architecture and Design* (New York: Phaidon Press, 2002), 168–84. Frampton points out that Cret appreciated both the "structural rationalism of Viollet-le-Duc and de Baudot"—which I interpret as primarily empiricist or "Baconian," based on scientific method—and the "classicism of Durand's permutative system," by far the boldest statement of the rationalist tendency of the Beaux-Arts. Cret, whose writing neatly balances ideas from both camps, nevertheless was, in Frampton's words, "understandably skeptical about the capacity of construction to constitute the sole basis for formal order and cultural significance."

9. This quote and Cret's description of the Beaux-Arts method are taken from Paul Philippe Cret, "Ecole des Beaux-Arts: What Its Architectural Teaching Means," *The Architectural Record* 23 (May 1908): 367–71.

10. Kahn in William Jordy, "The Span of Kahn," *Architectural Review* 155, no. 928 (June 1974): 318–24.

11. Ibid.

12. Frampton, "Louis I. Kahn and the French Connection."

13. Louis I. Kahn, "1973: Brooklyn, NY," in *Writings, Lectures, Interviews*, ed. Latour, 329.

14. See Frank Skinner, "The Sesquicentennial Exposition, Philadelphia," *The Architectural Record* 60, no. 1 (July 1926): 1–17. Originally planned as a linear garden city along the Schuylkill River, the Exposition ended up being staged between rail and Navy yards in South Philadelphia on the site of Veterans Stadium.

15. Ibid.

16. Esther Kahn in Richard Saul Wurman, *What Will Be Has Always Been: The Words of Louis I. Kahn* (New York: AccessPress/Rizzoli, 1986), 283.

17. George Howe, address at the Town Hall Club, 14 November 1930, quoted in Robert A. M. Stern, *George Howe: Toward a Modern American Architecture* (New Haven: Yale University Press, 1975).

18. Ibid., 137.

19. Kahn's article is reprinted in *Writings, Lectures, Interviews*, ed. Latour, 10–12. For Howe's debate with Frank Lloyd Wright, see Stern, *George Howe*, 141–45.

20. "Even I had I think too little of it now to expect others to judge my present capabilities by so naked a job as that one." Kahn to Hyman Cunin, 19 August 1947, Louis I. Kahn Collection, University of Pennsylvania and the Pennsylvania Historical and Museum Commission, Philadelphia (hereafter cited as Kahn Collection), LIK box 54.

21. "450 Permanent Units—Rental," *Architectural Forum* 76, no. 5 (May 1942): 306–7.

22. George Howe, Oscar Stonorov, and Louis I. Kahn, "Standards Versus Essential Space: Comments on Unit Plans for War Housing," in *Writings, Lectures, Interviews*, ed. Latour, 14–15.

23. "Carver Court, Coatesville, PA," *Architectural Forum*, December 1944, 116.

24. "In the Forum," *Architectural Forum*, December 1944, 28.

25. "New Buildings for 194X," *Architectural Forum* 78, no. 5 (May 1943): 69.

26. Oscar Stonorov and Louis I. Kahn, "Hotel," *Architectural Forum* 78, no. 5 (May 1943): 74–79.

27. Kahn, "Monumentality," 18–19.

28. Ibid., 20.

29. Ibid., 27.

30. Isadore Rosenfield, "Philadelphia Psychiatric Hospital, Philadelphia, PA," *Pencil Points*, November 1946, 81–88.

31. "Glass-Front Store in Philadelphia," *Architectural Forum* 91, no. 6 (December 1949): 94–96. This forgotten elevation still exists, in altered form, on Chestnut Street in Philadelphia, a remarkable testament to its continuing vitality in so transient an environment as retail design. The project was not completed until after the split between Stonorov and Kahn.

32. Nicholas Gianapolus and Thomas J. Leidigh, interview by the author, Keast & Hood offices, Philadelphia, June 2004.

33. Interview with Anne Griswold Tyng in *Louis I. Kahn: l'uomo, il maestro*, ed. Latour, 41.

34. "Philadelphia Plans Again," *Architectural Forum* 87, no. 6 (December 1947).

35. Tyng, *Rome Letters*, 18–23.

36. William Huff, "Kahn and Yale," *Journal of Architectural Education* 35, no. 3 (Spring 1982): 23.

37. Kahn's studio for UNESCO headquarters in Fairmount Park, Philadelphia, cotaught with artist Jean Charlot, was featured in "Student Architects, Painters, Sculptors Design Together," *Progressive Architecture*, April 1945, 14–18.

38. "Howe has accepted Yale Appointment will come here January first many thanks for your efforts." Charles H. Sawyer to Kahn, telegram, 29 August 1949, Kahn Collection, LIK folder 60.26 ("Yale University").

39. "Windows Insulated by 2 Sealed Panes: Dehydrated Air Space Reduces Heat Loss Up to 50%," *New York Times*, 30 April 1944, RE1, 1.

40. Maron J. Simon, ed., *Your Solar House* (New York: Simon and Schuster, 1947). The office's entry, attributed to "Oscar Stonorov and Louis I. Kahn," appears on pages 42–43.

41. "One thing I learned from that job [the Weiss House] was what Lou called the 'shadow joint' detail. He became very famous for that. The shadow joint is the idea of separation between materials so that if one has a door jamb in wood against rough stone work, rather than to try to scribe the wood to the stone shape, one actually lets it be separate, with its own straight edge away from the irregular edge of stone. The shadow joint is an indentation between them which would have depth at least equal to the distance between wood and stone." Inteview with Anne Griswold Tyng in *Louis I. Kahn: l'uomo, il maestro*, ed. Latour, 43.

42. The sociocultural foundations of Kahn's practice have been most clearly explored by Sarah Williams Goldhagen, *Louis Kahn's Situated Modernism* (New Haven: Yale University Press, 2001).

YALE UNIVERSITY ART GALLERY
NEW HAVEN, CONNECTICUT

While Kahn spent the fall and winter of 1950–51 in Rome, events in New Haven transpired to provide him with his first opportunity to build a major institutional building, one that would earn him a global reputation while giving him a chance to explore the combination of technology and monumentality of which he had written in the 1940s. To this point, Kahn's career had been productive. He was a valued teacher at Yale and, at fifty years of age, at a point in his career where he could have simply coasted on his considerable achievements as a modestly influential American modernist. His time in Rome, however, energized him, rekindling his love for ancient monuments. His visit to the construction site of Corbusier's Unité d'habitation in Marseilles spurred his thinking about the architectural possibilities of concrete as a technological yet historically allusive material. All of these factors—his career of designing for utmost efficiency, his desire to translate the gravitas of antiquity into modern techniques, and the revelation of concrete's expressive potential—came together in the Yale University Art Gallery.[1]

It was pure chance that the commission fell to Kahn in the first place. Yale's Gallery at the time consisted of a half-built collegiate gothic structure designed by Egarton Swartout and Evarts Tracy, which was begun in 1926 but abandoned halfway through construction in 1928.[2] Swartout and Tracy had been asked by Yale to

Elevation of the original scheme. Egarton Swartout and Evarts Tracy, 1926

provide a building for the fine arts to match its neogothic campus. Weir Hall, their first structure on the site, was a studio building designed to resemble Magdalen College at Oxford and was funded by benefactor Edward Harkness.[3] It was built on property abandoned by the Skull and Bones Society and included a generous courtyard space that opened through a block of commercial buildings onto Chapel Street, which then formed the Yale campus's southern edge. Swartout and Tracy's plan for the Art Gallery was to have enclosed this courtyard, providing a long, symmetrical façade of arcaded windows and a formal entry along Chapel Street. In the original plan, this façade would have fronted two major galleries for sculpture, taking advantage of the southerly light through the window arcade. Above the sculpture rooms were attic galleries for paintings that used daylight controlled by skylights and adjustable louvers. In addition to a central staircase connected to the slightly elevated courtyard behind, Swartout and Tracy planned stair towers at either end, encased in oval spaces with gently curved treads at the top. Only the eastern five bays of the Swartout and Tracy scheme were built, leaving the western two-thirds of the site untouched.

Following key donations of twentieth-century art in 1941, Yale considered ways that the gallery might be extended while taking on a new exhibition philosophy more in harmony with these recent modernist acquisitions. The University turned to Philip

49

Perspective of the proposed extension. Philip Goodwin, ca. 1947

Goodwin, who had designed the well-known Museum of Modern Art in New York with Yale critic Edward Durrell Stone. In the thirteen years since the original gallery's construction, Yale's appetite for continuing its gothic style had withered. The housing of twentieth-century art, much of it abstract, provided an opportunity for the University to take an early lead in matching progressive architectural ideas to its leadership in modern literature and sciences. Goodwin's schemes for the Gallery done throughout the 1940s show confidence in the possibilities for a genuine International Style approach, with crisp volumes, large planes of glass, and a relentless avoidance of ornament, in juxtaposition to the original building's more florid and massive approach. The contrast with the original building could not have been greater, but while the administration was enthusiastic about Goodwin's modernist approach, the project was stalled for lack of sufficient budget and a wartime ban on major construction.

A. Whitney Griswold became Yale's president in 1950 and quickly established his commitment to modern architecture on campus, in particular for the Gallery, whose prominent site offered a public face for the University. In fall 1950, Goodwin was asked to revise his earlier work in conjunction with George Howe, then the newly appointed chair of the Architecture Department, and with Charles H. Sawyer, the director of Yale's Division of the Arts. Griswold tightened the project's budget in late November and asked as well that the program be reconsidered. Whereas Goodwin's earlier schemes had been entirely based on the display of artworks, Griswold's overriding mission gave greater weight to buildings and programs with a dedicated educational function. Sawyer in particular was asked to push for a new scheme that could provide flexibility, allowing not only for gallery space, but also for classrooms, drafting areas, and undefined spaces for "visual laboratories." Sawyer concurred with Griswold's direction and suggested that a new architect associate with Goodwin to "bring a fresh eye to the drastic changes in thinking which these revisions will demand."[4] Sawyer also suggested making George Howe a member of the Building Committee, both because of his architectural expertise and for his department's likely tenancy in the completed building. The Yale Corporation, which oversaw all building funds, approved a construction budget of $1.5 million for the extension to the Gallery on 9 December 1950.[5]

Yale's request to associate may have disheartened Goodwin, as he resigned from the project in early January 1951, citing upcoming cataract surgery and the "necessary conditions of speed" stipulated by the project. In his resignation, he warned of a difficult road ahead. The United States was once again at war, this time in Korea, and while building construction was permitted, war material such as steel and copper was tightly rationed. While wishing Sawyer and Griswold luck, Goodwin noted that these war conditions would require a devoted effort by the project's new architect. In closing he recommended that the commission be given to either Howe himself or to Yale alumnus Eero Saarinen. Howe politely recused himself, but he and Sawyer contacted Saarinen, who "reluctantly concluded" that he could not take on the project due to other commitments.[6] Sawyer and Howe, with the recommendation of Saarinen, settled on Kahn as a second choice. "While Kahn has less of an international reputation than Saarinen," they wrote to Griswold, "he is widely respected in the architectural profession. He has worked with Howe, has served as a very effective member of our teaching faculty and is thoroughly familiar with the particular and very complicated problems involved in this building.... We think he would make an effective collaborator...and would give this building the imaginative thinking it is going to require."[7]

Griswold agreed immediately. Sawyer and Howe wrote to Kahn in Rome to offer him the job in association with Douglas Orr, a New Haven architect who had worked on several projects at Yale. While Kahn's remaining time in Rome would present a challenge, Howe felt that the University needed that time to prepare not only a program—which would remain vague throughout the project—but also a sense of what sort of building was required.[8]

51

Griswold's insistence on an educational function was not merely pedagogical; it was also practical. The rationing of steel and copper meant that construction had to be justified to the Department of Defense, which was unlikely to see the esoteric merits of a traditional art gallery in time of war. There was, however, a dedicated channel in the government's process for educational buildings, particularly those that supported the American government's cold-war emphasis on industrial production and infrastructure. Thus, Howe and Sawyer began to chart a strategy that involved programmatic flexibility. If the building were designed to accommodate a range of functions, its initial use might be tuned to gain a favorable reception from the government. Over time, these uses might decamp to other dedicated buildings, leaving the Gallery free for its initially intended purpose. In fact, though never explicitly mentioned in the project's correspondence, this appears to be exactly how the project transpired.

Such flexibility, however, could come at the expense of architectural clarity, and for several weeks Howe and Sawyer, with the assistance of Orr, looked at "loft" construction as a balance between complete functional openness and the desire for an expressive statement. While modernists led by Corbusier had championed the *plan libre*, or "free plan," as a fundamental precept of contemporary architecture, this was in most cases a spatial pretension. Taking advantage of columnar construction, Corbusier had called for buildings to adopt planning dialogically related to—rather than confined by—their structures. This led to explorations in the separation of wall from structure, as in Mies van der Rohe's 1929 Barcelona Pavilion, or Corbusier's own Villa de Monzie of 1927 in Garches, France. However, in these and other *plan libre* buildings there was no intention of actually changing the layout of the walls. Rather, the composition was considered permanent: a freely conceived, though functionally fixed, conversation between plane and column. Meanwhile, factory and warehouse construction had pioneered the structural frame as a means to a real, functional flexibility, where machinery, fixtures, and partitions could be moved to suit evolving assembly line and storage requirements. In particular, the early twentieth-century buildings of Ernest Ransome and the wartime work of Detroit architect Albert Kahn had presented an unselfconscious deployment of reinforced concrete frames designed with nothing more than flexibility as their prime goal. Yet these buildings had an undeniable power, one born of their rigor, their logic, and their frankly expressed construction and structure. Mies, famously, used photographs of Albert Kahn's work as a backdrop for his spatial experimentation, and he was also influenced by the unintentional aesthetic power of images of factories and warehouses that were published, alongside emergency housing work such as Kahn and Howe's, throughout the war.

Sawyer and Howe were explicit in recommending that the Gallery adopt factory-like loft construction, allowing for rooms, exhibits, and functions to be changed as the times demanded. This was communicated to Kahn in letters from Sawyer and Howe, with Orr's office providing some very basic sketches of the options being proposed. Kahn responded from Rome with sketches of his own, struggling to make sense out of the fluid program by dividing various footprint sizes into functions—drafting rooms for the architecture department, exhibition spaces and offices for the Gallery—in a methodical, but not yet inspired, manner.

The connection to the original Swartout and Tracy building was a major concern. The Gallery was crudely truncated due to the sudden abandonment of construction in 1928. The courtyard in the block's center required acknowledgment, and for a time the team considered ways to connect it with Chapel Street. This involved pushing the new building's mass to the site's western edge, replacing a line of deteriorated shops, and finding a way to connect the two buildings, covering the blank wall of the original while allowing the courtyard to spill down to the street. Kahn, Howe, and Orr considered schemes for gardens, bridges, and stairs, all of which connected the new pavilion to the old and the courtyard to the street. However, these seemed contrived and unwieldy. Furthermore, Sawyer worried about continuity between the old and new galleries, as bridges would emphasize the separation between them.[9] To connect with the original building's upper-floor galleries, Sawyer proposed that the new galleries be arranged on a ramp, bringing patrons in at ground level and gradually moving them up to the height of the toplit painting galleries.

Schematic Design

Following Kahn's return from Rome in March 1951, he spent six weeks commuting between New Haven and Philadelphia with Anne Tyng. Together with Orr's staff, they first explored Sawyer's ramp idea, which was quickly rejected because of its vast scale.[10] In order to provide a comfortable slope, the length of a ramp up to the old sculpture galleries had to double back on itself, traversing the length of the new building's site twice. They followed with somewhat less grand schemes for simple concrete frames, with loft bays sized according to the assumptions of Sawyer's curators, ranging from a 20' square to 23' × 25'.[11] By the end of April 1951, Sawyer's ramp had been replaced by a grand staircase, expanded by matched seating to fill two structural bays that provided access to split levels of loft space, eventually leveling with the third-floor

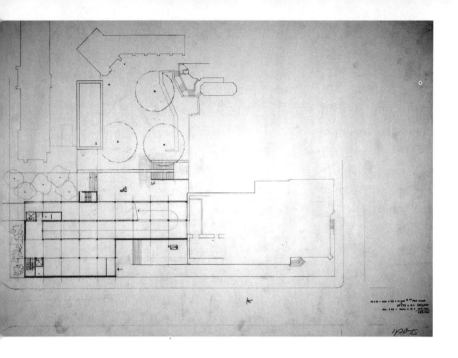

Plan of the early ramped scheme.
Office of Douglas Orr and Louis I. Kahn, Associated Architects, 1951

gallery in the original structure. Next to these stairs, Kahn wedged a core precisely into a single structural bay, an optimistic assumption as it provided room for only a single exit stair, a small passenger elevator, and one toilet room. Because of fire codes requiring two exits from a large space, this scheme placed a second stair outside the gallery block's north corner, stuck on to the exterior much as metal fire escapes were tacked onto the outside of factory structures.

54

Other variations on this scheme followed, as Kahn, Tyng, and Orr struggled to reconcile a pure structural grid with the increasingly refined requirements of circulation and servicing.[12] In hindsight, it is apparent that Kahn was operating under what he would come to see as a false pretense. In these early schemes, the structural grid is relentless, forcing some elements (e.g., the grand staircase) to expand to its dimension and others (e.g., the core) to contract beyond any reasonable size in order to fit within the grid. To borrow Kahn's later phrasing, the design's correct Order was yet to be found: the structural system was dominating all others, and there was no room for the orders of circulation and servicing to assert themselves. Nevertheless, under Howe's guidance, Kahn began to develop this loft structure within a carefully conceived container. The exterior began to emerge as a solid wall along Chapel Street, with a deep setback between the new building's mass and that of the old, and various

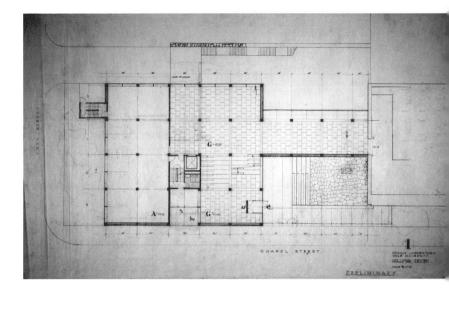

Plan of the staircase scheme.
Office of Douglas Orr and Louis I. Kahn, Associated Architects, April 1951

ideas—bridges, galleries, and sunken plazas—linking both galleries while connecting Chapel Street and the courtyard behind. This large-scale articulation between the new and old structures was an elaboration on the shadow or light gaps that Kahn first articulated in Weiss House. With vertical windows, Kahn suggested a careful expression of the old compositional system's limitations and the new loft scheme's promise; each was set at a respectful distance from the other and brought to logical conclusions at an intentionally neutral detail.

In May, Kahn and his collaborators developed a scheme that for the first time broke the square structural grid's tyranny and proved a crucial first step in the final scheme's rapid evolution. Realizing that the bay sizes proposed thus far were an imperfect interpretation of the "ideal" gallery or office size, they tried a double-bay scheme, 20' × 40', set parallel to Chapel Street. These bays were arranged in a rectangular grid, three bays deep by four bays long, providing a narrow footprint and a directional grain that emphasized the circulation connecting the new and old buildings. Kahn strengthened this initial gesture by organizing rooms and galleries on the upper floor en suite, with a corridor that ran the length of the new building and connected by a bridge on the third floor to the upper galleries of the Swartout and Tracy building. This bridge was to pass through a full-height atrium that provided an entry and a clear—

55

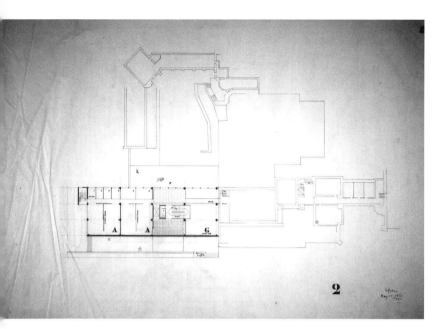

Plan of the double-bay scheme.
Office of Douglas Orr and Louis I. Kahn, Associated Architects, May 1951

though internal—connection to the garden courtyard behind. Offices and rooms that required compartmentalization were placed to the north of the main circulatory spine, while the larger gallery spaces were placed to its south, each occupying two parallel bays with clear, column-free floor space. Sliding between the middle bay's columns, overlapping the structural grid into the atrium, a grand staircase called out a core that now had a clear organization and order that was—tentatively—independent of the structural grid though still functionally too small. Nevertheless, the new bay configuration and the core's gentle slide out of the grid's confines opened up new possibilities. If the original scheme had been overdetermined by assumed bay sizes, this transitional scheme began to modify cautiously that structural order in light of programmatic and site constraints.

The August 1951 Scheme

By the end of August 1951 a scheme emerged that in its basic layout and intent would prove definitive, if open to major reinterpretation in its realization. In this iteration, which was approved by Yale in September 1951, the May scheme's double bay was maintained but was arranged in two large gallery lofts per floor composed of four parallel bays each. Between these, a narrower central precinct was wholly devoted to a service core and a grand scissor staircase, relocated from the May scheme's atrium, with operable partitions that could close off the circulation stack from the galleries. A third, smaller gallery provided the transition to the Swartout and Tracy building, with a narrow end piece containing a fire stair and, where levels met, access to the older painting galleries. The second fire stair was initially located at the Gallery's extreme northwest corner, similar to the early loft schemes, though in the alterations requested by Yale this was moved to become an integral part of the central service core at the plan's north edge.

While this basic arrangement is recognizable as the final scheme, its proposed concrete structure differs entirely from the structure as built. Given the restrictions on steel, concrete was the only remaining choice for the Gallery's structure, although even the steel reinforcement for its concrete needed to be cleared with the Department of Defense. Efficiency was, therefore, paramount. Kahn, Tyng, and Orr worked closely with Henry Pfisterer, a New Haven engineer, to develop a structure for the August design that would minimize reinforcing steel tonnage while expressing the building's loftlike rhythm and accommodating mobile partitions for changing exhibitions. The 20' × 40' bay size was, Pfisterer believed, best supported by a one-way pan joist system. In this type of structure, metal pans are laid across a formwork deck perpendicular to the location of major girders. When the concrete slab is poured, gaps between the metal pans form narrow joists, monolithic with the slab above and the girders to either side. The pans are then pulled away, and can be reused on floors higher in the construction sequence. Kahn recognized the potential in this system to integrate mechanical and lighting systems within the spaces between concrete joists. A lightweight ceiling system, hung below the rough concrete structure, could conceal ducts and, if shaped properly, act as an integral lighting fixture within the beam's depth, curved to reflect and diffuse light onto the walls and floors below. In the revised scheme of September 1951, conditioned air was to be distributed by a pair of main supply ducts on each floor, running north–south and concealed by a plaster ceiling between the core and the concrete girders. Smaller ducts were to drop from these main trunks, passing underneath the main girders and popping up into the void spaces between the concrete joists, diffusing air down the surface of curved ceiling panels to slots arranged along the joists' lower edges. Spotlights concealed within each reflector were to be tuned to illuminate particular works of art, while strip lighting along the edge of each reflector was to bounce diffused light off their surfaces, providing background illumination throughout the galleries.

57

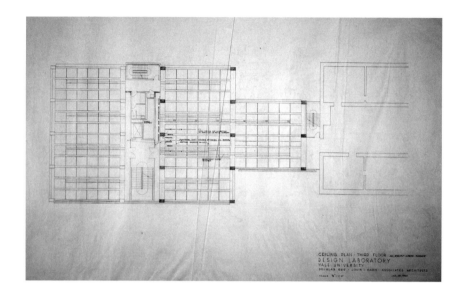

August 1951 scheme, plan (above) and section (opposite).
Office of Douglas Orr and Louis I. Kahn, Associated Architects, 1951

While efficient, this scheme did not quite rise to the level of Kahn's earlier writings about the integration of structure and services. On the one hand, the scheme was a remarkably well-integrated design from a functional standpoint. It took advantage of voids in an efficient structural system to distribute services and additionally found a way to use these voids as large-scale lighting reflectors. From the point of view of simply "harboring" the mechanical systems and thus avoiding their intrusion on the spaces below, this scheme would have worked quite well. But as Kahn would point out later, this came at the expense of the structure's legibility. Some measure of the building's structural grain might have been made legible by the reflectors' edge details, where the ceiling panels were held back just enough to permit a glimpse of the concrete joists' bottom surfaces. But the building's constructional and structural logics would have been concealed by the dropped ceiling panels, invisible to the casual patron and thus lost as an opportunity to convey the building's structural order. Speaking shortly after the Gallery's completion, Kahn critiqued himself for having even considered such a design:

> We should try more to devise structures which can harbor the
> mechanical needs of rooms and spaces and require no covering.

CHAPTER TWO

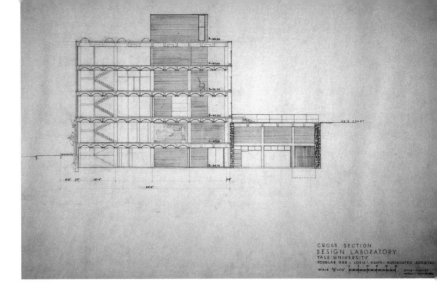

CROSS SECTION
DESIGN LABORATORY
YALE UNIVERSITY
DOUGLAS ORR · LOUIS I. KAHN · ASSOCIATED ARCHITECTS

> Ceilings with the structure furred in tend to erase the scale....
> It would follow that the pasting on of lighting and acoustical
> material, the burying of tortured unwanted ducts, conduits, and
> pipelines would become intolerable.[13]

Here we find Kahn accepting the challenge of his own "Monumentality," recognizing the need not only to solve the intricately knotted problems of support and service, but to reveal the ordering of each in relation to the other. After all, if ductwork or structure can be simply concealed, then it requires no integration and no
effort to understand its internal logic or its place in the constructed order of a building. The unkempt, unconsidered sprawl of ductwork and framing that would result
would be invisible, "buried" by architectural "covering." However, if—as Kahn suggested—the mechanical and structural systems were to be expressed or "harbored"
in architecturally significant elements, then their logic would be open to judgment.
Their designs would need to be considered not merely in terms of their performance,
but also in terms of their contribution to a larger architectural order. Revealing or
expressing these elements and systems *requires* that the architect fully consider them
in relation to the whole. In his preliminary scheme for Yale, Kahn must have eventually felt that its concealment of structure and ductwork was deadening to the space,

creating reasonably good galleries but being untrue to his developing vision of "perfecting" construction by fully working out its order and leaving nothing to be concealed. The August 1951 design would have failed to reveal its causes and purposes, and its ornament would have lain in its finish materials, not in the more challenging, cruder stuff of structure and air distribution.

Nevertheless, Kahn had fulfilled his obligations to Yale's program, schedule, and budget. Work proceeded on construction documents in Orr's New Haven office. Anne Tyng traveled back and forth to New Haven, coordinating efforts there with the main office's direction. The Philadelphia office continued to execute studies in support of Orr's efforts, including a cross section of 28 January 1952 that clearly shows the proposed floor configuration in detail—a simple concrete frame with curved ceiling reflectors hiding conduits and ductwork. Construction documents continued through March, with structural work expedited in order to apply for an allocation of reinforcing steel.[14] As drawings were completed, Yale planned to send drawing sets out for bids in late March, with construction expected to begin on 1 May.

The Tetrahedral Grid

From accounts by Kahn and Tyng and correspondence among the project's principles, it is apparent that in late March 1952, just as construction drawings were being finished, Kahn proposed a wholesale change in the gallery's floor structure based on experiments in space-frame geometry by Tyng. In 1951, she had prepared a conceptual design for an elementary school similar in appearance to the contemporary explorations of Octet-Truss frames by Buckminster Fuller. In 1950, Fuller had led a studio at North Carolina State University in the design of an Automatic Cotton Mill using a lightweight floor system made of short steel members arranged in a three-dimensional truss. Though unpublished until 1952, Fuller apparently presented a similar idea while lecturing at the University of Pennsylvania in 1949. Fuller would later take indirect credit for Yale's floor system, but Tyng's interest in space frames may have been sparked by her brief employment with Konrad Wachsmann, who had developed a Mobilar structural system in which mass-produced tubular members and connections created three-dimensional trusses with a basic tetrahedral module.[15]

Tyng's project for the elementary school adopted and expanded Wachsmann's and Fuller's principles, creating a lightweight flat structure triangulated in all three

Project for an elementary school. Anne Tyng, 1951

dimensions. While it remained wholly conceptual, without cladding or an environmental system, Tyng's design represented a sophisticated structural idea. Fuller's development adopted the logic of a two-dimensional truss, which separates top and bottom chords by diagonal bracing, building up a resisting moment from the compressed top chord and the tensioned bottom chord, while resisting internal shear between these chord forces by dividing the space between into triangular panels. Trusses had been used extensively for bridges since the nineteenth century, but Fuller's and Wachsmann's innovations expanded the triangular geometry of a typical truss into three dimensions. Now a two-dimensional floor system—not merely a one-dimensional road or walkway—could be supported using the same basic principle. The truss as Fuller developed it was essentially a lightweight sandwich of small steel members, with a solid plane at the top and a field of tetrahedral shapes below. Tyng's major improvement on this was to consider the method of the frame's support as integral to the truss itself. Whereas Fuller's Mill was supported by a conventional concrete core, Tyng's elementary school project created supports by continuing the truss geometry in a tapered "column" that used the same elements and tetrahedral geometry as the roof.

61

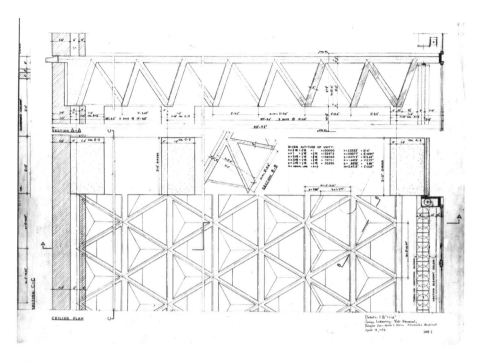

Reflected ceiling plan and section details. Office of Douglas Orr and Louis I. Kahn, Associated Architects, drawing by Anne Tyng, 1952

Tyng's project was exhibited in Philadelphia in late 1951 and early 1952. She was by then at work on the Gallery full time and apparently growing frustrated with the Gallery's conventional construction. As drawings were being finished, Tyng recalls asking Kahn, "Why bother to build [the Gallery] if you don't use an innovative structure?"[16] Kahn shortly thereafter found himself threading pencils through Tyng's model, noticing that the triangulated members' minimal dimensions offered clear routes for ductwork and cabling. At the same time, the geometry of the truss's bottom frame offered a provocative rhythm and pattern as a ceiling, repeating a statically efficient triangle across the sweep of the overhead plane. Changing the building's material to steel in a wartime economy was unthinkable, however. Kahn and Tyng thus proposed a tetrahedral grid made of concrete—essentially a layer of three-sided concrete pyramids, joined at their bottom corners and supporting an overhead slab at their top vertices. The concrete's solidity offered greater visual concealment for lights and ductwork as well as natural fireproofing. It also lent the ceiling a gravitas that light steel would have lacked, and Kahn assumed that the grid's porous nature would provide some measure of acoustic baffling. Kahn suggested this radical change just as the final construction drawings were about to be released, believing that the new structural idea would provide an expressive solution, while the approved concept would yield only efficiency.

CHAPTER TWO

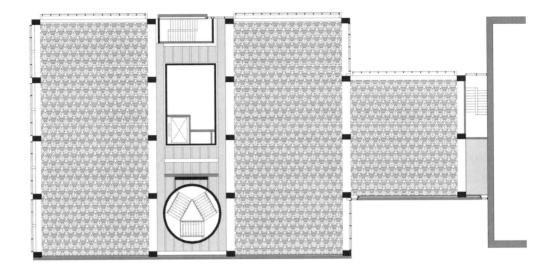

Reflected ceiling plan, final scheme

The suggestion came at a delicate moment. By February 1952, Yale had formally applied to the Defense Department for the quantity of reinforcing steel required by the August scheme. The 40'-0" bays shown in this version had already added significantly to the reinforcing requirement; even after careful engineering by Pfisterer, the required quantity had gone from 225 tons in May to 325 in September.[17] Extensive politicking on Yale's part had been needed to sell the project to the Federal Government.[18] Having conveniently renamed the project the "Yale Design Laboratory," Griswold emphasized the Department of Architecture's space requirements, noting in his application its importance for "training young men [*sic*]...engaged in important research projects in Hospital Planning and Administration [and] engaged in research projects for city and state planning commissions."[19] In the midst of this delicate process, Kahn's proposal nearly doubled the proposed reinforcing steel allocation, according to Pfisterer's calculations. After discussing the tetrahedral grid in early March with representatives from the George Macomber Company, a Boston contractor in the running for the job, Yale initially rejected the change.[20] Kahn, however, campaigned heavily for the revised system on the basis of its mechanical efficiency and its architectural effect. While the steel allocation was being approved on 18 March 1952, Kahn and Orr met with Charles H. Sawyer, again presenting the tetrahedral system along with a revised main

63

stair that now adopted the ceiling's triangular geometry. Housed in its early stages in a round brick silo, the new stair design provided three dramatic, angular flights between floors while adding a sculptural presence between gallery spaces.[21] The spatial impact of this silo and the powerful order of the new ceiling grid evidently swayed Sawyer, for he approved the revised structure's inclusion as an alternate in the bid documents, which as a result were not sent out until 21 March.[22] While this complicated the bid process, Sawyer quickly became a staunch advocate for the tetrahedral grid, appreciating both its aesthetic potential and its ability to provide truly flexible planning on each floor. However, he found himself defending it to a skeptical administration as initial costs suggested that it might represent a $50,000 increase over the more conventional beam-and-slab system. Writing to Kahn in mid-April, Sawyer asked for help in explaining the system's perceived advantages:

> I have promised the Treasurer that I would give him a written statement in four-letter words as to why the revised ceiling construction was worth the additional cost and the structural complications involved from our standpoint.... The three reasons that have occurred to me are:
>
> a) The lighter construction giving a greater sense of space which we need in the Gallery spaces because of the low ceiling heights.
> b) The better acoustical properties inherent in the nature of the construction itself....
> c) Better distribution of the general illumination without any diminishment of the opportunities for specific illumination....
>
> I think we can resolve the honest doubts if we have a clear statement of the facts. On the other hand...the building will simply not afford any further tangents or major experiments no matter how potentially valuable they might seem to be. We have spent two months which ought to have been available for careful and reasonable interior planning on these structural problems....[23]

Macomber provided a bid on 29 April, including the tetrahedral ceiling's cost and the round stair tower. While the bid was over budget, it was within a few percent of the target cost, and with additional savings in the curtain wall the construction cost was reduced to a mutually acceptable figure of about $1.25 million.[24] Macomber had large stockpiles of reinforcing steel on hand, obviating any delay in the requisitioning process and easing the possible increase in steel tonnage, if not reducing its price. The floor system was accepted and included in Macomber's contract, which was formally awarded on 26 May 1952.[25]

While cost was a primary consideration, the new floor system presented two additional challenges for Pfisterer and Macomber: how would the floor system's shapes be cast and how would they carry the Gallery's floor loads? These were no small problems. The efficiency and economics of space-frame structures had relied on their assembly out of mass-produced metal elements. While experiments by Pier Luigi Nervi had by this time successfully introduced triangulation into concrete shell structures, these patterns were two-dimensional, analogous to simple beams and slabs. Pfisterer was thus faced with an engineering problem of daunting proportions, as the tetrahedrons presented a fully three-dimensional structure in concrete. Space frames and trusses in an era of manual calculation could only be analyzed by assessing each strut and joint as discrete linear elements in order to find the axial force within them, and even this method required extensive mathematical effort. What Kahn and Tyng had proposed was not, however, a system of discrete elements with identifiable stresses in tension or compression. Rather, the faces of each concrete tetrahedron were actually concrete diaphragms capable of tension, compression, shear, and bending in multiple directions. The integral slab atop these pyramidal shapes would sit on them as on a bed of nails, with literally hundreds of points of connection. While Pfisterer could estimate the gross scale stresses in the system, how floor loads would actually be transferred from slab to tetrahedron, and thence throughout the network of concrete diaphragms and steel reinforcing, was far beyond his—or any other engineer's—abilities in 1952.

The system's basic engineering was solved in meetings and discussions as the tetrahedral idea took shape in March and April 1952. Pfisterer had warned Kahn and Orr of the difficulties in calculating the transfer of loads into the system, and Kahn had sought the assistance of William Gravell, an eminent Philadelphia engineer and longtime adviser. Gravell, then in ill health, recommended junior engineers to Kahn's office to discuss the system. Nicholas Gianopulos and Thomas J. Leidigh, both of whom would go on to work with Kahn in the firm of Keast & Hood for more than twenty years, met with Kahn and Tyng in April 1952. Gianopulos recalls seeing the mechanical layout for the first time at this meeting; the layout had not changed substantially from the system woven through the August beam-and-slab scheme.[26] Its major

65

supply ducts still ran north–south from the mechanical space on each floor, with minor ducting running exclusively east–west, passing through sleeves in the major girders and then passing between the concrete tetrahedrons' sloped surfaces. Cabling for light fixtures within the voids of the slab likewise ran only east–west. While the tetrahedral slab offered clear runs in three directions, the mechanical and electrical systems were only using one. The difficulties in calculating the load transfer would be eliminated, Gianopulos realized, if the tetrahedrons' faces in the east–west plane were connected to one another, essentially creating long, inclined beams that would connect continuously with the slab above instead of at discrete points. This would allow them to be calculated as simple beams and slabs, a shortcut to understanding the system's overall performance. At the same time, ducts would have a natural path alongside the inclined joists, and the ceiling pattern below would remain unchanged. The only drawback—other than the obvious compromise of the "pure" space-frame system—was that the additional triangular portions of concrete necessary to transform the pyramids' faces into continuous joists would add weight to the system.

Pfisterer agreed with Gianopulos's suggestion. Writing to Kahn, Orr, and Sawyer on 8 April, he described the serious problems with the original model—the pure space frame—and added his thoughts on the suggested reconfiguration. Pfisterer's best guess had been that the space frame as originally conceived would act very much as a beam-and-slab system anyway, because of the 20' × 40' column bay. The east–west chords would, in his view, have become primary members no matter how they were connected to the rest of the system. Likewise, he viewed the original proposal as an essentially steel scheme because of the extraordinary reinforcement it required. "The floor construction," he wrote, "ends up as *fireproofed steel* rather than *reinforced concrete*." He proposed, instead, essentially what Gianopulos recalled:

> a modification which would overcome some of the above objections— provide for construction as reinforced concrete, express the structural skeleton more significantly, and provide a ceiling pattern retaining the tetrahedron form with alternate openings.

> One of the ribs is made a continuous sloping joist 4 inches wide spanning between girders. Two sides required to complete tetrahedron are made 2½ inches thick. Clearance for duct passage is provided parallel to main joists only. Girders are expressed with solid soffit.[27]

Pfisterer has never been properly credited for suggesting that the concrete plates' dimensions be varied, which would have accurately represented the revised slab's structural hierarchy. This arrangement was, in fact, shown in the definitive drawing of the scheme by Tyng on 18 April, priced by Macomber, and accepted by Yale. Subsequently, however, the combined need for sufficiently fireproofing the reinforcing in all bottom chords and Kahn's interest in maintaining the ambiguity of the ceiling's directionality led him to standardize the widths of all truss members. Thus, the floor system's actual performance, which is indeed similar to a one-way joist system, would be concealed by the appearance of the nondirectional triangular grid on the ceiling.

Macomber was responsible for one final twist in the structural design, which had been at least partly anticipated by Pfisterer. While the joist construction eased the structural calculation considerably, it did not alleviate the difficulties of constructing such an intricate geometry in liquid concrete. Formwork for the tetrahedrons' "walls"— their joists and smaller inclined triangles—had to be built with both inside and outside surfaces, and it became quickly apparent that the upper panels forming the tetrahedrons would be stranded once the slab was poured. For economic reasons, this custom formwork had to be reusable, and Macomber suggested that each floor slab be poured only after its joists had cured. The upper formwork could then be lifted up while the bottom formwork could be pulled down. Permanent acoustic paneling could be laid flush with the top edge of the resulting structure, and the top slab could then be poured with robust connections created by dowels and rebar cast into the raw tetrahedral grid. Seen this way, the floor system's actual logic is revealing. It consists of three components: long joists inclined at about 20°; folded triangular "struts" on which these joists lean and which hold the bottom chord of each joist in place; and a slab on top of this system. Pfisterer and others would remain critical of the structure's efficiency. However, the resulting system was Kahn's first major step toward finding an architectural order for the combined challenges of structure and mechanical elements, a "hollow stone" that for all its contradictions nevertheless revealed its systematically formed hollows to the spaces below.

Pfisterer wrote to New Haven's Building Department in May informing them of Yale's intent to construct the tetrahedral grid, describing it in terms that revealed its actual structural performance and architectural intent:

> A special type of cast-in-place concrete joist floor system involving
> the use of deep inclined primary ribs with auxiliary bridging

diaphragms has been developed to provide for desired architectural, lighting, and acoustic effects.

This floor system cannot be designed and constructed on the basis of complete conformance of the New Haven Building Code. To serve as a basis for final approval by your department, we propose to construct a sample panel to determine the adequacy of the construction by test....[28]

While it has been claimed that New Haven balked at the original, pure space frame and thus forced the change to a hybrid structure, the Building Department was, in fact, surprisingly supportive.[29] They acknowledged that the structure was technically in violation of the code, but admitted that this was due more to the code's failure to keep up with "generally accepted regulations covering beam and slab construction."[30] Rather than force the approval process through the city's Board of Examiners, the Building Department encouraged Pfisterer to construct a proposed test panel. Macomber scheduled the test for late August, by which time the site would be fully cleared, and the resulting—successful—test drew attention not only from the local community, but also from a number of architectural journals.

Architectural Forum devoted two pages in its November 1952 issue to the design and included a picture of the test being carried out, perhaps not coincidentally adjacent to the spread on Fuller's Octet Truss.[31] Whatever its structural quirks, the Gallery's triangulated ceiling generated immediate enthusiasm even prior to its construction, challenging not only orthodox assumptions about rectilinear composition, but also the propriety of creating space and form out of mechanical and environmental needs. "Even return air ductwork is observable," *Progressive Architecture* remarked on the building's completion, a heresy that presaged two decades of Kahn's work to find the proper expression for this usually ignored aspect of building engineering.[32]

Detailing and Construction

If the spatial, structural, and mechanical integration in the Gallery's ceilings was a blend of Fuller's and Tyng's influences, the building's execution in poured concrete practically shouted its Corbusian precedents, particularly in the sculptural main staircase. Kahn originally proposed building the triangular staircase in brick but changed it during the summer of 1952 to raw concrete. The handling of this spatially important volume and other nearby core elements borrowed directly the expressed *béton brut*—literally, "rough concrete"—that Kahn had seen used in the construction of Corbusier's Unité d'habitation at Marseilles. To realize the stair silo's fairly tight radius, Kahn and Orr specified vertical board forms, each only a few inches wide, that could break down the circular plan into numerous tiny facets. As the concrete was poured, however, these vertical boards required framing to hold them in place and to prevent their bowing out under the wet concrete's hydrostatic pressure. Typically, these problems are solved by connecting the two skins of formwork, letting the outward pressure of the concrete on one side pull against the pressure on the other side by using steel wires that pass through the poured wall. These wires are clamped against an outside layer of timber bracing by steel cones, which grip the wires more tightly as the formwork is wedged against them. Because the cones need to penetrate the formwork, the resulting surface in a concrete wall is left with circular voids, usually about 1" in diameter, where the cones were during the pour. When concrete walls are covered with plaster, stone, or brick, these marks are hidden, as are the rough edges, where concrete seeps between boards and leaves projections, and the concrete's texture itself, which takes on the boards' patterns. However, drawing on Corbusier's acceptance of poured concrete's raw appearance at the Unité, Kahn wholeheartedly accepted the marks, imperfections, and roughness of the material in the stair silo and the exposed beams and girders at Yale. These records of "how it was done" became part of a dialogue, as at Marseilles, between the coarse and the honed. The concrete's appearance drew on Kahn's belief that the joint—in this case, that which was left between pieces of wooden forms—could become the "basis of ornament," telling a more interesting story than the contrivances of neogothic detail or the more Miesian refinement of abstract prisms of metal and glass.

69

It is often pointed out that Kahn's almost obsessive use of concrete belied his modernist side, favoring an archaic atmosphere over technological statement. However, this assertion was confounded in the Yale project by two factors. First, Kahn's use of concrete as a resolutely technological material added a mathematical precision to the Gallery's spaces that was utterly modern in conception despite its rough texture and larger scale. Second, in all of Kahn's concrete buildings the dialogue between coarse, poured structural material and honed, polished attachments to it meant that his statements in raw, unfinished concrete were always met by a balance of extraordinarily refined, lightweight work in metal, glass, and timber. If steel was not a legitimate structural material for Kahn because of its lack of gravitas, it was certainly capable of adding a delicate skin or of inserting a precise railing or light fixture that would express the provocative ambiguity of mass and delicacy.

At Yale, Kahn used metal for three major elements—the curtain walls, the service zone's ceilings, and the staircase handrails. These elements, like most metalwork in Kahn's designs, were set against raw concrete elements or attached to them in a way that highlighted distinctions in material, texture, and finish. Tyng recalls that Kahn developed his thinking about shadow and light gaps here, ideas that had begun with the Weiss House in emphasizing the separation between elements made of different materials or with different processes. Connections between steel handrails and concrete stairs, for example, were left with bolts and fixings completely exposed so that there would be no confusion about which material was doing the heavy work and which was there for human comfort. Likewise, the steel and glass curtain wall, though not as customized as Kahn would have liked, was consistently pulled back in one direction or another so that the building's columns could be visible to the outside—sheathed, admittedly, in blue stone, but nonetheless clearly stated. On the west façade, the curtain wall was nestled in among the five main columns, visually emphasizing the structural grid on that side. On the north façade, though, the broad stretches of curtain wall revealed the long dimensions of each bay, while the service zone was clad in solid brick, explaining the functional and spatial ordering of the interior and, again, resolutely demonstrating an architectural blend of timeless atmosphere with modern technology.

This, of course, leaves the south façade to be explained. Undoubtedly the Gallery's most famous—and notorious—elevation, this long, unbroken rectangle of brick and stone clearly explains the structure's horizontal stratification beyond. Stringcourses of blue stone at each floor level candidly tell us that. But the position of the vertical columns behind is left unspoken, hardly characteristic of Kahn's desire to tell us frankly about all aspects of the building's construction and structure. How can this be reconciled with Kahn's stated interest in revelation? There are clues in the elevation's configuration that suggest a twofold explanation. On a strictly functional level, the south façade's execution in solid brick keeps out direct sunlight that could damage fragile artworks. New Haven's street grid is actually nearly 45° off true cardinal directions, and the "south" façade actually faces southwest. The southeast façade is generally in the Swartout and Tracy block's shadow, but the solid façade along Chapel Street dispenses with troublesome south light, while the more open façades on the northeast and northwest elevations allow indirect daylight when desired.

But this does not fully explain why the brick wall has only horizontal divisions. Surely it could still let us know, as does the north elevation, where the structural and service bays are located. If one imagines the façade composed like this, however, a problem emerges. The galleries' mechanical logic is this: two wings are served by a central core through which all vertical service elements pass. A long section of the building shows a treelike servicing strategy with a main central trunk and minor horizontal branches, all of which thread through a minutely detailed structural frame. Were this to be expressed on the south elevation, we would get an overwhelming sense of the newer building's centrality and its dense central bay. Instead, the Swartout and Tracy building farther east on Chapel Street gives an impression of structural rhythm, of movement along the galleries' axis.

If there is a "center" to the site, it is right where it was in the original 1927 scheme: in the middle of the block, where Kahn located the wing's new entry. The brick wall is, therefore, essentially a graphic plane, seeking to carry on the original building's horizontal stretch without asserting the contradictory logic inside. Kahn reconciled these competing desires to express and conceal on the northwest and entry elevations, where the brick wall's depth is clearly shown, with a distinct shadowgap between it and the exposed column. The brick façade, this detail tells us, is exactly that—an applied façade. Once we've seen this, it is apparent that the wall purposefully conceals the new gallery's self-contained logic. That story is more fully told on the north façade, where the courtyard's focus is exclusively on the new building, which can thus be clearly expressed without interrupting the old building's existing logic. The brick wall is a balance between the desire to produce an ideal, logical element and the realities of the circumstances in which the building finds itself, a compromise that only reads as "pure" in its acknowledgment of the site's contingencies of mass, elevation, and orientation.

Macomber built the Gallery in a burst of activity between June 1952, when excavation commenced, and the building's dedication in November 1953, an astonishing accomplishment considering the complexity of the concrete floor system. While the tetrahedral grid proved to be a challenge, the construction of the structural test panel in August 1952 allowed Macomber to experiment with steel formwork, and the typical module's repetition allowed them to refine and perfect the placement of concrete within the forms' tight confines. Presaging a common occurrence on later projects, Macomber was allowed to experiment on the tetrahedral grid's first pour, which took place in early October 1952.[33] Concrete in this pour, which formed the basement's

Construction views of the tetrahedral floor grid

ceiling, had a rough, mottled appearance that was corrected by altering the placement technique of the upper floors, showing that the iterative process of construction allowed for considerable refinement in technique as the building progressed.
Concrete is a notoriously fickle material, sensitive to minute changes in temperature,
humidity, and the conditions of its forms. Its color, texture, and surface can change
radically with only a small variation in the mix—be it in the coloring, aggregate,
or sand. Likewise, the smoothness of the forms and the friction between the setting
concrete and the formwork walls must be carefully controlled. Forms are often oiled
to permit easy removal; oil, however, can discolor the concrete surface or, if applied
improperly, cause poorly bonded pieces of the set concrete's matrix to come loose as
the forms are pried away. Like the layout of exposed ducts, concrete demands care on
the part of the contractor if it is to be presented as an architectural finish. Kahn's confidence in the material would grow to the point where the Salk and Kimbell buildings
displayed large swaths of unfinished concrete fresh from the forms, but here Kahn
relied on the formwork marks and the ceiling grid's triangular voids to break up distinctions in color and texture.

While the concrete placement proceeded smoothly, problems developed with the
mechanical system's integration. The tetrahedral grid allowed space between its

Detail view of the ceiling showing ducts,
conduits, and the acoustic liner

joists and triangular diaphragms for small round ductwork. However, in order to
get air to these small ducts from the mechanical spaces in the core, a connection to
the main distribution trunks was necessary. These ran along the core's face, on the
opposite side of exposed concrete girders from the triangular ceiling grid. In the
preliminary scheme, this connection had been handled by introducing false ceilings below the girders. Kahn's desire to express the concrete, however, had eliminated all hung ceilings in the galleries and made these girders key visual elements
in separating the grid from the metal mesh ceilings in the core. The only way to get
air from one side of these girders to the other was to go through the concrete itself.
Such penetrations are not as great a structural problem as they might appear. The
central portion of any simply loaded girder, whether it be the web of a steel shape or
the middle of a concrete section, does not perform the work of the outer edges. Thus,
it is usually possible to take away material toward the center of such structural elements, and in fact, this is the very logic that allows the Vierendeel truss, which Kahn
had explored in conjunction with the 1944 Parasol House, to work. On that earlier
project, Kahn explored a rudimentary Vierendeel—a top and bottom chord separated
by vertical members with robust connections. To call the girders at Yale Vierendeel
trusses is, perhaps, a bit too charitable, yet this is exactly how the mechanical system is distributed: it punches through the center of the main girders to run between

73

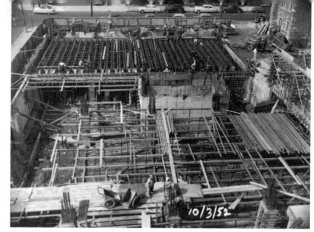

Left: View of the main concrete girder during renovation showing the location of the embedded ducts
Right: Construction of the first-floor slab

the sloped joists and the ceiling grid's folded tetrahedrons. Small ducts branch off
from the main trunking, passing through sheet-metal cylinders cast into the girder's
depth and then running east–west through the ceiling's interstices. The containment
of these ducts within the structure and the need to coordinate the sheet-metal workers
with formwork crews and concrete pours proved problematic. The sheet-metal workers, unaccustomed to working on so raw a site so early in the construction process,
held up progress considerably during the first six pours.[34]

From this point forward, though, the concrete work proceeded without incident, each
floor taking about eight weeks to have its formwork placed, its mechanical systems
installed, and its concrete poured and cured to working strength. Work on each floor
was staged with the west half typically being formed first. Masons and glaziers followed the concrete's progress, working two months behind the concrete pours to install
the building's skin, all of which was completed by March 1953.

Because of limitations in manufacture, the Gallery's curtain walls and windows were
relatively small, and their fine grain across the elevations was highlighted by careful attention to the steel subframes' detailing. Each panel was set atop a horizontal
steel angle. Vertical mullions within window panels were run between these, so that

74

View of construction from the west

the windows' major directionality was horizontal, mimicking the stringcourses on the south elevation, but with a clearly expressed vertical cross grain set back slightly from the horizontals, clearly announcing its place in the built order. Distinctions between floors were further emphasized by the layout of the cladding panels themselves. Each was composed of three glass panes, two vertically oriented at floor level and a clerestory panel that runs the panel's full width. The result is, again, that each floor level is clearly distinguished on the elevation.[35]

75

If the exterior was designed to reveal the loft structure's horizontal logic and its ambiguous relationship to the original building, work on the interior focused on emphasizing the concrete frames and the floors' heavy, load-bearing nature. Developed to contrast with the concrete structure, gallery display walls, office partitions, and stair rails again emphasized, through lightweight material and detailing, the "distinction between things" that Tyng noted. Of particular interest were the display walls, designed to attach to the floor and ceiling beams by means of spring-loaded poles. These 5'-0"-wide pogo panels were conceived by George Howe, and they took advantage of the galleries' totally free space by attaching anywhere there were solid floor and ceiling surfaces. This enabled exhibits to be changed rapidly and allowed designers to tailor the Gallery's spaces to diverse shows and displays. Elsewhere, on floors with

View of the completed interior showing the pogo panel display walls

administrative areas, simple, low file cabinets partitioned open office spaces, while classrooms and private offices relied on full-height gypsum board or masonry partitions, depending on how permanent the enclosure was likely to be. Even these were carefully detailed; plaster walls were given deep shadowgaps at the floor and ceiling lines to demonstrate their infill nature, and the masonry walls were built with a custom-sized brick, whose square proportions suggested that they did not have the traditional bearing function of a standard, rectangular brick.

Perhaps the most dramatic contrast to the heavy concrete structure was the main triangular staircase, which Kahn and Tyng redesigned several times during construction. The final scheme employed poured concrete stringers and landings, monolithic with the surrounding silo. Precast black terrazzo steps were then placed atop these structural members, leaving the concrete supports' undersides exposed. The stair's handrail was detailed in stainless-steel pipe, with balustrades made of woven metal mesh, a conveyer belt fabric discovered by Tyng late in the process. The resulting composition is iconic, providing a clear history of the stair's construction by segregating materials spatially according to their chronology. The rough concrete stringers are visible only from below, while the handrail is very obviously bolted onto the terrazzo treads, the most condensed statement yet of a material hierarchy in Kahn's work.

CHAPTER TWO

View of the main staircase

Opening and Reception

> I believe I have done a complete architectural job....
> Everything here marches together for the solution.
> —Louis I. Kahn

The Gallery opened in early November 1953, gaining great attention from both the Yale community and the architectural press. Locally, the building was recognized as the first major modernist statement on a campus that would soon become synonymous with architectural innovation. The flexible, compact gallery spaces were reviewed as worthy successors to the formal but functionally dated galleries of the Swartout and Tracy building, and the new structure averaged nearly four hundred visitors a day during its first month.[36] Speaking at the formal dedication, the chairman of the building's donor committee added that the Gallery represented "an expression of the wholesome balance between respect for tradition and willingness to pioneer," a neat summary of the architectural press's reaction to follow.[37]

The Gallery was a major story in the development of a scientifically literate, though monumentally inclined, architectural approach in postwar America. In late 1953,

Frederick Gutheim, critic for the *International Herald Tribune*, led the analysis of the building's bold pronouncements and subtle ambiguities, declaring the Gallery to be "the outstanding academic building produced by the modern movement."[38] Anticipating Kahn's later musings, Gutheim noted that, despite the technical conception of the building's ceiling, it was nevertheless part of a humanely conceived design:

> Fully mechanized, it is not mechanical. One of the highest functions
> of modern building design is to liberate technology, to enlarge its
> possible applications. When that is done, a high technology of itself
> does not destroy human values or human scale. The demonstration
> at Yale, however, argues that to allow men [*sic*] to make the most of
> their technology art must control and qualify.

> Rarely is a building of such technical interest realized with such
> refinement. Here structure is so integral with architecture it has
> acquired the value of ornament.[39]

Other critics offered a more balanced assessment. *Progressive Architecture* featured the Gallery in May 1954 and invited prominent deans of architecture programs to assess the building via letter.[40] The Gallery received high praise from most. G. Holmes Perkins, the University of Pennsylvania's dean of fine arts, who was soon to hire Kahn, echoed Gutheim, saying that "here art is in control of the technologies of building." The ceiling he described as a "superb unifier of space as well as an efficient machine."[41] Robert McLaughlin, then director of Princeton's School of Architecture, was more critical, however, noting that while the space's flexibility was an inherent good, the "noble discipline" of Kahn's honest deployment of materials and structural systems went too far. "I find it hard to be noble for so long," he opined, believing that the ruggedness of the materials in particular would wear thin for the occupants over time.

Oddly, C. Clark Macomber, president of Macomber Builders, sounded the most negative note in *Progressive Architecture*'s coverage. While acknowledging that the Gallery's construction was "a privilege given to few builders," Macomber attributed much of the building's success to Douglas Orr's "tempering" of Kahn's "forward looking and experimental theories." Macomber took direct issue with the tetrahedral ceiling's complexity, citing the complex formwork required and noting that, while the construction ended up being "practical and economical...these spans and wide open spaces may be obtained with any standard construction." Furthermore, Macomber believed that Kahn's use of vertical board formwork on columns and stairs "recall[ed] methods of the past but do[es] not provide the functional boldness or sincerity of structure developed by the normal large sheet of plywood or metal form." Board forms belonged, he felt, to "the field of special veneers rather than honest fundamental expressions of structural elements used for finish surfaces."[42]

Henry Pfisterer expressed similar sentiments regarding the ceiling structure. As the scheme was being developed, he and Kahn had discussed the tetrahedral grid with Vernon Read of *Architectural Forum*, who drafted an article for their review. Read's comments incensed Kahn, who found the article "dull...confused [and] negative."[43] In particular, Kahn was troubled by the fact that Read, quoting Pfisterer, remarked that the slab was 60 percent *heavier* than a conventional beam-and-slab system.[44] Kahn and Sawyer delayed publication of this article on the design's progress until November 1952, and while Read reported honestly on the weight issue, he also noted the slab's unique appearance and suggested that it would be "an instructive challenge to budding architects studying beneath it."[45] Following the Gallery's completion, however, Pfisterer wrote a complete description of the floor system that was no less damning. While hoping that Kahn, in particular, would "not find it too negative," his conclusion was that "the depth–weight ratio is high and...forming and placing costs are very high." Pfisterer did, however, acknowledge that "the structure is stimulatingly controversial and will serve to portray the possibilities and limitations of *in situ* concrete to future Architects from Yale."[46] In other words, the floor system was, in Pfisterer's view, largely architectural, not structural, a line of comment that Kahn's future engineering collaborators would repeat to great effect. Such assessments did not dampen enthusiasm for the structural concept, which was featured again in a special issue of *Progressive Architecture* in June 1954, along with an article on "stereo-structures" by Felix Candela and structurally advanced work by Mies van der Rohe and others.[47]

Such critical apologia for the floor system's questionable efficiency stemmed in part from the growing sense that postwar construction in Europe and the United States suggested a coming together of contemporary technique and timeless architectural principles, as Kahn himself had predicted in his 1944 "Monumentality" essay. The Gallery's tetrahedral grid in concrete, with masonry and glass wrapping, set out in an axially disposed floor, but with an asymmetrical entry seemed to be a statement of the

View of the main entrance

postwar vacillation between modernism's claims on technical efficiency and continuity with tradition. Vincent Scully, Kahn's contemporary at Yale, wrote in 1954 on this
reemergence of "archetype and order" in American architecture. Scully's argument
focused on Philip Johnson and Paul Rudolph and their reintroduction of "vaults and
domes" into the discourse of modernism, but the Yale Art Gallery came in for particular mention, being "symptomatic of the new direction in design."[48] Scully saw in its
dialogues between the technically progressive and the archaic a "search for the integral, complete and generalized form"; this search was part of the overall movement
"toward order and clarity in design...a release from many of the curious academ-
icisms and cliches of the recent past."[49] No one reading this could mistake Scully's
target. His was a careful shot fired over the bow of the late International Style, whose
precepts of forced asymmetry, volumetric expression at the expense of mass, and the
eschewing of all things ornamental had begun to be rejected even by its founders. For
Scully, Kahn was one of the first to apply the "abstract anti-romantic classic order"
to the sudden advancements in building technology after World War II, suggesting
a rapprochement of modernism's empiricist, technical interest with its rationalist,
Beaux-Arts heritage, whether fully disinherited or not. The heavy though porous
slab had value not only as a technical achievement, however dubious, but also as an

View from the west

evocative one, a balance between technologies and traditions that would continue to be a fundamental precept in Kahn's work.

Reyner Banham, then a young critic for *Architectural Review* in Britain, offered a parallel, though more technically inclined, interpretation of the Gallery in his 1955 essay "The New Brutalism."[50] Banham's rise as one of Britain's top architectural critics and provocateurs would turn, in part, on his becoming Kahn's most astute critic. For Banham, the "formal legibility" of the Gallery's plan could very well have been classical in nature. He noted that the appearance of Kahn's design occurred only four years after Rudolf Wittkower's seminal book, *Architectural Principles in the Age of Humanism*, which, in Banham's words, laid out an architectural theory "in which function and form were significantly linked by the objective laws governing the cosmos."[51] Such an obvious rationalist agenda and its growing influence in Britain and the United States certainly permitted deviance from the International Style's law of asymmetry. Whether Kahn was directly influenced by Wittkower's book is open to debate, though it certainly would have been a topic of discussion among architects at the Academy in Rome in 1951.

For Banham, however, the Yale scheme's genius was that its axiality, symmetry, and formal order were only parts of the Gallery's importance. Even these statements of planometric and formal legibility were, Banham noted, compromised by the off-center entry and by the complete veiling by the south wall of the symmetrical layout. Rather, Banham pegged Kahn's work, as well as contemporary work by Alison and Peter Smithson, as part of the New Brutalism, a movement that stressed the unselfconscious acceptance of the brute facts of construction as inherently important to a building's aesthetic. This phraseology was in part polemical. The image of a brutal building suggested the mechanistic piling on of system and material without regard to its visual import, but the term also echoed the French phrases *art brut*, which championed an anticompositional primitivism, and Corbusier's *béton brut*, rough concrete with its wooden form marks left exposed. For Banham, Brutalism was really another name for what the *Review* had, a decade before, termed the "New Empiricism," a move away from the latent reliance on composition in modernist designs toward an expression of techniques, requirements, and structure. While resisting any formula, Banham claimed that Brutalism as generally understood relied on three key factors for its aesthetic impact: the aforementioned "formal legibility," a clear expression of structure, and "a valuation of materials for their inherent qualities 'as found.'" In the movement's ultimate monument, Alison and Peter Smithson's Hunstanton School, this resulted in intentional "ineloquence" and "underdesigning" to generate the work's aesthetic. Banham found these somewhat dubious qualities lacking in Kahn's architecture, which was both eloquent and heavily "designed," but he recognized that the Gallery was "uncompromisingly frank about its materials...inconceivable apart from its boldly exhibited structural method...[and] formal in the disposition of its main elements."[52] Perhaps more importantly, Banham identified a fourth brutalist characteristic that the Yale Gallery exhibited in no small measure: "bloody-mindedness," a relentlessness in the detailing and expression of the building down to its smallest components.

Scully and Banham's related but ultimately divergent criticisms marked Kahn's preliminary achievement in reconciling rationalist and empiricist modes of architectural design. Both acknowledged the power of the building's "image," its immediate apprehension in the mind's eye or, in Wittkower's words, a "man-created harmony" as a "visible echo of a celestial and universally valid harmony." On the other hand, Banham's linking of the Gallery to the Smithsons and their disciplined acceptance of materials and components "as found" suggested an opposite, worldly empiricism to the lofty formality of Scully's intimations of transcendental order. In this light, the development of the Gallery's plan can be interpreted as a weaving together of these two processes. Kahn's early struggles with the prematurely imposed bay sizes, the difficulties of the core, and the desire to relate to the existing building all suggest the building up of a balance between the Gallery's own internal logic and the complexity of the site surrounding it. In August 1951, the first major step toward asserting a singular image that nonetheless solved problems of function and context was taken, and its "imageability," that is, its ruthless logic and legible planning, then established itself as a nearly incontrovertible asset. The execution of this rigorously conceived scheme remained open to debate, however, and the weak rationale for the beam-and-slab construction—its convenience given the controls on steel—did not survive Kahn and Tyng's continuing scrutiny. When a structural system presented itself as an ordering device equal to the overall plan's clarity, even its questionable efficiency was less important than its ability to continue the building's visual and spatial hierarchy down to the smallest scale. From that point on, Kahn and Tyng's process was purely rationalist, as details and elements, in particular the main staircase, were revised or reconsidered based on their expression of the overall order. Among its many powerful connotations, surely one of the primary sensations in the Gallery is the appropriateness of the basic gestures to the site and the program, and of the parallel "bloody-minded" consideration of even the minutest details in relation to the whole. Rational and empirical, inductive and deductive, balanced and woven together, the Yale Art Gallery's construction and performance and their intertwined expression mark this building—as much as its dubious archaic qualities, its formalist planning, or its abstract expression—as Kahn's first major statement of belief in an architecture of orders and of Order.

83

Postscript: City Tower

The Yale Art Gallery was by far Kahn's most important work at the time of its completion, and it would define the major themes of his later career. It also signaled two important transitions. The first was an unhappy one. Yale took to the new building enthusiastically but with some hesitation about the floors' total flexibility. While the Department of Architecture settled into its temporary quarters on the top floor, the exhibition spaces and their pogo panels proved challenging for displays of large artworks and sculpture. George Howe's declining health led him to resign as department chair in 1953, shortly before his death in 1955. Howe offered the position to Kahn, who refused it, and the chairmanship instead passed to Paul Schweiker for a brief and troubled two years.[53] However, the departure of Schweiker and Charles H. Sawyer in 1958 brought in new administrative figures, in particular Paul Rudolph and Gibson Danes. Their indifference to the previous regime nudged Kahn out of the Department of Architecture's inner circle. While retaining his connections at Yale, Kahn accepted temporary positions beginning in 1955 with the Massachusetts Institute of Technology and the University of Pennsylvania, where G. Holmes Perkins recognized the potential for integrating Kahn's practice and teaching. Meanwhile, the Gallery suffered a major renovation under Rudolph's direction, in which the pogo panels were discarded and permanent plasterboard display walls installed even as Kahn was teaching one of his last studios in New Haven in spring 1958. Kahn wrote to President Griswold, asking for the opportunity to meet and explain why these new panels were at such odds with the space's conception, but Griswold dismissed his "picayune" comments and pointed out that the building had long since ceased to be Kahn's.[54]

Kahn and Tyng's continuing interest in the tetrahedral grid's possibilities, however, made two final, dramatic appearances. In June 1954, the Yale ceiling shared a spread in that month's *Progressive Architecture* with Kahn and Tyng's proposal for a new City Hall in Philadelphia. Kahn's continuing interest in urban planning and his devotion to his home city led him to work with civic groups in replanning a large swath of downtown Philadelphia. Among the various schemes, a new building to house city offices was proposed. It adopted the three-dimensional truss of Tyng's elementary school, but on a far larger scale, rising fourteen stories. Within the large interstices of this angular structure, lightweight floor slabs modeled on the Yale example—though never thoroughly detailed—provided space for city offices and were pulled back in key areas to open up floors to larger meeting spaces and public forums. This scheme was developed further in 1957 for the Universal Atlas Cement Corporation, whose advertising campaign sought innovative uses for structural concrete. Undoubtedly impressed by Kahn's achievements in New Haven, the company asked him to propose a bolder, taller City Hall, using the basic strategy of the original City Tower proposal. Kahn commissioned a detailed model that showed the powerful main structural members and the more delicate tetrahedral floor slabs within, a graphically elaborate public plaza, and connections between columns and floors that used ornamental tetrahedrons to provide a visual transition from structure to slab. While Kahn claimed that the structure provided an efficient means of resisting both gravity and lateral loading, in reality the tower's structure, like that of its predecessor at Yale, would have been an extraordinarily expensive way of achieving what could be done with simpler rectilinear steel frames. That, however, was hardly Kahn's point. Earlier, he had

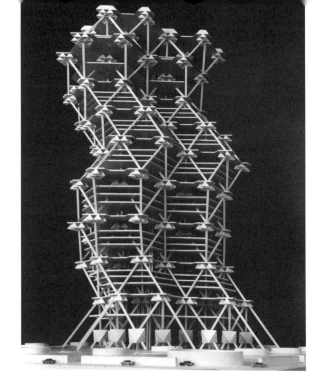

City Tower project, Philadelphia, Pennsylvania. Louis I. Kahn, 1952–57

critiqued Mies's Seagram Building as a "bronze lady in corsets," whose lateral bracing was concealed by pretentious marble panels on the core's exterior.[55] To Kahn, the City Hall Tower's angular structure was more than simply an efficient way to resist the wind; it was a way of telling a more complete structural story, a design derived from banal requirements that nevertheless resulted in a compelling vision. It would remain, of course, just an image, perhaps fortunately so, as the challenge of integrating cladding and circulatory systems, both hinted at in the final model, seems intractable in hindsight.

The City Tower marked another key transition for Kahn, as Anne Tyng, then pregnant with Kahn's daughter, departed for Europe in 1953, leaving the office as a full-time partner and taking with her much of the office's interest in mathematical geometry as a generative force. At the same time, the Tower featured the draftsmanship of Robert Venturi, recently arrived in Philadelphia and soon to be a demonstrable influence on Kahn's growing interest in conceptual and physical layering. Kahn's buildings from this point forward never completely rejected the Yale ceiling's mathematical methodology, but they immersed this geometrical logic into a much broader context, one that began to pay particular attention to the contingencies of sites and precedents. This, of course, is where Scully and, for that matter, Venturi begin their assessment of Kahn's importance as a forefather of postmodernism. However, Kahn's career from this point forward also sought to correct some of the conceptual shortcomings that had been manifest in the Yale Gallery, in particular the falsity of the free plan, which had been fundamentally rebuked by Paul Rudolph's intervention. This unhappy incident would lead Kahn to seek gradually a balance between functional flexibility and spatial definition. He would also seek to expand on the theme of systems and structural integration that had provoked such a powerful aesthetic presence in the Gallery's ceiling. Perhaps stung by criticism of the tetrahedral grid's inefficiency, Kahn sought out new engineering partners, new techniques, and new principles throughout the following decades that would further develop the idea of "hollow stones," arriving eventually at a rich interweaving of architectural structures and systems. At the same time, Yale represented the provocative knitting together of architectural gravitas, advanced technique, fertile historical reference, and expressed logic that would provide the basis for much of Kahn's career and philosophy over the next twenty years.

The Yale Gallery remains a powerfully stated synthesis of the progressive and the archaic. Its singular brick façade is, fifty years later, still a provocative foil to the original Gallery building, and it remains a lesson to architects long after that department decamped to Rudolph's art and architecture building across High Street in 1963. But it is perhaps most interesting as a defining moment in Kahn's career, in which one can see the crystallization of the themes that would dominate his later work. There is a slightly uneasy relationship between the technical conception of the floor slab and the archaic forms of the stairs and front façade that would give way later to a more complete integration of these two sensibilities. But the spaces remain compelling, markers of a developing fluency in structural and constructional languages. At Yale, Kahn began several dialogues that would preoccupy his most productive years, and the weavings of structure, skin, services, and space that are nascent in the Gallery would become the conceptual language from which his final works would spring.

Endnotes

1. A complete history of the Gallery project is included in Patricia Cummings Loud, *The Art Museums of Louis I. Kahn* (Durham, N.C.: Duke University Press, 1989).

2. Ibid., 43–46.

3. Weir Hall was completed by Dean Everett Meeks in 1924. See Patrick Pinnell, *Yale University*, Campus Guides (New York: Princeton Architectural Press, 1999), for a complete history of the site and surrounding campus.

4. "The justification from an educational standpoint for a laboratory or center of visual material for teaching in all the humanities and for courses in the visual arts is far greater and its appeal far wider than a justification based solely on additional room for exhibitions and art collections." Charles H. Sawyer to A. Whitney Griswold, 27 November 1950, A. Whitney Griswold Collection, Manuscripts and Archives Department of Yale University's Stirling Library, New Haven, Conn., record unit 22, box 27 ("President's Office: Records of A. Whitney Griswold as President, 1950–1963"), folder 247 ("Art Gallery Extension: New Wing [1950–1954]").

5. Notes from a meeting of the Yale Corporation, 9 December 1950, ibid.

6. Sawyer to Griswold, 8 January 1951, ibid.

7. Ibid. Kahn apparently never learned he was Yale's second choice. Despite their professional rivalry, he and Saarinen enjoyed a close friendship until the younger architect's death in 1961.

8. Howe to Kahn, 8 January 1951, Louis I. Kahn Collection, University of Pennsylvania and the Pennsylvania Historical and Museum Commission, Philadelphia (hereafter cited as Kahn Collection), LIK box 107, folder 107.42 ("Correspondence with Yale University").

9. "The whole success of the project from the Gallery point of view seems to me to rest on these two factors: a) A magnetic attraction into the Gallery section of the new building through changing exhibitions; and b) Easy access and some logical sequence from floor to floor and section to section of the exhibition sections of both new and old buildings." Sawyer to John Phillips and Lamont Moore, memorandum, 6 February 1951, Kahn Collection, LIK folder 107.42 ("Correspondence with Yale University").

10. The description of the schematic design process up to and including the approved August 1951 scheme is based on a set of recently found drawings and sketches now in the Yale University Art Gallery's Prints, Drawings, and Photographs Department.

11. Orr to Sawyer, 12 April 1951, Kahn Collection, LIK folder 84.1 ("Yale Art Gallery").

12. Anne Tyng's work on the Gallery is confirmed not only by her memoirs, but also by cost account sheets of the project submitted to Yale on 1 September 1951, showing that she had worked 152.5 hours on the project between March and August, more than anyone in the office but Kahn—who had logged 585 hours. Also interesting is that Tyng was paid more than other staff architects, with the exception of David Wisdom. Internal office memorandum, "Cost Account to Sept. 1, 1951—Design Laboratory," Kahn Collection, LIK folder 84.1 ("Yale Art Gallery").

13. Louis I. Kahn, "How to Develop New Methods of Construction," in *Louis I. Kahn: Writings, Lectures, Interviews*, ed. Alessandra Latour (New York: Rizzoli, 1991), 57.

14. Sawyer to Laurence Tighe (Treasurer, Yale University), 18 March 1952, Kahn Collection, LIK folder 107.42 ("Correspondence with Yale University").

15. Konrad Wachsmann, *The Turning Point of Building* (New York: Reinhold, 1961), 161–63. Wachsmann points out that it was Alexander Graham Bell who first built a lightweight tetrahedral truss structure of any scale in about 1900. See ibid., 29–34.

16. Anne Griswold Tyng, ed., *Louis Kahn to Anne Tyng: The Rome Letters, 1953–54* (New York: Rizzoli, 1997), 47.

17. Pfisterer to Orr, 21 October 1952, Douglas Orr Collection of the Yale Manuscripts and Archives Department of Yale University's Stirling Library, record unit 241 ("Office Files of Douglas Orr Associates, Records of Yale Art Gallery Expansion, 1951–1954").

18. Sawyer enlisted the aid of Yale alumnus Juan Trippe (CEO of Pan American World Airways), who wrote to the Defense Department in February on behalf of the project.

87

19. Griswold to E. V. Hollis (Chief of College Administration, Federal Security Administration), Griswold Collection, record unit 22 ("President's Office: Records of A. Whitney Griswold as President, 1950–63").

20. "There is no justification for the proposed new system on the basis purely of structure…. It uses 90% more steel…it requires about 3 times as much form work…it would cost five to six times as much…[and] in view of yesterday's word from Washington that we will shortly get approval on our steel, we cannot afford the weeks or months that it would take to resolve all the problems that the proposed new system raises." H. D. Palmer to Howe, Solomon, et al., memorandum, 11 March 1952, Kahn Collection, LIK folder 84.1 ("Yale Art Gallery").

21. The initial presentation of this stair tower in brick gives some credence to the idea that Kahn may have borrowed this form from Philip Johnson's Glass House. Johnson and Kahn were both critics at Yale at the time. See William Huff, "Kahn and Yale," *Journal of Architectural Education* 35, no. 3 (Spring 1982): 24. See also the minutes of a meeting held 18 March 1952, Kahn Collection, LIK folder 107.42 ("Correspondence with Yale University").

22. "Because of the nature of the structure, the character of the concrete work is of extreme importance as much of it will be left exposed….The manner of pouring each floor with particular reference to the exposed concrete will be a matter of extreme interest and will require the utmost cooperation from the contractor to produce 'Architectural' concrete." Orr to various contractors, 21 March 1952, Kahn Collection, LIK folder 107.45 ("Correspondence with Douglas Orr").

23. Sawyer to Kahn, 17 April 1952, Kahn Collection, LIK folder 107.42 ("Correspondence with Yale University"). Simultaneously, Orr's office consulted with acoustical engineers Bolt, Beranik, and Newman, who advised that the shape of the slab itself was unlikely to provide any reverberation control and that acoustic lining be placed on the soffit of the flat slab itself at the tops of the tetrahedrons. Robert B. Newman, Bolt Beranik, and Newman to H. D. Palmer, 17 April 1952, Kahn Collection, LIK folder 107.45 ("Correspondence with Douglas Orr").

24. This figure is conjectural, as Macomber's original bid does not exist in any of the archives reviewed for this chapter. In October 1952, Sawyer reported to Griswold that "the actual contractual figures are exceeding the original estimates by approximately eight per cent, or in terms of the total cost of the building by about $100,000." Details on the scope of Macomber's bid do exist in a cover letter sent from Charles B. Solomon (Vice President, George B. H. Macomber Co.) to Orr, 29 April 1952, Orr Collection, record unit 241 ("Office Files of Douglas Orr Associates, Records of Yale Art Gallery Expansion 1951–1954").

25. Orr to George B. H. Macomber Co., 26 May 1952, Kahn Collection, LIK folder 107.45 ("Correspondence with Douglas Orr"). Agreed revisions, including the depth of the floor system, were included in the final agreement dated 9 July 1952, also in LIK folder 107.45.

26. This meeting is recalled by Gianopulos in Richard Saul Wurman, *What Will Be Has Always Been: The Words of Louis I. Kahn* (New York: AccessPress/Rizzoli, 1986), 274. Mr. Gianopulos emphasized the role that the preexisting mechanical layout played in conceiving the alternative idea in an interview by the author at Keast & Hood's offices, Philadelphia, 9 June 2004.

27. Pfisterer, 8 April 1952, memorandum, Kahn Collection, LIK box 107.

28. Pfisterer to Henry G. Falsey (Building Inspector, New Haven Building Department), 21 May 1952, Kahn Collection, LIK box 107.

29. Falsey to Pfisterer, 18 June 1952, Kahn Collection, LIK box 107.

30. Ibid.

31. Burton Holmes (Technical Editor of *Progressive Architecture*) to Orr, 7 August 1952, Kahn Collection, LIK folder 107.45 ("Correspondence with Douglas Orr").

32. George Sanderson, "Extension: University Art Gallery and Design Center," *Progressive Architecture*, May 1954, 100.

33. "At the meeting on November 11th [1952] we discussed in considerable detail with Mr. Macomber the necessity of keeping a substantial sum…for continued experimentation in the betterment of pouring of the tetrahedrons. The methods now adopted on the form placement and concrete pouring is apparently developing very satisfactory finished concrete." Orr to Sawyer, 24 November 1952, Kahn Collection, LIK folder 107.45 ("Correspondence with Douglas Orr").

34. "We are very much dissatisfied with the progress being made by the sheet metal man in connection with the installation of his circular ducts. In every one of the six pours made to date he has delayed us anywhere from three to five days…. As you know, these ducts are an integral part of the building, and any delay in them delays our entire concrete progress." George Macomber to Buckingham and Routh, 19 November 1952, Orr Collection, record unit 241 ("Office Files of Douglas Orr and Associates, Records of Yale Art Gallery Expansion 1951–1954"), folder 4.

35. Condensation both within the insulating glass panels and on the steelwork proved to be a major problem, particularly as the building aged. Seals on this first generation product failed over time, and the renovation being carried out at the time of this writing seeks to correct flaws in these panels, which have over time led to many of the windows becoming clouded.

36. News release, Yale University News Bureau, 7 March 1954.

37. Remarks by Robert Lehman (Chairman, Associate in Fine Arts, and Member of the committee representing the donors) at the dedication of the Yale University Art Gallery, 6 August 1953, Griswold Collection, record unit 22 ("President's Office: Records of A. Whitney Griswold as President, 1950–63"), folder 248 ("Art Gallery Extension [New Wing] Dedication Nov. 1953").

38. "Letters," *Progressive Architecture*, May 1954, 16.

39. Ibid.

40. Ibid., 15, 16, 22, 24.

41. Ibid., 16.

42. Ibid., 24.

43. Typescript of an article by Vernon Read for *Architectural Forum*, marked by Kahn, Kahn Collection, LIK folder 107.44 ("Yale Art Gallery").

44. Ibid.

45. [Vernon Read], "Building Engineering: Tetrahedral Floor System," *Architectural Forum* 97, no. 3 (November 1952): 148–49.

46. Pfisterer to Kahn, 23 February 1954, Kahn Collection, LIK box 107.

47. "Toward New Structural Concepts," *Progressive Architecture*, special issue, June 1954. Kahn's work was featured on pages 102–3. Candela's essay contained extensive illustrations of curved and folded plates, including diagrams remarkably similar to those consulted in early phases of the Kimbell Art Museum's design. See chapter 5.

48. Vincent Scully, "Archetype and Order in Recent American Architecture," *Art in America* 42, no. 4 (December 1954): 250–61.

49. Ibid., 257, 250.

50. Reyner Banham, "The New Brutalism," *Architectural Review* 118, no. 708 (December 1955): 355–61.

51. Rudolf Wittkower, *Architectural Principles in the Age of Humanism* (1962; repr., New York: W. W. Norton & Co., 1971).

52. Banham, "The New Brutalism," 357.

53. Schweiker's tumultuous term of service was, however, notable for the institution of *Perspecta*, the Yale journal that would publish Kahn's first major philosophical statements since "Monumentality."

54. Kahn to Griswold, 30 July 1958, Kahn Collection, LIK folder 60.25 ("The Yale University Correspondence").

55. Louis I. Kahn, "1959: New Frontiers in Architecture," in *Louis I. Kahn: Writings, Lectures, Interviews*, ed. Alessandra Latour (New York: Rizzoli, 1991), 91.

89

RICHARDS MEDICAL RESEARCH LABORATORIES
UNIVERSITY OF PENNSYLVANIA, PHILADELPHIA

One day I visited the site during the erection of the prefabricated frame of the building. The crane's 200-foot boom picked up 25-ton members and swung them into place like matchsticks moved by the hand. I resented the garishly painted crane, this monster which humiliated my building to be out of scale. I watched the crane go through its many movements all the time calculating how many more days this "thing" was to dominate the site and building before a flattering photograph of the building could be made.

Now I am glad of this experience because it made me aware of the meaning of the crane in design, for it is merely the extension of the arm like a hammer. Now I began to think of members 100 tons in weight lifted by bigger cranes. The great members would be only the parts of a composite column with joints like sculpture in gold and porcelain and harboring rooms on various levels paved in marble.

—Louis I. Kahn

Like most medical schools in the United States, the University of Pennsylvania underwent dramatic changes in the 1950s. Foreseeing rising enrollment and the growing importance of technically advanced laboratory work to medical education, the University of Pennsylvania looked to ease its space problems in the late 1950s with new laboratory buildings that would pull research-intensive functions out of obsolescent space, allowing other departments to fill these older buildings. One major development involved the construction of a new wing for the University Hospital; however, nonclinical departments, including physiology, microbiology, public health, and an experimental surgery group did not require such proximity to hospital facilities. In 1956, the medical school put together a conceptual plan to accommodate these departments in a modular, eight-story tower to the west of the main hospital building along Hamilton Walk. The site was surrounded by buildings housing the departments of zoology and biology and a quadrangle of dormitories, all designed by Cope and Richardson in a powerful collegiate gothic style.

Kahn received the commission for the project, eventually named the Richards Medical Research Laboratories, in February 1957. A commission for a second phase to the west of the first followed shortly thereafter. At the time, Kahn had completed the Yale University Art Gallery and was in the final stages of completing the American Federation of Labor Building in Philadelphia but had built neither a laboratory nor a high-rise structure. His name arose in discussions led by G. Holmes Perkins, head of the University of Pennsylvania's fine arts program, again alongside that of Eero Saarinen's, as possible architects for projects on campus. Kahn was a familiar name, with an established practice near the campus and a growing connection to the University of Pennsylvania's architecture department. Publicity for the Yale Art Gallery had been extensive, with good reviews in *Progressive Architecture* and Architectural Forum, and the City Tower proposal had gained local and national press around the same time. Yet his limited experience on a large scale meant that he was still something of an unknown factor, and the commission for a high-profile women's dormitory went to Saarinen. The laboratory building was seen as a relatively utilitarian project, and the selection of Kahn seemed a calculated risk on the part of Perkins and the University.

Trenton

While Yale and City Tower were the best known of his projects, Kahn himself believed that one of his most important commissions of the 1950s had been for the Trenton Jewish Community Center, on which he worked from 1954 until 1958. Although the

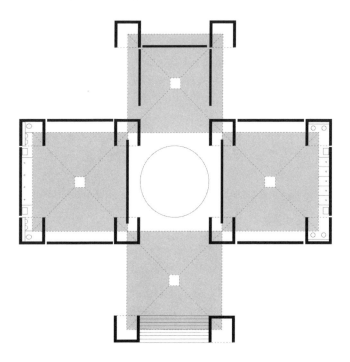

Plan (above) and view of the interior (opposite) of the Trenton Jewish
Community Center Bath House, Trenton, New Jersey. Louis I. Kahn, 1954–58

majority of the project was eventually abandoned, a set of small pavilions on the site
were built to house a day camp run by the Center and to provide changing rooms for
a swimming pool. This latter structure represented for Kahn the refinement of a new
ordering principle, one that would to some extent find itself deployed in all of his subsequent work. Kahn had, by the time of the Yale Gallery, already described in detail
the notion of "hollow stones," structural elements whose *poche*, or cross section, was
scooped out and inhabited by mechanical systems, leaving a structurally efficient outer
skin. This, however, had been only partially explored at Yale. The Gallery's mechanical systems in plan were still confined to an all-but-invisible core, and the connection
between its precisely conceived floor system and this core—through the major concrete girders—was awkward to say the least. Perhaps influenced by Wittkower, Kahn
noted in the early 1950s that the houses of Palladio, in particular the Villa Rotunda,
contained a hierarchical grid, one in which the major thematic spaces occupied larger
modules, and minor supporting spaces occupied smaller ones. These minor spaces
often contained secondary circulation or storerooms, in each case weaving space
for mechanical "servants" between the houses' served spaces. Kahn noted the validity of this idea in modern architecture, though he recognized that mechanisms—
ductwork, piping, and cables—had replaced the human servants of the late
Renaissance. Nevertheless, the Palladian plan, with its rich interplay of differently

sized grid modules, served as a useful analogy for Kahn's conception of mechanical "servant" spaces. Writing in 1955, he set this idea against the pure grid modules of his contemporaries: "Mies' order is not comprehensive enough to encompass acoustics, light, air, piping, storage, stairs, shafts, vertical and horizontal and other service spaces. His order of structure serves to frame the building but not harbor the servant space."[1]

It is useful to see this realization set against the conception of the Yale Gallery's plan. During that project's early phases, Kahn obviously struggled with the bay size that had been imposed on the project by the building committee, unable to meaningfully express the core, "servant" space within its universal grid. The first key moment in the Gallery's realization had arrived when Kahn conceived of the entire central bay as a servant zone, containing all core services but rigorously asserting itself in space as an auxiliary to the two primary gallery wings. At Trenton, Kahn explored this principle in three dimensions. The Bath House is composed of four large pyramidal roofs— originally intended in concrete but in fact made of wood—each of which sits on four hollow square columns, arranged in a diamond pattern. In some instances, the hollow columns serve as pass-through entrances, shielding the changing rooms from view. However, at the structure's edges these columns contain toilets and sinks, and elsewhere they harbor chlorination equipment for the pool and a ladder to the basement mechanical pit. The plan is essentially a superimposed square grid—the roofs atop a tartan grid with two modular dimensions, the smaller of which is dedicated to subsidiary functions, either mechanical or circulatory. It is here, in the weaving together of Kahn's "hollow stones" with the Palladian distinction between "servant" and "served" spaces, that a full dialogue between the modern concerns for structure and servicing first appears in Kahn's work, fulfilling the Yale Gallery's embryonic promises. Kahn would later explore the notion of combining these principles in a pair of residential commissions—the Adler and DeVore houses, both of 1954–55 and both unbuilt. But the idea of weaving together structure and mechanical systems provided an obvious theme for the construction of a laboratory, given its heavy reliance on piped and ducted services. Kahn instantly recognized the potential for this approach at Richards.

Early Designs

Kahn engaged the services of several familiar consultants to work on Richards, including landscape architect Ian McHarg and mechanical engineer Fred Dubin. McHarg was on faculty at the University of Pennsylvania and thus a natural collaborator, while Dubin had quickly developed a reputation as one of the top mechanical consultants in the northeast. Perhaps seeing the limitations of his experience at Yale, Kahn added to his roster of consultants a New Jersey–based structural engineer, August Komendant, who was to become his most important collaborator after 1958. Like Kahn, Komendant was a native of Estonia; however, he had been educated in Germany, receiving his doctorate in engineering from the Technical University of Dresden.[2] Following World War II, Komendant worked on the reconstruction of German bridges that had been destroyed by Allied bombing, a task that required rapid design, fabrication, and construction. Faced with a continuing shortage of steel, which had been the preferred material for long-span bridges prior to the war, Komendant was instrumental in developing a hybrid type of construction known as prestressed concrete. Concrete had generally performed poorly in bridge construction because reinforced steel often failed to bond properly with the material surrounding it. Komendant helped to perfect a sort of superreinforcing called *pretensioning*, in which concrete was poured around steel rods or bars that were tensioned by anchors and jacks. As the concrete cured, the steel would be released from its anchors, snapping tight against the solid concrete and thereby inducing a large compressive force into areas of the element that would

Engineer August Komendant

otherwise be in tension. If located accurately, this compressive force could eliminate the need for extensive areas of reinforcing, thus giving concrete the tensile capacity of steel while using only minute amounts of the scarce metal. Komendant was also a pioneer in the use of posttensioning, in which concrete was cast around loose strands of steel that were then tightened after the concrete had cured, with the same effect. Prestressing proved efficient in precast members, where the jacking could be done in the factory, while posttensioning could be done on site, using power tools to manually tighten the slack strands. Komendant often explained both principles by demonstrating how one could pick up a row of books by simply applying pressure on both ends, adding compression to the lower third of the row to cancel out the books' tendency to "bend" and fall apart. Komendant emigrated to the United States in 1950, setting up a consulting practice in Upper Montclair, New Jersey, and capitalizing on his expertise by authoring the first major manual on the technique he had employed and improved; *Prestressed Concrete Structures* established Komendant as the leading expert on the subject.[3]

 97

Kahn first contacted Komendant about a prestressed concept for the Enrico Fermi Memorial competition at the University of Chicago in early 1957.[4] The two formed a fast friendship, based on their shared ancestral roots in Estonia and a collaborative

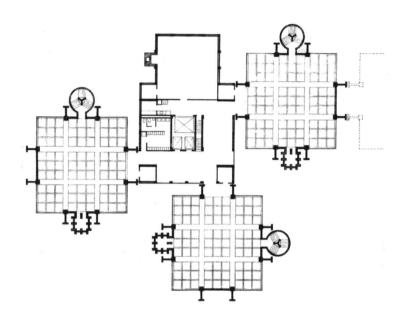

Early plan showing the nine-square grid structure, ca. 1957

dynamic that would prove extraordinarily productive—if often tense—over their eighteen years of work together. Komendant was neither a form-giver nor a designer, limitations that he reluctantly admitted. Kahn, on the other hand, despite his exquisite attention to detail, did not possess the mathematically analytical mind that had won Komendant acclaim. Each needed the other's sensibility, and the results of their collaborations would be flawlessly integrated meshes of structure and architecture, inconceivable without their stormy partnership's long arguments and impassioned debates about space and structure. Following their unsuccessful work on the Fermi competition, Komendant hosted Kahn's students at a prestressed concrete plant in Lakewood, New Jersey, where he was a consulting engineer. Kahn rhapsodized about the plant and its equipment, which suggests that the idea of prestressed members was firmly planted in his mind as the Richards project was in its early design stages.[5] Komendant was brought on as a consultant shortly thereafter to assist Kahn's Philadelphia engineers, Keast & Hood.

By June 1957, a mere four months after the commission, Kahn and his consultants developed a layout for the laboratories that would stubbornly resist alteration throughout the project. Unlike the Yale Gallery's, the basic scheme for Richards came together quickly, based on the absolute requirements of a single mechanical system. Yet this

98

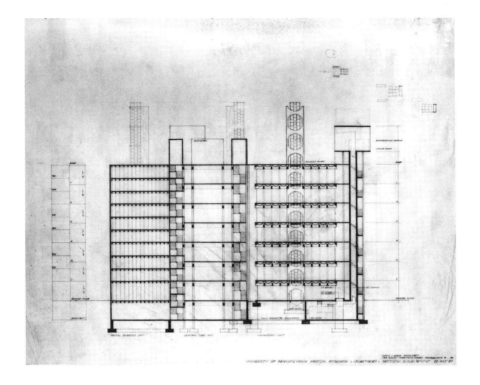

Section through the laboratories, ca. 1957

single generative issue sparked a rich hierarchy of service and served spaces in a rigorously conceived and executed design that expressed completely the synthesized logic of its parts and their integration.

The plan for Richards was radical. Instead of large horizontal expanses of loft-type floors or repetitive laboratory benches, the team's proposal involved trays of "studio" space, stacked in towers rising well above the surrounding neogothic campus buildings. Based on Fred Dubin's initial consultations regarding plumbing lines and code-required falls, the design team proposed a single standard module for the laboratories, a 45'-0" square space free of columns or walls. This permitted a central pipe loop that would service the entire floor plate, while permitting maximum flexibility for bench and partition locations. The standard module was to be replicated in three towers of eight floors each, clustered around a central nine-story core containing mechanical systems, animal quarters, elevators, and stairs. From the beginning, the site arrangement placed the laboratory towers in a pinwheel formation around the core, or Tower X. This created offsets in the overall site massing, allowing each tower a three-sided exposure to daylight. The arrangement also played on the fine distinction between the building as a single mass and as a collection of independent

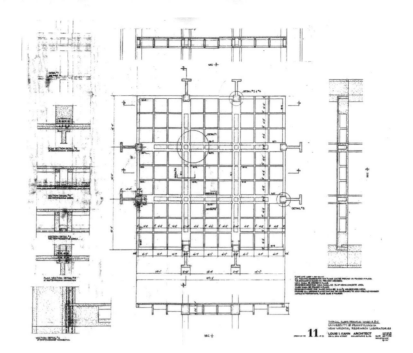

Detailed schematic structural plan, ca. 1957

tower elements, an articulation that would form the basis for a much finer ordering of the building's systems and details as the design progressed.

On the laboratory towers' exterior, preliminary designs showed subsidiary service runs including exhaust air, secondary plumbing, and fire escape stairs housed in towers that formed the dramatic, vertical massing that would become the project's signature. In July 1957, the first drawings of these towers showed ladder trusses, hollow and presumably open air, harboring smaller ducts and stair towers within. The trusses' circular openings formed doorways to the laboratory floors, a trope that was repeated in the cantilevered beams extending from the truss and forming the laboratory floors themselves. One sketch in particular shows these cantilevers spanned by ersatz Vierendeel trusses, with arced openings allowing the passage of pipes and, presumably, ductwork.[6] While statically imperfect as drawn at this point, it is apparent that Kahn recognized the potential for efficient laboratory servicing in the porous truss elements that he had first explored in the 1947 Parasol House.

In August 1957, the towers and their structural elements were refined aesthetically and functionally. Drawings during the late summer show a distinction between stair and flue towers, with the former terminating in rectangular capitals, and the latter

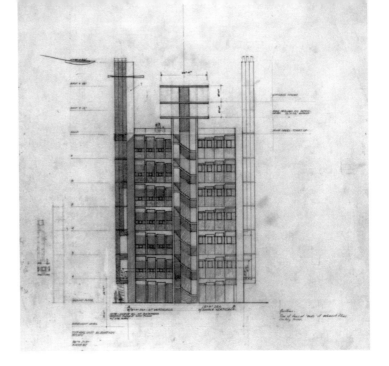

An early elevation, ca. 1957

in flat cornices, each tower with vertical striations on the exterior indicating their status as vertically oriented ducts.[7] The laboratory floors themselves were shown with a nested concrete structure. Each consisted of large, interconnected beams on a nine-square grid, with a finer grain of interior trusses that repeated the grid on a smaller scale. The concrete structure was now conscientiously divorced from the service towers and expressed separately, in pairs of concrete columns flanking the service towers at one-third points along the edge beams. Kahn continued to experiment with the service towers' articulation, developing a system of clay flues that gradually filled out the volume of each exhaust tower as it rose up the side of the laboratory, adding flues at each floor to represent the accumulation of exhaust. Meanwhile, Komendant's work on the concrete structure focused on prefabrication strategies, developing a kit-of-parts approach to provide large cross-and-edge beams that could be craned into place like steel. Once in position, these large members would form the support for the filigree of lighter members and trusses, all of them using Vierendeel principles to allow integral open space for mechanical and plumbing systems.

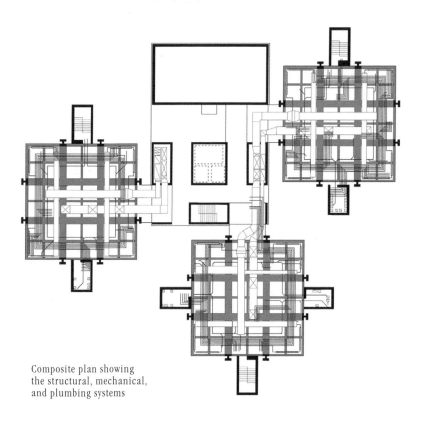

Composite plan showing
the structural, mechanical,
and plumbing systems

Structure, Services, and Cladding: A Woven Fabric

While the developing scheme for Richards was radical, it was by no means unprecedented. In particular, Chicago's Inland Steel Building, completed in 1958 but published as early as May 1955, displayed a very clear hierarchy among its vertically finned service tower, its outboard structure, and its clear-span office space.[8] Contemporary laboratory design was not this articulate in its expression of structure and service, although laboratories at Washington University in St. Louis, designed in 1956 by Harris Armstrong, expressed a similar interplay between reconfigurable laboratory space, a cast-in-place structure, and a compressed core.[9]

The synthesis achieved by Kahn, Komendant, and Dubin, however, went far beyond these forerunners. Richards's structural scheme was designed to be manufactured with dowels, seats, and rebar connections that would form a monolithic floor system when complete. The nine-square grid was reflected in the shape of the cantilevered edge beams, which gradually stepped up toward their corners at each intersection with an intermediate cross member. At each of these changes in section, a downstand piece was included on the outside beam to provide a seat for intermediate trusses. On the exterior, the columns were also designed as precast members, shaped to sit on the column-and-edge beam of the floor below. Three sets of posttensioning cables were located in a vertical duct running through each column—one each in their inboard and outboard segments and through their centers—aligning with cable ducts cast through the edge beam. Upon tightening, these cables provided a firm connection between the precast parts, which relied on friction induced by the tension in the cables to lock the precast members in place. The same technique was employed on the interior members. Prestressing in the main spanning beams allowed Komendant to reduce their overall depth, while intermediate beams running between the main spans and the columns were connected to the main beams and to one another with posttensioning cables. After tightening, the precast frame would be stressed along all three axes, forming an extremely rigid system, much like a circus toy whose limbs are connected by loose threads that, when tightened, make the toy stand rigidly. The cast-in-place floor slabs provided additional stiffness in both horizontal directions, with monolithic connections to the precast beams created by wire loops and metal studs, which became embedded in the poured concrete slab above.

Essentially a hybrid system of concrete and steel, the structural system arrived at by Kahn and Komendant used a language of jointing throughout to express the building's overall order, demonstrating the scale of its assembly. Expressed joints between members delineated the individual pieces and their interface. No attempt was made to hide or conceal these joints; instead, where necessary, grout or caulk was colored to contrast with the surrounding material. At the ground level, the entry porch in the central tower purposely eschewed dropped ceilings or infill panels, presenting the visitor with a clear exposition of the modular, skeletal floor system.[10] At every opportunity, the design was developed to visually and tactilely "speak" about its construction and performance. The building's aesthetics were thus intentionally built up from its practicalities, the overall intent being not merely to solve the difficult issues of servicing, structure, and integration, but to record and explain the complexities of the problems and the rigor of the solutions. This didactic intent existed in the concrete formwork at Yale, but it took on a new importance at Richards. Kahn seemed to be pushing further now, intent on achieving a richer visual and spatial experience based on the program's added complexities—a clutching at the immeasurable, woven together out of the pedestrian realities of ductwork, assembly, and circulation.

Dubin's mechanical system played a key role in this process. The air supply and return strategy took advantage of the structural system's porous nature; however, it maintained its own geometric logic, deferring to and subtly transforming the reading of the

103

Detail of the exterior and cladding

building's major ordering principles.[11] Tower X, the main core, was largely given over to vertical shafts, including four ground-level "nostrils" on the building's south side. Air was ducted from these to a penthouse on the core tower's roof, where it entered four air-handling units, one for each laboratory tower and one dedicated to animal quarters in Tower X itself. Conditioned air was then directed down two major supply ducts, along the core's east and west sides. At each floor, supply trunks branched off from these vertical shafts to the laboratory ceiling voids, entering through the Vierendeel-edge beams on axis with each laboratory tower's connection to the core. Typically, supply air was brought to the center of each floor plate, where branches distributed it to each quadrant of the floor. Exhaust air was removed from the main laboratory spaces by a parallel system of exhaust ductwork and taken back to the main core; however, this was supplemented by the large volumes of air drawn out by fume hoods, which were exhausted directly to vertical ducts in the service towers.

Drawings by Dubin show a refined set of rules for duct placement within the trusses, with supply ducts always occupying the void's lower half and exhaust ducts occupying the top, ensuring a coordinated system that could cross over itself where required. Hot and chilled water, gas and vacuum, and waste service to each floor were supplied in a racetrack layout. Pipes entered through the center of the Vierendeel frames

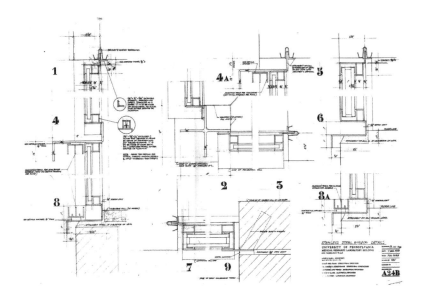

Details of the stainless-steel window framing

on either side of the main ductwork, turned 90°, and ran in the laboratories' outer third, orbiting the central precinct of each floor, crossing supply and exhaust ductwork as those elements tapered toward the floor edges. Each system thus interpreted the typical laboratory floor's shape differently—a simple grid (structural), a radial scheme (mechanical), and an orbital plan (plumbing)—weaving structure, function, and services together in a system of elements that were conscientiously exposed to view in the laboratories below.

Architecturally, Kahn developed the exterior of the complex to reflect the various functions of its structural, mechanical, and circulatory systems, again pursuing the goal of a building that spoke of its own constructive and functional hierarchies. The precast structure itself provided a robust exterior finish and could thus be expressed plainly, while infill elements were detailed to communicate that they provided simple enclosure, lower in the hierarchy of expressed performance and later in the sequence of construction. Brick walls were precisely in plane with the precast beams' exterior surfaces, graphically emphasizing the structure as in the Radbill Building, and large sheets of plate glass clearly emphasized the horizontal reach of the precast cantilevers above and below.

These windows were held in place by a system of brake-shaped stainless-steel mullions. Kahn had used standard steel sections at Yale for the curtain walls and windows, but was not happy with the results. His attempt to redesign that system came too late, and the rolled and bent steel shapes that formed the Gallery's window walls seemed to him to be inarticulate. The alternative to steel at the time, box sections of aluminum, seemed to Kahn to deceive the eye—one saw a solid box, when in fact they were hollow, their structural performance achieved by a thin skin of metal. Such a system failed to speak of its making or its function, lacking didactic potential (and thus honest visual interest), and Kahn sought instead a solution that would express the curtain wall's functions—resisting gravity and wind loads and forming an environmental seal—while articulating its fabricational process.

Curtain wall development by 1957 had pursued several alternatives to rolled-steel sections and to the eventually ubiquitous extruded aluminum box. Among the earliest experimenters was, of course, Mies van der Rohe, whose designs for the Illinois Institute of Technology and for 860–880 Lake Shore Drive in the 1940s and 1950s featured glass walls supported by customized steel sections, panelized and inserted into a rolled steel frame. As Edward Ford has pointed out, Kahn's approach to curtain-wall detailing owed more to Eero Saarinen, whose designs for the General Motors Technical Center's shop buildings used a more subtle system of rolled steel sashes, closures, and frames. Unlike aluminum, steel is not ductile enough to extrude—friction between the metal and the die leaves a rugged surface that is visually unacceptable for high-end locations. Rolling steel while it is still cooling is, on the other hand, quite common, producing shapes with relatively thin walls. Because of the process's geometry, however, corners are left rounded and can only be sharpened by hand-grinding after the rolling process. Steel's use in precise curtain walls was, therefore, aesthetically problematic, as the material invariably seemed cruder than the finely honed, polished glass that it held. Saarinen used aluminum cover plates for his more formal buildings at General Motors, disguising the steel connections and rolled surfaces, and Mies, in fact, had reverted to aluminum casings on his curtain walls by the mid-1950s, both masters betraying a frustration at the standard approaches to glazing with steel.

There was, however, another process by which steel could be formed into structural shapes. "Braking" steel sheets involves folding thin-gauge steel on a brake press and making precise bends that hold their shape. Through a combination of these folds, a brake press can form an approximation of a hollow section manually, a "hollow stone" of metal that, because the process has to leave an open side, is naturally

Exterior view of the American Federation of Labor Medical Services Building. Louis I. Kahn, 1957

expressive of the void within. This is a labor-intensive process, as it requires a skilled workman to operate the press, and typically involves several folds to make a single piece. While the corners on a brake-pressed piece are rounded, these have a tighter radius than those of rolled sections, and the piece's edges can be quite precise—the width of the thin-gauge sheet.

Kahn first explored the idea of a brake-shaped cladding frame on the American Federation of Labor (AFL) Medical Services Building, designed and built between 1954 and 1957. This structure relied on a Vierendeel frame designed by Keast & Hood for its primary structure—a nine-square grid that was a direct precursor to Richards but constructed out of poured, not precast, concrete. The Medical Services Building's exterior skin provided a noteworthy contrast to this bulky concrete structure. Full-story glass and solid panels were arranged in four simple bands around the building's edges, with expressed horizontal drips at the floor lines—and little else. Vertical mullions between the cladding panels were initially designed to be similar to Mies's details, with exposed steel angles and glazing stops holding the sheets. However, Kahn redesigned this system out of brake-shaped stainless steel, with a deep U-shaped section providing structural depth against wind loads. These sections contained continuous vertical tabs at the ends of the U against which glass could be set from the

Interior view of the American Federation of Labor Medical Services Building.
Louis I. Kahn, 1957

inside, with stops installed behind. Kahn was thus able to reduce the depth of the exposed metal substructure on the exterior from that of a stop to that of a steel sheet, pushing the glass as far out to the edge of the building elevation as possible. The resulting appearance was, as Edward Ford describes it, "taut" rather than deep, precise rather than fussy, and minimal in the sense that there are very few vertical lines where glass meets glass. Mies and Saarinen had emphasized their corners with reentrant elements, but in Kahn's AFL building the corners seemed intentionally insubstantial, which presented the glass corner in a way that lessened—rather than deepened—the visual gravitas of the building's skin and thus emphasized the structure's weighty drama within. The attention to the structure and detail of this skin system emphasized an aesthetic of precision. Its tightly built, honed set of components contrasted broad planes of stark material with intense, expressed connections contained in minute channels and shadowgaps between elements.[12]

In conversation with William Jordy, Kahn spoke of the rationale for the brake-shaped system, noting the technological "falseness" of stock-aluminum members, and the "suspicion" he had of hollow metal members.[13] The system developed at AFL, he thought, was more "insect-like, terrifically light, but tenacious." The fact that stainless steel requires no paint and that it could be expressed in the condition in which it arrived on the site was also important for Kahn. Crucially, the system's precision could be played off the concrete's rough texture—an incomplete dialogue at AFL, as the concrete was not expressed on the exterior. At Richards, however, the opportunity for this contrast presented itself as the structure developed. "A very sharp edge," such as the stainless-steel mullion's blade, "and shadow joint against concrete...tells you the limits of the concrete, the limits of the steel."[14] Kahn's didactic intent here is apparent—the "truth" of the building and its interrelated systems were to be conveyed through the experience of each system's limits, through the visual language of cast, rolled, brake-shaped, and assembled components and their natural textures—rough, finished, and honed.

The glass system at Richards was developed to elaborate on this contrast with its heavy concrete. Razor-thin stainless-steel shapes were brake shaped and used to set the glass apart from the concrete frames at the top of each window by shadowgaps similar in spirit to those in the Weiss House and at Yale. At the windows' bases, continuous stainless-steel drips performed the same visual task atop a low brick wall. Large panes of glass were set into Z-shaped subframes, again glazed from the interior to provide a crisp, taut exterior with virtually no relief. At the corners, these Z-bars met up with a cruciform stainless post that provided structural continuity and added vertical shadowgaps at the corners. This post extended through only the main window light; the clerestory light above, set within the precast structure's depth, was designed with simple glass-to-glass clips, its corner panes siliconed together but otherwise unemphasized. The resulting composition is complex, but immediately noticeable is the fact that all surfaces in the external wall—precast structure, brick infill, and glass cladding—are precisely in plane with one another. The Richards's wall surface is thus almost purely graphic, with only the drip edges at the windows' bases offering any relief. The vertical corner post effectively contrasts with the sharp brick corner below, providing a slight reentrance that distinguishes the zones of infill and cladding. However, stopping this post short of the structure above emphasizes the distinction between the window and the cantilevered span. The precast trays' carrying action is thus made clear, though their intricate relationships with the glass and brick walls are not overly simplified. Rather, the visible distinctions between these three systems together illustrate a very clear construction sequence—concrete, then brick, then steel, then glass— while emphasizing the integration of these into a precise assembly of systems. Kahn would return to this window system often, refining details but keeping the flush exterior and the revelation of the stainless-steel sheet's folding process—a unique curtain-wall system whose conception has gone largely unnoted.

109

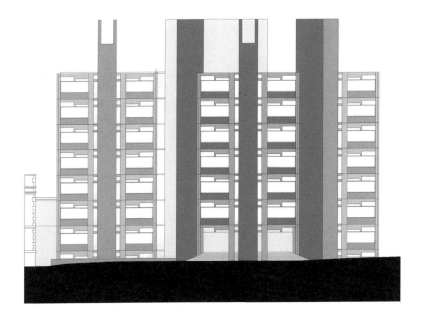

Elevation from Hamilton Walk as built

On the roof, the parapet line was emphasized with a double line of flashing, and columns were topped with a finial-like device, incorporating a round top profile that visually matched the proportions of finials on the surrounding Cope and Stewardson buildings.[15] At this stage, the flues were still designed as crenellated, vertically striped tubes, while fire stairs were shown as rectangular or cylindrical shafts, recalling the core zone in the Yale Art Gallery, which played a rectangular service shaft against a cylindrical circulation stair. Connections between the laboratory towers and Tower X were articulated by large sheets of plate glass, and Tower X itself was clad in brick with plate-glass windows revealing the locations of corridors within.[16] The laboratory towers' internal planning was largely left to the departments. Kahn's office provided a list of "rules" for the layouts, particularly noting that walls should align with the positions of small beams above.[17]

Production and Assembly

Construction drawings were issued in May 1958 and sent out for bids that June. The final year of production was largely spent cutting costs, in particular altering Tower

X to simplify its sectional layout and finding savings on air conditioning, finishes, and laboratory equipment.[18] However, by the time the construction drawings were made, there had also been significant cutbacks in the architectural scheme. Most importantly, the crenellated towers were abandoned in favor of the plain brick shafts that were eventually built, leaving only the device of extended planar walls at the top of the stair towers to distinguish the shafts' various functions. The project was once again threatened after the bids arrived. Joseph R. Farrell, a Philadelphia contractor, was awarded the job despite a bid of more than $3 million, or about $500,000 over the planned budget. In August 1958, additional cuts were made to reduce the cost of construction to $2.5 million.[19] Caissons were substituted for deep footings, ceiling heights were standardized in the core tower, and the structural scheme was changed to reduce the number of intermediate trusses and joints on each floor, transforming the secondary, nested structural grid from a nine-square to a smaller four-square grid. This last change seems in hindsight quite obvious, as it reduced the number of truss members per tower floor from 72 to 27 and likewise reduced the number of labor-intensive joints in each floor's structure from 144 to 54. This change had consequences for both the partition layout and the duct and pipe runs. The former was redesigned by Kahn's office by November 1958. However, it was decided not to alter the extensive mechanical drawings, saving time and design fees. The drawings were issued based on the old scheme as scope documents, leaving the precise locations within the new grid to the contractor's discretion. The structural change also simplified the exterior expression considerably. The University of Pennsylvania had raised objections to the cluttered elevations that resulted from the expression of the nested nine-square grid in small sheets of glass, a visual problem that was eliminated by the new layout.[20] While the revised scheme remained slightly over budget, the project proceeded even before the reissue of drawings on 13 November 1958. Excavation commenced in August, and foundation walls were poured by December.[21]

With construction underway, the building schedule relied on the manufacture and assembly of the precast structural system. The story of the precast beams has often been alluded to; however, the rarely examined engineering, manufacture, and installation of these elements demonstrates the intensity of thought and integration that would become characteristic of Kahn and Komendant's subsequent collaborations. These fabrication and assembly processes were conveniently summarized by J. B. (Sandy) Smythe, Chief Engineer for Atlantic Precast Corp., in a paper delivered to the Precast Concrete Institute and recounted by Komendant in his 1975 memoirs.[22]

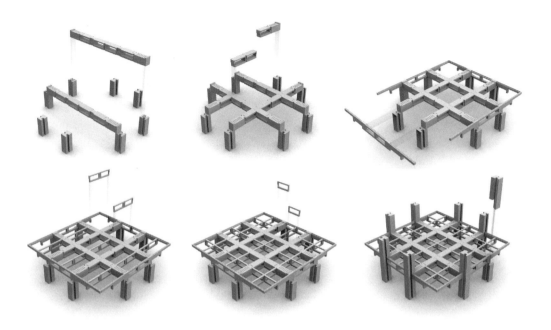

Smythe's paper pointed out that the job's fundamental problem was the precise alignment of three different varieties of concrete—the poured-in-place Tower X, constructed by a different subcontractor; the pretensioned main beams at each floor; and the posttensioned minor trusses, beams, and columns. While standard tolerances called for up to ⅜" offset between various concrete elements, such imperfections would have been visually jarring and, in some cases, would have prevented the jointwork of Richards's concrete structure from fitting together properly. Similarly, Kahn's expression of the columns as primary elements in the façades meant that they had to be absolutely plumb to bear the visual emphasis that was placed on them. To win the contract, Atlantic guaranteed perfect shape, flatness, and alignment, relying on steam curing, metal formwork and jigs, and extremely tight production control. Primary attention was given to the spandrel beams and columns, the most visible elements in the structure. These were cast with a flat pallet and laid on their side with the exterior face at the bottom. Metal formwork was used for its ability to withstand the heat and moisture of steam curing as well as to achieve the precise tolerances demanded by Kahn and Komendant. Because of the pretensioning cables, the main structural members had to be cast upright, with complex voids formed by extensive steel formwork and bracing.[23]

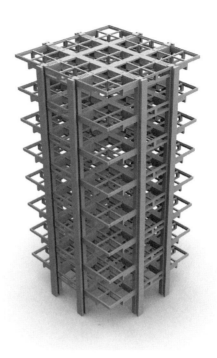

Sequence of precast-beam construction
(opposite) with the fully assembled
tower structure (right)

The exterior columns posed particular casting problems. Because of their exposed nature, Atlantic advised that they be poured vertically, so that any settling of aggregate would form horizontal, not vertical, striations. Further refinements included altering the column shapes slightly to include a tapering in the outer flanges, permitting forms to slide out as single pieces and avoiding the use of awkward collapsing forms. Ducting throughout the members used flexible hose tubing, protecting posttensioning cables from snags and friction from the surrounding concrete. Following the curing process, the columns were laid flat for storage on a bed of white sand, thus eliminating the need for patching. As a result, Atlantic reported that of the 168 columns cast, not one required remedial work.[24]

Atlantic did extensive production studies, determining that the use of reusable forms, an assembly line workforce of sixteen, and a dedicated casting bed would allow eighteen minor trusses or six main trusses to be poured at once. A separate team of nine ironworkers set to work fabricating reinforcing cages for the posttensioned members. Like the concrete, the reinforcing had no tolerance and was fabricated using identical jigs in the steel shop and on the factory floor to ensure a perfect fit. Beginning on 3 April 1959, Atlantic produced an average of two spandrel beams and four minor trusses per day, finishing production in mid-June. The work was scheduled

Precast girder being hoisted into place (left) and posttensioning being applied (right)

to overlap with the erection process, and the first precast frames, originally scheduled for delivery to the site on 4 May, were craned into place on 26 May following three weeks of final costing and minor redesign.[25]

The installation process did not start well. Atlantic contracted directly with a steel erector, Cornell and Company, to place the precast elements, and their unfamiliarity with the material combined with logistical problems to slow construction to a crawl through June. Additional coordination was required among the ironworkers erecting the pieces, masons from Atlantic responsible for grouting and packing the beams in place, and supervising engineers from Keast & Hood responsible for ensuring that the posttensioning was done to specification. There was no storage at the site, so members had to be shipped exactly on time by truck from Atlantic's plant in Trenton through downtown Philadelphia. Access to the site was possible only from the winding service drive to the rear, and the need to preserve adjacent trees and buildings meant that every crane lift had to thread a careful path from the rear of the site to the towers.[26] To maximize efficiency under these difficult conditions, the towers were carefully sequenced to ensure that concrete-floor pours occurred early enough to form a rigid frame for the continuing sequence overhead. Typically, structural members would be craned into place on two towers while grouting and pouring occurred on the third.

114

Construction view

Despite this extensive planning, on 16 June Joseph Ferrell, the contractor, wrote to Smythe to complain about the work's pace.[27] To that point only three floors—one in each tower—had been completed, raising concerns that delays would push the structural portion of the construction into October. As the masonry knee walls were to follow the completion of the concrete work, the cold weather could cause more delays throughout the winter.[28]

The pace picked up quickly, however, as the ironworkers warmed to the new material and the complex ballet of cranes, jacks, and concrete pours became routine. By July, Cornell and Atlantic were averaging one finished floor per week, three times their starting pace, and the work was completed by 14 August 1959; in all, 1,019 precast pieces were fabricated, shipped, and erected without major incident.[29] The team had finally adopted a mass-production strategy on the site, with teams of two workers riding structural pieces and using custom-made jigs and tools to align columns and trusses prior to the arrival of the tensioning jacks. This was matched by close cooperation from Kahn, Komendant, and Keast & Hood, and Smythe recognized them for their work. While some postinstallation patching was necessary, Smythe reported that the largest offset between pieces was within $\frac{1}{16}$"—virtually perfect given the state of the industry and the confined site.[30]

115

Construction view (above) and the interior of a typical laboratory studio (opposite)

Construction of the exterior wall, mechanical systems, and interior fitout continued into 1960. The building was dedicated in May, and researchers occupied laboratory spaces as work was completed. Their first impressions of the building were not good, and for a design that had claimed such explicitly technological underpinnings, the problems that occurred during the opening of Richards were both frustrating and embarrassing. The large plate-glass windows, installed without the specified shading screens on the east and west façades for budgetary reasons, caused intense glare in many of the laboratory spaces. Worse, several panes actually cracked, leaving researchers worried about the safety of the design itself. Investigation revealed that the cracked panes had been improperly supported and that some had been clipped to accommodate bolts that were installed in the wrong location. But the cracked glass was only the most visible issue. The solar-gain problem was exacerbated by a lengthy and troublesome balancing process, and researchers sweltered throughout the summer of 1960. Finally, ominous cracks appeared in the brickwork towers, and the University of Pennsylvania went behind the designers' backs to commission a report from United Engineers, a construction management firm that was then bidding on the construction contract for the second phase of the project, the Biology Building. Kahn, Komendant, and Keast & Hood were incensed at what they perceived as

116

a conflict of interest on United's part, and further study revealed that the cracks had a relatively benign cause linked to the differential in load on the towers' roofs and floors. But the University of Pennsylvania had been sufficiently alarmed; they removed Kahn from any position of authority on the Biology Building project, handing control of the design's execution solely to United and effectively blocking any future appointment of Kahn to build on his home campus.

Richards's troublesome reception suggests that Kahn may have exceeded his own grasp in designing such a technically advanced building. A full reading of events during the final cost cutting and construction, however, reveals that the University of Pennsylvania bore a great deal of responsibility for the solar-gain problem, having removed the exterior screens from the budget. Kahn remained diplomatic about his ouster and about the ongoing complaints from users, but more importantly he learned some very difficult lessons. The elimination of glare, for example, would become a preoccupation in his subsequent work; indeed, his project for an American consulate in Angola would be conceived around an architectural device to diffuse harsh sunlight. Perhaps even more importantly, Kahn's fascination with building technology would be productively tempered from this point forward by a concern for the quality of the spaces contained. At both Yale and Richards, the quality of the architecture is

RICHARDS MEDICAL RESEARCH LABORATORIES

A completed exterior porch (above) and the interior of a laboratory
studio prior to occupation showing the plumbing and structure (opposite)

largely in the execution; one is a brilliant statement about triangular geometry and
integrated services and the other, a fluent integration of precast construction and daring glass detailing. After Richards, these aspects became important primarily as they
related to qualities of human space. Kahn's attention shifted, and while the use and
expression of advanced construction and structural engineering remained a primary
theme, these were part of a mix that included conceiving the spatial design from first
principles, seeking essences not only in how a thing was done, but increasingly in why
that thing was being done. Richards was thus an important turning point for Kahn, as
his enthusiasm for pure building technology was balanced by his quest to understand
in greater depth the essential needs of the functions for which he was designing.

Assessment

Despite its mixed reviews in Philadelphia, worldwide reaction to the Richards building was overwhelmingly positive and, with the exception of at least one major dis-
senting voice, enthusiastic. The project was published in more than fifty international
journals and magazines, ranging from *Architectural Record* to *Vogue*.[31] The building's appearance in such a range of outlets suggests its powerful allure, both as an

architectural achievement and as a popular icon that expressed the technical nature of building in a hyperactively scientific age. Richards appeared alongside highly engineered, technically advanced structures that had primed the public for a building that teased visual interest out of technological requirements. A one-building show at the Museum of Modern Art in spring 1961 sealed Richards's status as an iconic example of this approach.

Two analyses in particular addressed the "unusual degree of interest" aroused by Richards and pointed to its challenging position as a paragon of technologically expressive design. Writing in *Architectural Review* in 1961, William Jordy saw in Richards's planning and massing the stark juxtaposition of solid and void or, in his words, the "drama of being and nothingness."[32] Describing the concrete, Jordy noted the visual language of the rough, form-finished, poured-in-place stairwells, which recalled the stark finishes of the earlier Yale Gallery's core elements, and their contrast with the precast members' "smooth surfaces, sharp edges and precise tolerances."[33] That a third type of concrete—masonry that formed the partitions—was a part of this material narrative was proof for Jordy that a primary function of the building's fabric was, in fact, the "fullest revelation of its construction." Jordy acknowledged the building's well-documented flaws—inadequate sun control, dust collection on the exposed pipes, and the lack of spatial clarity inside. But he suggested that its "meticulous differentiation," "passionate logic," and interest in not merely "containing" but also in "disclosing" would make Richards the "most influential American building" since the Mies trio of the Illinois Institute of Technology, the Farnsworth House, and 860–880 Lake Shore Drive. "The ultimate challenge" of Richards, Jordy wrote, "is nothing less than the fluid fusion and integration as an entity of what is here eviscerated.... Its archaic quality stems from the search for an unaffected reconciliation of the complex technology of the modern world with the primal elements of building, and these with the primal human responses to shelter."[34]

That an historically minded critic such as Jordy would note the knitting together of the measurable (complex technology, the modern, measured world) and the immeasurable (primal human responses, archaic quality) pleased Kahn,[35] but this assessment was matched by the criticism of Reyner Banham, whose wary praise of the Yale Gallery's brutal honesty evaporated in what he saw as fundamental contradictions at Richards. Writing for the *Architectural Review* a year after Jordy, Banham began a five-month indictment of contemporary architecture's technological shortcomings by precisely dissecting Kahn's "problem of services."[36] Comparing Kahn's hierarchical disposition of served spaces and the servant "harbors" provided for pipes and ducts, Banham found Kahn's approach to be a "cruder" version of that proposed by Corbusier in the Pavilion Suisse, where each element in the composition described an overriding functional hierarchy of dormitory, circulation, and meeting. Banham attacked the functionality of Kahn's solution, noting that the "functionally neutral" approach of moving the stacks outside of the laboratories was an incomplete articulation. Most of the ducting and piping occurred in the core tower, as was described above, making the external brick towers more gestural than strictly expressive. Noting that humans and pipes both occupied similarly scaled and detailed towers, Banham pointed out the confusion presented by these monumental forms located adjacent to the visually lighter precast structural cage and finally alighted on Kahn's incomplete understanding of the mechanical system as his ultimate critique of the work.[37] Because of their fixed but distributed nature these systems must, Banham noted, be delivered "via a permanent grid of ducts, pipes or wires." While Kahn's plan expressed the vertical distribution of these services, the ultimate question posed by comparatively recent developments in air and fluid supply was, for Banham, "in the first instance, a problem of the section of the building."[38] Richards was, if anything, a building conceived in plan—in fact, there is no recorded publication of the overall building's section. Banham felt that Richards represented a "section/plan paradox"—a "frank exposition" of tubes and ducts as they were horizontally distributed on each floor, but an "abhorrence" of their vertical expression in each tower and thus the psychological need for monumental brick "harbors."

This was, of course, part of a larger agenda on Banham's part to move architecture away from its monumental traditions toward a more ephemeral conception of highly serviced spaces for living, surrounded by an anonymously conceived and (according to Banham's logic) aesthetically compelling servicing tissue.[39] Whereas Jordy saw in Richards a finely honed balance between past and present, monument and machine, Banham bemoaned the fact that Kahn had not pushed past this balance and abandoned entirely the mythology of the architectural monument, resulting in the underfunctional but emotionally satisfying brick towers. This is not quite a fair criticism, given the cost-driven evisceration of Kahn's original ideas for the more articulate air "schnorkels," and it is difficult to know what Banham would have thought had the much more expressive weavings of concrete and clay pipes been built as originally proposed. That scheme, along with the one-time rendering of the Richards stair towers as cylindrical elements, would surely have ameliorated Banham's major criticisms regarding legibility. Given the project's history, this article must have been extraordinarily grating, but Kahn took Banham's criticism with good humor.[40] Kahn never addressed these issues publicly, instead, perhaps, taking some comfort in the fact that Banham also noted that the contemporaneous scheme for the Salk Institute seemed to be a step forward in the synthesis of structure, services, and architectural form.

Banham would eventually concede the global importance of Richards as a "legitimization" of the idea that services could form the basis of architectural conceptualization, though he remained critical of the building's "beaux-arts crudity" and its nervous stuffing away of aesthetically compelling pipes and ducts into "monumental cupboards."[41] Compared with Mies, of course, whose pursuit of the open plan stuffed pipes and ducts into cramped, invisible floor and ceiling spaces, this seems a bit overstated. However, what is more striking about Banham's critique, given the building's actual history, is that it focused on only one aspect of the design—the organization of its services—while ignoring the structural and fabricational advances occurring in such close proximity to the heavily critiqued ductwork harbors.[42] However one might feel about the towers' appropriateness—and Banham later admitted their eventual influence on architects as diverse as Ulrich Franzen, Mike Webb, and Richard Rogers— they occurred within a fabric of material and systems innovation that was, at the time, unmatched. Richards did not merely propose a new (albeit, *pace* Banham, widely

121

RICHARDS MEDICAL RESEARCH LABORATORIES

Exterior view

anticipated and occasionally attempted) strategy for housing ductwork and pipes in an architecturally legible composition. It also explored a new, untested method of building prefabrication; formed the second in a series of experiments that reconceived the glass curtain wall as a tightly stretched, minutely detailed surface; and marked a refinement of Kahn's effort to weave environmental systems into an overall architectural conception. The building's technical multivalence, its appeal to a wide range of interests in building assembly and performance, was its primary significance, not—as Banham seems to have suggested—the mere fact of its solution to the problems of ductwork's proper position in the built hierarchy of a laboratory.

Perhaps the most cogent assessment of Richards came from Vincent Scully, who in 1960 positioned the new laboratories at the forefront of what he called the American "Precisionist Strain."[43] This short-lived formulation described for Scully a tendency in American architecture toward "purity of shape, linearity of detail, and, at times, compulsive repetition of elements" and included works as early as the "taut, hollow boxes" of seventeenth-century Massachusetts, the "clear, sharply separate geometric shapes" of the University of Virginia, and Louis Sullivan's "active statement[s] of human force."[44] For Scully, the ultimate expression of Richards was its interchange between crisp, precisely delineated steel, glass, and precast concrete and the rougher,

CHAPTER THREE

coarser finish of its poured concrete structures. The precision of its "brittle planes" with its glass, concrete, and brick stretched to a common boundary plane, suggested both a mastery of technique and a compulsive cleanliness—modernist goals in themselves but pushed to unusually evocative limits at Richards.

The challenges of the building's "precisionist" ideals in its expressed logic and pithy detailing seem to have been, in fact, the defining conditions of Richards's conception and reception. The intensity of praise from Jordy, among others, suggests that the tortuous process of the design's execution, its struggles against cost and technical hurdles nevertheless led to a work of supreme legibility and craft, as the "precise" nature of its assembly mirrored the sharp logic of the design's genesis. The realization that an integrated approach to the wide variety of problems posed by its amorphous but demanding program could create a building of such revealed clarity may have been Richards's greatest achievement. In fact, while the building spawned outright imitations, many on the University of Pennsylvania's campus, its pristinely expressed sense of order and orchestration can be seen in the work of a subsequent generation of architects who were at an impressionable point in their careers. In particular, the Yale thesis project done jointly by Richard Rogers and Norman Foster in 1961 shows direct affinities to the *parti* and handling of vertical service runs in Richards, an influence since acknowledged by both.[45] Likewise, work by Rogers + Piano on the Centre Georges Pompidou in Paris shows a clear exposition of servant and served spaces, while their proposal for a demountable hospital for the Association for Rural Aid in Medicine of 1971 reads as a tribute to Richards in its plan and section.[46] Rogers designed the most overt manifestation of Richards's servant/served plan at Lloyd's of London (1986), where the brick harbors of Richards were stripped off to reveal a rich tangle of stainless-steel ducts, fire stairs, and elevators wrapped tentacle-like around a rectangular prism of open-plan office space.

123

Forty years after its completion, Richards's bold articulation seems quite subtle compared with the overtly expressive buildings it inspired, but the appearance of such a finely honed, well-ordered, and rigorously conceived structure against the ornamental backdrop of the University of Pennsylvania's neogothic campus is still provocative. Richards was a touchstone for the postwar debate on the proper roles of technology and tradition. While much has been made of its references to medieval towers, the brute force of the Richards complex was a strong argument in favor of a progressive, confident technology against the more purely compositional approaches of an earlier era. The Yale Art Gallery had been a tentative first step in Kahn's reconciliation of archaic atmosphere and modern technique, suffused in a language of modernist abstraction, but Richards went further, dramatically contrasting complex systems with monumental, calm masses.

Richards marked a turning point in Kahn's career, as the intensity of this technical experimentation was increasingly tempered in his later works with a concern for the monumental apparent in smaller doses at Richards and Yale. While the Salk Institute and the Kimbell Art Museum in particular employed innovative solutions to mechanical, structural, and constructional issues, neither project pushed the technological envelope in as many directions as Richards had. Kahn's reach may have slightly exceeded his own grasp and that of his clients, but this fact would be moderated by the extraordinary, nearly flawless technical successes that would follow in La Jolla and Fort Worth and by the continued usage of the laboratory building today. In reaching for the precisionist goals of perfect tolerance, ultimate flexibility, and aesthetic refinement, Richards was undoubtedly doomed to fall short. That it arrived so close to its ideals, and that it did so by transforming ordinary materials into a well-integrated and legible whole, remained a powerful indictment of less rigorously conceived architecture, laboratory and otherwise. But the debates that it inspired and the legions of designers who sought to learn from its example made Richards—for all its well-documented flaws—among the most influential of Kahn's works. The precision of its execution and the richness of its conception combined to define and transcend the tenets of the "precisionist strain," hinting at a synthesis between technique and experience, concept and detail that nearly two generations later remains an elusive, though inspiring, goal.

124

Endnotes

1. Louis I. Kahn, "The Mind Opens to Realizations," in *Louis I. Kahn: In the Realm of Architecture*, eds. David B. Brownlee and David G. De Long (New York: Rizzoli, 1991), 78–79.

2. "A. E. Komendant, 85, A Structural Engineer," obituary, *New York Times*, 18 September 1992, A26.

3. August Komendant, *Prestressed Concrete Structures* (New York: McGraw-Hill, 1952).

4. August Komendant, *My 18 Years with Architect Louis I. Kahn* (Englewood, N.J.: Aloray Press, 1975), 1–4.

5. "In the future...tremendous cranes will characterize our construction sites." Kahn, as quoted in Komendant, *My 18 Years*, 5. It is intriguing to compare this experience with the well-known quote about the crane on the jobsite that opens this chapter.

6. Drawing DD-118, n.d., ca. 22 July 1957, Louis I. Kahn Collection, University of Pennsylvania and the Pennsylvania Historical and Museum Commission, Philadelphia (hereafter cited as Kahn Collection), LIK folder 490.001.

7. Drawing DD-113, n.d., ca. 22 July 1957, Kahn Collection, LIK folder 490.001.

8. James S. Hornback, "A Review of the New Skyscraper," *Architectural Record*, March 1957, 228–49.

9. Armstrong's building was well publicized, appearing in *Architectural Record* in 1957. Herbert L. Smith Jr., ed., *Buildings for Research: An Architectural Record Book* (New York: F. W. Dodge, 1958), 173–78.

10. This description is based on a review of Komendant's structural drawings for the project, contained in LIK folder 490.009 of the Kahn Collection. A clear summary of the structural scheme is offered by Robert M. Price (Inspector for the City of Philadelphia) in his report of August 1959 (see Kahn Collection, LIK box 25).

11. The descriptions of the mechanical system are based on a review of Fred Dubin's drawings, contained in LIK folders 490.010 and 490.008 of the Kahn Collection.

12. These details, along with a cogent summary of their assembly and importance, are included in Edward R. Ford, *The Details of Modern Architecture*, vol. 2, *1928–88* (Cambridge: MIT Press, 1996), 306–7. Ford, in quoting Kahn, notes the contradiction here between hollow structural members—which Kahn endorsed—and hollow framing members, which seemed somehow suspect.

13. "What the Building 'Wants to Be': Louis I. Kahn's Richards Medical Research Building at the University of Pennsylvania," in William H. Jordy, *The Impact of Modernism in the Mid-Twentieth Century*, vol. 5 of *American Buildings and Their Architects* (New York: Oxford University Press, 1976), 361–426.

14. Kahn quoted in Richard Saul Wurman, *What Will Be Has Always Been: The Words of Louis I. Kahn* (New York: AccessPress/Rizzoli, 1986), 237.

15. Drawing A17, 16 October 1958, Kahn Collection, LIK folder 030.I.C.490.005.

16. Kahn's final construction drawings for the project are contained in LIK folders 490.006 and 490.005 of the Kahn Collection. As noted below, numerous important changes to the layout of the structure were made between the first issue of construction drawings for bidding in May 1958 and the set that was incorporated as the contract drawings in September–November 1958.

17. "Using these [other departments'] plans as examples please lay out your own quarters on the vacant half of floor 5B as indicated in the ¼" scale drawing. The partitions should always fall immediately under a beam, hence the pattern of beams overhead is faintly indicated on the plan." Thomas Vreeland (Louis I. Kahn office) to Dr. Theodore Ingalls, 15 November 1957, Kahn Collection, LIK box 9.

18. Kahn to Dr. Norman H. Topping (Vice President for Medical Affairs, University of Pennsylvania), 20 December 1957, Kahn Collection, LIK box 9.

19. "Meeting of the Planning Committee, 11 September 1958," Kahn Collection, LIK box 25 ("Alfred Newton Richards Medical Research Laboratory, University of Pennsylvania").

20. "The elevation of the building indicates that the windows have increasing heights from the center to the outside corner. Mr. Kahn agreed to endeavor to work out the elevation so that the two inner windows would be the same height with the outer of greater height." Ibid.

21. Photograph taken 1 December 1958, Kahn Collection, LIK cat. no. 490/K12 8p.1.

22. J. B. Smythe, "Concrete Results," *PCI Journal*, September 1961, 86–91. Smythe's paper is summarized in Komendant, *My 18 Years*. Also see Thomas J. Leidigh, "From Architect's Conception to Concrete Reality," *PCI Journal*, September 1961, 80–85.

23. Atlantic refined Komendant's shapes slightly to enable them to reuse the formwork on other projects, offsetting the significant tooling costs for such an intricate job. Komendant had no objections, and the formwork found later use for bridge girders and rectangular columns. J. B. Smythe (Chief Engineer, Atlantic Precast Corp.), untitled paper, 1962, August E. Komendant Collection, Architectural Archives of the University of Pennsylvania, Philadelphia, copy in box 8.

24. Ibid.

25. An undated chart from Atlantic in LIK box 25 of the Kahn Collection details the start and end dates for frame erection, in addition to the time required to cast the various pieces.

26. In particular, Cornell realized late in the process that the reach of the crane would put the long main beams into close proximity with the old Medical School Building during their crane flight. The direction of their span was changed during the construction process to minimize the extension required of the crane to move these eighteen-ton members at the seventh and eighth floors.

27. "The progress on the job has been extremely disappointing. It has taken three weeks to erect three floors, which means that if there is no improvement, we are going to be erecting precast concrete into the end of October.... In the three weeks you have been on the job there has been no improvement in methods or time in the erecting of each of the three floors which are done." Joseph R. Farrell to Smythe, 16 June 1959, Kahn Collection, copy in LIK box 25 ("Alfred Newton Richards Medical Research Laboratory, University of Pennsylvania"). This copy is marked in pencil "show to Lou."

28. For a complete description of the construction process, see Leidigh, "From Architect's Conception."

29. Daily reports on the construction sequence filed by Thomas J. Leidigh of Keast & Hood are contained in LIK box 25 ("Alfred Newton Richards Medical Research Laboratory, University of Pennsylvania") of the Kahn Collection.

30. Smythe, untitled paper, 1962.

31. "Are You Illiterate about Modern Architecture?" *Vogue*, 15 September 1961. See also "Form Evokes Function," *Time*, 6 June 1960, 76; Ada Louise Huxtable, "In Philadelphia, An Architect," *New York Times*, 11 June 1961; and, overseas, James Baker, "The American Argument," *The Guardian* (Manchester), 3 July 1961. The Architectural Archives at the University of Pennsylvania has records of more than 250 citations of the building in the local, national, and international press.

32. William Jordy, "Criticism: Medical Research Building for Pennsylvania University [*sic*], Philadelphia," *Architectural Review*, February 1961, 100.

33. Ibid., 104.

34. Ibid., 106.

35. Kahn to Jordy, 21 October 1961, Kahn Collection, LIK box 9, folder "Master File 10/2/61 to 12/31/61."

36. Reyner Banham, "On Trial 1: The Situation. What Architecture of Technology?" *Architectural Review* 131, no. 780 (February 1962): 99.

37. "What it comes to is this: Kahn has dramatized the fact that his building is mechanically serviced, but he seems to be pretty insensitive to the nature and functions of those services...." Reyner Banham, "On Trial 2: Louis Kahn and the Buttery-Hatch Aesthetic," *Architectural Review* 131, no. 781 (March 1962): 205.

38. Ibid., 206.

39. Reyner Banham, "Stocktaking," *Architectural Review* 127 (February 1960): 93–100.

40. "I appreciate your letter about the Reyner Banham-Johnson tilt.... I am sure you will have a fine time. I am sorry that I must miss the jousting and then the swords. I am also quite sure that both knights will be unhorsed and shake hands and find that they are really brothers." Kahn to Doug Haskell (Editor, *Architectural Review*), ca. March 1961, Kahn Collection, folder "Master File 3/1/61 to 5/31/61."

41. A reference to the title of his piece "On Trial 2: Louis Kahn and the Buttery-Hatch Aesthetic." "Buttery-hatch" is a butler's cabinet in public-school residences and country houses into which plates are put after a meal, or a cabinet in which liquor is hidden.

42. Reyner Banham, *The Architecture of the Well-Tempered Environment* (Chicago: University of Chicago Press, 1969), 246–55.

43. Vincent Scully, "The Precisionist Strain in American Architecture," *Art in America* 48, no. 3 (1960): 46–53.

44. Ibid., 46, 47, 49.

45. This project is published in both *Richard Rogers + Architects* (London: Academy Editions, n.d.), 20, and in *Norman Foster: Sketches*, ed. Werner Blaser (Boston: Birkhauser Verlag, 1992). In remarks that accompany the thesis drawings, Foster points out that Kahn was a "strong influence at the school; for me Kahn gets better all the time as an architect and I still make pilgrimages to look at his buildings." Foster also includes in this volume a Yale project for an office building that has a crenellated duct tower with obvious affinities to Kahn's earlier scheme for Richards: "The stepped profile reflected varying space needs alongside the diminishing bulk of service ducts and structure" (pp. 20–21).

46. Peter Buchanan, ed., *Renzo Piano Building Workshop: Complete Works* (London: Phaidon, 1993), 44.

SALK INSTITUTE FOR BIOLOGICAL STUDIES
LA JOLLA, CALIFORNIA

Jonas Salk's announcement in April 1955 that human trials of a new vaccine against polio had been successful helped to usher in an era of profound scientific optimism. Polio had infected nearly thirty-eight thousand Americans in the year prior to the introduction of the vaccine. Reaction to the new treatment was immediate, and its apparent triumph crowned the scientist who developed it with lasting celebrity. The vaccine was named after Salk, who had worked on typing the polio virus and tracking the body's reaction to it for eight years, and he became the new face of a humane scientific culture.

Salk was an unlikely candidate for such fame. Born to Russian-Jewish immigrant parents in 1914, he grew up in relative poverty in East Harlem and the Bronx.[1] His father, a factory worker, pushed him toward academic achievement, and Salk attended the City College of New York and New York University (NYU) Medical School. He eventually followed his mentor, Dr. Thomas Francis, from NYU to the epidemiology department at the University of Michigan and later accepted an opportunity at the University of Pittsburgh to lead research on viral epidemiology. It was at Pittsburgh that Salk began experiments on the polio virus, isolating its three strands and studying the effects of neutralized viruses.[2]

CHAPTER FOUR

Jonas Salk as featured on the cover of *Time* in March 1954

This research was funded as part of a nationwide campaign by the National Foundation for Infantile Paralysis. Led by Father Basil O'Connor, there had been little progress in the 1940s, which spurred a younger generation of scientists to pursue unconventional research. Salk quickly became the leading voice in the typing program. Other researchers, in particular Alfred Sabin at the Rockefeller Institute, pursued parallel tracks, but Salk's work led the field.[3] While Sabin's approach would be more effective in the long run, Salk's was completed first, and the successful field trial for his vaccine commenced in April 1954.

With Salk's help, the National Foundation for Infantile Paralysis had, by 1956, largely achieved its goal of eradicating polio. Its original mission now accomplished, the Foundation possessed a generous endowment that required a purpose morally equivalent to the fight against polio that had inspired its original benefactors. In the late 1950s, Salk and O'Connor began discussing the establishment of an institute that would foster the type of research Salk had done at Pittsburgh, with the intent of addressing the social context of biological science while seeking new medical advances. Salk and O'Connor laid out four primary principles that formed the basis for subsequent planning:

That the pursuit of knowledge through scientific research is a
constructive human activity in itself;

That the most effective means for the maintenance and enhancement
of health as well as for the prevention and cure of disease will derive
from fundamental advances in the life sciences;

That the growing knowledge of the behavior of cells and of the
molecules of which they are composed promises to effect a
fundamental change in man's view of himself as he interacts with his
external environment and in the possibilities of control over himself
and over that environment;

That in order to assure the maximum contribution to human welfare,
the scientist must be concerned with men not only as biophysical
organisms but as unique individuals and as social beings.[4]

Salk and O'Connor's mission stands out from other scientific ventures of the era by
virtue of its focus on qualitative, in addition to purely quantitative, results. Set against
other cold-war research, the work for which Salk sought a place would be holistic,
with biomedical research seen as part of a sociocultural fabric into which its fit was
as crucial as its achievements. In addition to prominent scientists, the support of
writers and humanists was enlisted; these included Jacob Bronowski, whose 1956 book
Science and Human Values decried the brutality of the atomic bomb, proposing a
value-rich dialogue between the arts and sciences.

132

By 1959, the idea of an institute had solidified to the point where, with promised fund-
ing from O'Connor and others, Salk began the process of selecting a site. The City of
San Diego, then planning a research district in suburban La Jolla to complement the
University of California campus, offered land overlooking the Pacific that Salk visited in September 1959. Initially, he was skeptical of its appropriateness for a "serious institute" but upon seeing the location he was moved and planned a second visit
for January. Between the two trips, colleagues of Salk's reported on a lecture given by
Kahn at the bicentennial of Carnegie Mellon University; the talk featured the Richards
Laboratories then under construction in Philadelphia. They advised Salk to speak
with Kahn about the selection process for architects; Salk visited Philadelphia in

December 1959, meeting briefly with Kahn before visiting the Richards site, where the structure and stair towers had just been completed.[5]

Though he was intrigued by the Richards project, Salk was not immediately enthusiastic. Kahn, on the other hand, was sincerely moved by Salk's visit, and it is mostly in his recollections that the tenor of the conversation is recalled. Salk made it known immediately that the project would supercede simple quantities of space. He suggested that Richards's size—one hundred thousand square feet divided among ten research groups—would be a reasonable assumption for the institute, but further described his spiritual goal of linking science with the humanities by quipping that he wanted to invite Picasso to the laboratories. Salk also described the work as belonging not to researchers, but to the "population." Perhaps most importantly, Kahn recalls Salk making a distinction between the "measurable" and "immeasurable" work of the scientist, a description of the objective and subjective worlds that meshed well with Kahn's belief in architecture's ability to link the ineffable with the mundane.

Salk and Kahn formed an immediate bond following this brief encounter. They shared a common background: both came from Jewish immigrant families; had grown up in working class, urban neighborhoods; and had been encouraged by their parents to transcend their origins. And both had risen to prominence through public education and internal drive. Some combination of these experiences left them with a willingness to embrace the grinding day-to-day minutiae of their professions. Salk's primary achievement came about through the painstaking routine of viral typing, while Kahn's work to that point had involved the transformation of mundane programs into satisfying works of architecture. The public faces of their careers projected the transcendental, an image that both Kahn and Salk promoted, but their successes lay largely in their mastery of the numbing detail of architectural design and laboratory work. This shared appreciation for detail would define their collaboration and the building they would produce together.

Kahn accompanied Salk on his second visit to La Jolla in January 1960. San Diego and the University of California offered a twenty-seven-acre plot of land between U.S. Route 101 (Torrey Pines Road) and the Pacific Ocean, adjacent to the newly planned University of California at San Diego campus but bisected by a deep arroyo, making much of the land unbuildable.[6] In November 1960, the city formally approved the plan negotiated with the University and Salk; an additional significant piece of land

133

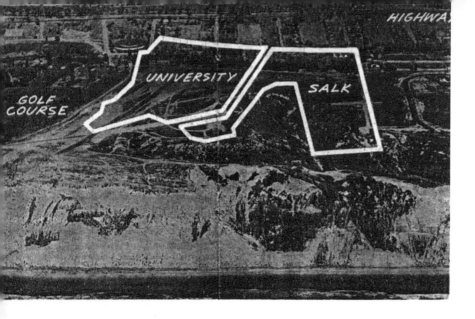

The site of the Salk Institute in 1960 showing adjacent University of California land and the site's challenging topography

in the burgeoning scientific community, albeit with a difficult topography, was given to the institute at no cost.

Initial Scheme

Following discussions with Salk, Kahn's office assembled a preliminary scheme, and by March 1960 the office had prepared a site model that was used by Salk to publicize his deal with the city.[7] Based on his conversation with Salk at the Richards jobsite, Kahn proposed a faithful rendition of that project's towers. On the much larger California site, the clusters of towers proposed by Kahn seemed lost, however, and the design compensated for this through an extensive provision for service routes, which formed intersecting lines crossing the broad plateau at the east end of the site. The laboratory clusters themselves were mounted atop round podia, forming tangential, pulleylike relationships with two service structures. Moving west, residential and recreational buildings were arranged on either side of the canyon, linked by separate roads that ran to the highway; a rectilinear meeting complex was joined to the rest of the site by a bridge over the northern branch of the canyon.[8]

134

Site model of the preliminary tower scheme

As Kahn would later admit, this initial scheme was unrealistic and inefficient.[9] While the tight confines of the Richards site had forced Kahn to build laboratory towers, the La Jolla site offered a vast expanse of flat land, suggesting a simpler, lower solution. The position of the towers on the site left a narrow strip of parking, and the service strategy was, despite its graphic interest in the model, inefficient, requiring separate loading areas for each of the eight towers. Views from the laboratories would have been distinctly unequal. The western half of the towers would have looked out over the Pacific, while those in the eastern half would have looked at the new campus— an inequality that would have belied the democratic ambitions of the institute. Finally, developing subdivisions to the south imposed a height restriction on the site that quickly nullified the tower scheme. This scheme was abandoned almost immediately after its presentation to the city, and Kahn even apologized to Salk for its too-rapid conception and lack of sensitivity toward the site.

Over the next twelve months, Kahn's work focused on developing a new solution. He again hired both August Komendant and Fred Dubin as consultants, then finishing their work on Richards. Work began in tandem with the institute's in-house laboratory planner, Earl Walls, on the first of two low-rise schemes that would integrate structural, functional, mechanical, and programmatic issues.

Program

Salk never formally issued a full brief for the institute, later named the Salk Institute for Biological Studies. Rather, its program evolved throughout the early stages of the design process and remained in flux even through the completion and occupation of the buildings in 1966–67. Salk's initial conversation with Kahn regarding the size and disposition of the Richards laboratories remained the clearest source of direction for the team. However, as part of a 1962 presentation, Kahn's office prepared a narrative, "Abstract of Program," that summarized discussions regarding the Institute's space requirements. This abstract formed the sole basis for work on subsequent schemes, and it went well beyond quantitative requirements for square footage. The language is recognizably Kahn's, yet it defines daily patterns in the laboratory that only Salk could have contributed, demonstrating the project's collaborative spirit at its earliest stages.[10]

The abstract laid out objectives for the site administration and support areas in detail. It began with the recognition that the site itself would be an integral part of the function and purpose of the laboratories:

> The choice of the site of Torrey Pines, La Jolla, San Diego,
> overlooking the sea and protected by surrounding park and University
> property is the first inspiring act towards creation of the environment
> for the Institute of Biology. From the presence of the uninterrupted
> sky, the sea and the horizon, the clear and dramatic configuration of
> weather-beaten land spare of foliage, the buildings and their gardens
> must find their position in deference to Nature.[11]

If this introduction suggests an attempt to play to the spiritual side of the Institute's scientists, the remainder of the program is remarkable for its thorough, efficient description. Laboratories were to be designed to service "any of the natural and physical sciences," not only biology. Column-free spaces permitting "complete flexibility of physical and mechanical layout" were specified, and high air quality and climate controls were dictated as well. Flexibility in space planning mandated a 50 percent overprovision for each research group, permitting both expansion and growth in staff or equipment. Service spaces such as "kitchens, storage [and] shops" were to be located in dedicated areas providing for "the most effective circulation."[12]

The Salk program suggested a further refinement to the servant/served dialogue that Kahn initiated at Trenton and Richards in that a new type of servant space was described at length in the program document. Office and study space in the Salk were to have dedicated zones of their own, rather than be carved out of working laboratory areas as had been done, to unsatisfying effect, at Richards. In this early definition, both office and study spaces were to be provided in separately defined areas. While being accessible from the laboratories, studies were to maintain separate entries, allowing scientists to separate the mental work of their research from the bench work. The recognition that research would proceed on two distinct paths led to one of the primary programming gestures of the project: the separation of studies from laboratory blocks.

Additional spaces lying outside the laboratory blocks were specified in the program abstract as well, most notably, meeting and seminar spaces that would become the ill-fated Meeting House planned for the north edge of the site. Just as the studies provided a retreat for the individual scientist, the meeting spaces were to provide for "discussion and exchange of ideas" among and between groups. Dining rooms, a large assembly space, and a communal library were to be part of this complex as well, while temporary residences for visiting fellows, an exercise spa, and administrative functions were to be housed in their own structures separate from the laboratories and the atmosphere of the meeting spaces.

It is apparent from this 1962 brief, issued nearly two years after Kahn had begun work, that the design of the Institute and its programming proceeded alongside one another, with architectural ideas informing the planning and vice versa. There is throughout the brief a distinction between the spaces that required numeric provision—such as administration—and those that required spatial or functional qualities, such as the separation of studies from laboratories. No piece of the program was ignored or cast aside as inconsequential; instead, there was an attempt to determine the character of each space both on its own terms and in relation to others. This was not, therefore, simply a space program; it was the description of an architectural and functional interweaving, already explored by Kahn at Yale and Richards, in which the goals of the Institute were approached by considering the role of each element and its position in the larger hierarchy. Kahn obviously relished the opportunity to introduce this sensibility into the foundational document of the project, as it allowed him to have a say in building up the definitions of the laboratory's spaces based on what was needed to do research. This process would continue through two major design

137

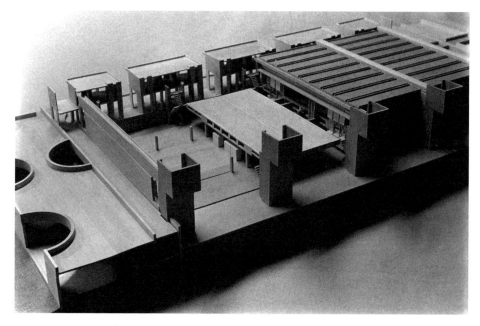

Model by Kahn's office (above)
and a section of the second folded-plate scheme (opposite), ca. 1962

iterations and would focus not only on the coarse grain of the site and laboratory programs, but also on such mundane details as curtain walls, concrete formwork, and stair handrails.

Second Folded-Plate Scheme

The second Salk scheme, developed alongside the program from 1960 through the beginning of 1962, deployed laboratory and ancillary functions in a more logical manner than the tower proposal. Writing in *Progressive Architecture* in April 1961, Kahn explained its division into three elements.[13] The "research and study group," or what came to be known as the laboratory block, occupied the flat area at the head of the arroyo perpendicular to Torrey Pines Road. Two-story laboratory blocks were arranged around a pair of garden courts, with a central alley for service and air intake to the two central blocks. At the west end of these courtyards, terraces with semicircular exedrae terminated the garden axes and provided patios from which to look over the bluffs beyond. At the north and south edges of the laboratory group, additional service towers mirrored the arrangement in the center alley, providing exhaust and mechanical services for the outboard laboratory blocks. A narrow band of personnel

138

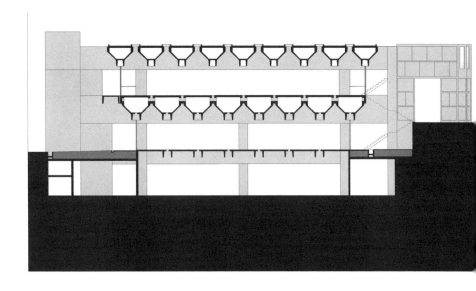

parking was provided to the east of the laboratories, leaving land between the laboratory block and Torrey Pines Road undisturbed for "future expansion."[14]

The remaining elements of this scheme—the Village and the Meeting House—took advantage of the flat areas along the arroyo's north and south edges. To the south, sixteen pavilions were provided to house visiting fellows, arranged in a casual pattern along the contours of the ridge. Parking spaces for these were provided off the southern access road, and a path connected the Village to the laboratory group, two hundred yards to the east. On the north side of the arroyo, the Meeting House was connected to the laboratory block by a diagonal axis, following the edge of the site with allées of trees and additional parking. The coincidence of the site boundaries with a large expanse of flat topography made this area ideal for a large, relatively centralized element, and its distance from the laboratory group—three hundred yards—provided a sense of retreat from the bench into a communal setting. Its layout, suggestive of the plan of Hadrian's Villa, clustered conference, lecture, dining, and domestic elements around a central, covered hall. To either side, gardens suggested spaces for contemplation, while the interior planning was monastic, arranging platonic solids of meeting rooms around a central ambulatory.[15]

139

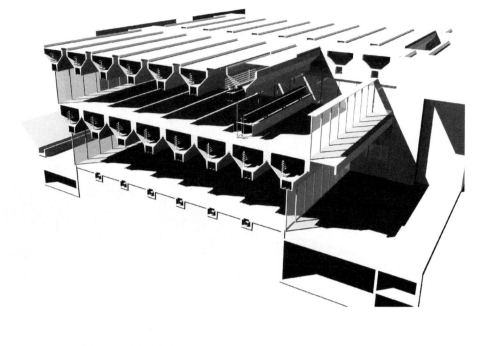

Reconstruction of the second folded-plate scheme

It is worth noting that Kahn's approach to historical precedent was, like his approach to services and structure, one of weaving and balance. It may well be that Hadrian's Villa served as the inspiration for the Meeting House plan. But this reference was not taken as an absolute, and in the face of various functional requirements, the floor plans and sections of the Meeting House evolved to accommodate these needs while echoing the Roman precedent. Historic reference was, certainly, one interest of Kahn's; however, it was hardly his only concern, and the appearance of recognizable precedents in his work is perhaps best seen as another dimension to the conceptual weavings that Kahn's buildings manifest—as intensely here as anywhere in his work.

Within the blocks themselves, laboratories were laid out in this second scheme to meet functional requirements, with 80' × 210' spaces slotted between the study areas and the service towers.[16] These open laboratory floors were free of columns on the upper level, permitting a flexibility beyond even that of Richards, while on the lower floors, the clear span was compromised by a single row of columns that provided support to the upper story. The floors and ceilings of this early scheme accommodated services in a deep ceiling above the main working spaces, allowing maintenance and refitting to occur with minimal disruption to the laboratory areas below.

CHAPTER FOUR

Each laboratory block in the second Salk scheme was separated into four masses. These sections were separated by 10'-0" service zones, "reserved for the positioning of all [fume] hoods and other large pieces of equipment" and aligned with the studies and service towers.[17] By corralling large, service-intensive equipment into dedicated, high air-volume zones, the laboratory spaces themselves could be reserved for benches, adding a programmatic rigor to the working environment.

Above the service zones, U-shaped beams—9'-0" deep above the lower level and 7'-4" deep above the upper—ran across the laboratory block, supported by the study and service towers.[18] On the garden side of each block, these beams were connected to fresh air intakes, while on the service-tower side they were connected to exhaust fans. Fume hoods were to be located directly beneath these high-volume "breathing beams" so that their formidable exhaust requirements could be handled directly, and the beams' large cross sections permitted space for workers to access these ducts along their entire lengths, over the laboratory spaces.[19]

The logic of the hollow beam was carried through to smaller-scale spanning members running parallel to the laboratories' long axes. These were designed to carry through ductwork and services from the main breathing beams above each laboratory space much like a folded piece of paper can carry heavy loads in its hollow. Designed as 40' extrusions, the folded beams consisted of upper and lower concrete flanges with diagonal webs canted at 45°, allowing significant reinforcing and post-tensioning in the areas of greatest structural efficiency while providing large spaces inside for piped services and access, albeit quite limited in height. A cross element at the springing point of the diagonal webs tied the two halves of each beam together structurally but could be punched through to bring services down from the main void. The bottom flanges tapered from this cross element to form a smaller void at the beam's base, accessible from the laboratory below.[20] The folded-plate beams were to be formed and placed without tops to facilitate access during construction, with floor and roof surfaces to be provided by 7'-9" wide precast planks placed later. On the roof, curbs along the edges of these planks were to form bases for skylights for the upper floor.[21]

At first glance, these beams look like they were designed to allow large-scale ductwork to run in the large upper voids, while permitting pipes to run in the more easily accessible lower hollow. Actually, the opposite was true. Exhaust and supply ducts were routed through the small slots at each beam's base, passing through square

141

Site model of the second folded-plate scheme

openings in the sides of the large breathing beams, and then turning upward to join the main supply and exhaust trunks contained therein. Because the main crossbeams took care of the volumes of air required by the fume hoods, this laboratory ductwork could be small. Splitting the lower void into dedicated exhaust and supply sides permitted partitioning systems to run down the center of each beam. The entire floor plate could thus be divided into 10'-0"-wide strips, which Kahn's office showed on experimental floor plans issued in late 1962.[22] More importantly, placing the pipe racks in the upper chamber of the beams allowed access to these services without disturbing the floor plates below. Piped services such as gas, water, and air were to be directed through holes in the bottom of the beams' upper voids, snaking between the ductwork in the lower section and dropping to sinks and benches on the laboratory floor below. Alterations to the laboratory floor plan could thus be serviced by reconfiguring piping, with simple reconnection the only task requiring workmen to enter the laboratory itself.[23]

This efficient scheme for laboratory planning and servicing had intriguing architectural implications. The sculpting of the ceiling into linear "bailiwicks" gave definition to individual laboratory aisles. On the upper floor, the voids between the V-beams permitted strips of daylight to illuminate the laboratories from above, while on the exterior edges the beams formed overhangs, shading the glass exterior walls from direct sun. Whereas Richards had relied on the perhaps too-subtle expression of the ceiling trusses, piping, and ductwork to define the spaces below, this scheme for the Salk proposed a bold linear grain of integrated structure and systems. This organized the laboratory blocks into well-defined interior spaces, with equipment areas separating laboratory modules and with a ceiling that would lend clarity, direction, and rhythm to the otherwise chaotic workspaces below.

The folded-plate scheme was developed during the final months of 1961 and presented at a meeting with Salk in Philadelphia on 18 January 1962. Detailed architectural plans and sections showed the folded-plate scheme in its final form and Komendant prepared forty pages of structural calculations demonstrating the performance and constructability of the scheme.[24] Salk, however, expressed a growing dissatisfaction at the January meeting, and work over the subsequent eight weeks revised the basement arrangement and widened the gardens between laboratory blocks.[25]

On 27 March 1962, Salk and Kahn met with potential contractors to select a construction management team.[26] Salk reported that after the day's meetings, he walked the site and "became terribly unhappy."[27] He would later say that he had been too preoccupied with financial matters during the development of the scheme to be critical of the emerging design. The morning of 28 March, Salk and Kahn flew to San Francisco to report on progress to Basil O'Connor, and much like the conversation between the two at the Richards construction site, this moment reset the direction of the project. Salk objected to the narrow gardens and depth of the laboratory spaces and told Kahn that, despite approvals given in the previous two months, the project needed to "start over."[28]

143

Kahn, while admitting that he "felt the loss" of the folded-plate scheme, would later say that this direction enabled him to build a greater building.[29] The folded-plate scheme had occupied more than eighteen months of his time, yet Salk's criticism rang true. The original pair of gardens had been, in Kahn's words, a "convenience," and Salk urged him to focus on one garden serving the entire complex, a true "place."[30] Subsequent comments by Kahn revealed other problems with the folded plates. Space for ductwork proved to be too small and access to the pipe chases would have been difficult for a workman equipped with large tools or replacement parts.[31] Most importantly, the laboratory spaces themselves presented problems, notably the 10'-0" grid of service connections. While this provided an abundance of opportunities to plug

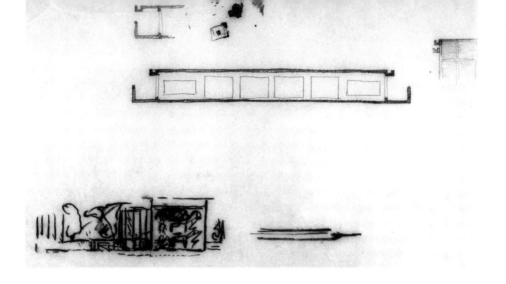

Sketch of a Vierendeel truss used as an interstitial floor by Kahn, ca. April 1962 (above)
and model of the Salk Institute's final scheme by Kahn's office (opposite)

into the interstitial pipes and ducts, the reality of laboratory work demanded a far
tighter grid—typical laboratory benches were often no more than 5'-0" long, a length
which would have left large dead zones between the overhead beams. Salk's demand
for flexibility meant that the grain of the service beams was too coarse, and their rigorous spatial definition to the laboratory floors below ended up being at odds with
his functional requirements.

144   In the weeks following Salk's change of heart, the design team pursued two paths.
Final studies of the folded-plate scheme were undertaken to see if Salk's objections
could be satisfied. For at least a month, Komendant refined calculations and worked
with Kahn's office on alternate arrangements of the breathing beams. Meanwhile,
Kahn, Dubin, and Salk examined options for completely reconfiguring the laboratory
block. Preliminary work on the new configuration appeared promising, and by 3 May,
the Institute officially instructed the design team to change course.

Final Scheme

Three weeks later, on 24 May, Kahn presented a new direction to Komendant and the George Fuller Company, recently appointed as contractor. The new arrangement would have two laboratory blocks, each with a smaller footprint than the previous blocks but would be three stories tall instead of two. The total footprint of each block would be 240' × 62', and to avoid blocking views from neighboring developments, the entire complex would be sunk into the site by one full-story height.[32] Between the laboratory floors, pipes and ducts would run in story-high boxes, interstitial floors allowing easy access to services within. To maintain the column-free laboratory spaces, Vierendeel trusses would run through these interstitial floors at 20'-0" intervals, their openings sized to admit the largest anticipated duct trunking. While much larger in scale than the trusses at Richards or the floor slab at Yale, the principle here was much the same: shaping structural elements not only to span, but also to harbor, complicated masses of ducts and pipes.

On either side of the laboratory blocks, towers again provided service and study facilities. Facing a yet-undefined courtyard, five study towers provided space for principle investigators to work away from the laboratory benches. These aligned not

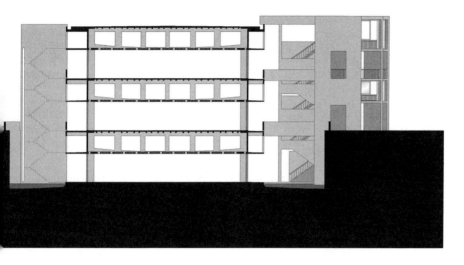

A section (above) of the Salk Institute's final scheme and
a combined plan (opposite) of a typical laboratory floor (top half)
and an interstitial floor (bottom half)

with the laboratory floors, but with the interstitial spaces, providing open areas below the towers at ground level and intermediate terraces at the upper laboratory. There would thus be a short stair required to link laboratories with adjacent studies, a distance that enhanced the separation of what Kahn called the "spaces of air handling and those of the oak table and carpet." Whereas earlier schemes had placed these studies directly across the courtyard from each other, the final scheme employed a formal sleight of hand that gave each room a view of the ocean. The towers were divided into two ranks of studies, each with an angled window bay that directed views toward the west. The eastern study in each tower was given a slightly larger bay to enable views past its immediate neighbor. Between the study towers and the laboratories, a light well dropped down to basement garden courts to provide daylight and access to the lower story.

On the outer north and south edges of the laboratory complex, service cores contained elevators, rest rooms, and escape stairs. These were to be simple concrete volumes, with openings at ground level to connect the stairs with public areas outside the complex. Between these towers, garden courts again provided daylight to the basement. At the west end of each laboratory block, additional office, administrative, and library spaces were accommodated in wings overlooking the ocean, while chillers, air

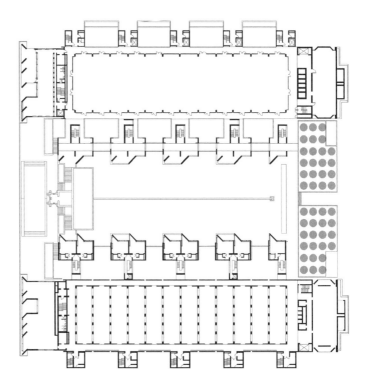

handlers, and utility connections were placed in rectilinear mechanical buildings to the east, connected to one another by an underground service tunnel. This later scheme thus adopted some of the expressive logic of Richards with a number of refinements. The studies, in particular, represented a servant space of a different order, while the provision of horizontal, rather than vertical, air distribution meant an altered approach to housing the major air-handling system. The result was a dialogue between served and servant spaces, between free-plan laboratories and harboring concrete structures that refined and enriched the initial experiments of Yale and Richards. Here, servant spaces were not only made distinct from served spaces in plan, but also in section, and the distinction between the two types, following Banham's critique of Richards, was made clear in both. Likewise, the experience of the mechanical harbors would become much stronger in the Salk, where public circulation would be defined constantly and modulated by a rhythm of service towers and interstitial floors, enriching the experience of the buildings' grain while providing a flexible mechanical strategy.

This scheme was presented to Salk on 9 June 1962, less than three months after his charge to redesign, and it received his approval on its general massing, revised dimensions, and mechanical systems. Salk asked the team to look at phasing the

147

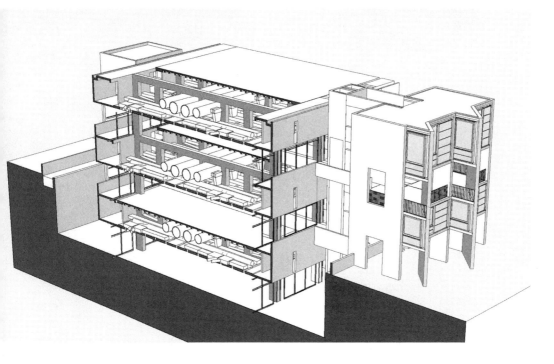

Cutaway view of one laboratory block

construction, a sign that there was deepening financial pressure on the Institute.[33] Komendant, whose contribution to the new structural arrangement had been limited, began detailed design on 9 July. The release of new construction drawings was staggered over the next several months to allow site work to begin, and clearing commenced on 15 July 1962, just five weeks after Salk's approval. While architectural changes, including revisions to the exterior corridor widths and the configuration of stair towers, delayed Komendant's work on the structure, his calculations were finished by 1 December 1962. The full architectural and structural package was released to the site before 18 January 1963.[34]

It is intriguing to note that the Vierendeel solution appears to have been Kahn's, not Komendant's. Komendant would later claim that he had not been informed of the new direction until late September 1962—a claim that would make his performance in finishing the structural calculations by December particularly impressive but that would also lay its authorship in May and June 1962 squarely in Kahn's hands.[35] Kahn's rationale for the change—that the budget had forced a simpler scheme on the project—might have been only partly true. Komendant deeply suspected Kahn and Salk of changing plans for philosophical and aesthetic rather than functional reasons, and no doubt Kahn would have raised objections had he continued to believe that the

CHAPTER FOUR

folded-plate scheme was the best alternative. "My structural engineer," he recalled, "was not for change." The Salk's trusses thus show Kahn adopting approaches from an earlier project—the floor trusses of Richards—and reconceiving them in a new context, a hallmark of an empirical design process in which each iteration builds and extends knowledge gained in earlier attempts. The literal translation of Richards to the first scheme on the La Jolla site did not recast its principles based on the unique circumstances of the new site. But here, the adoption of an approach, rather than a form or component, had broad applicability.

Whatever the system's genesis, the structural solution Komendant developed from Kahn's initial sketches was brilliantly executed. Despite his objections that the Vierendeel was a structurally "incorrect" hybrid solution, the Salk remains a textbook example of the potential for this structural type, and it was, perhaps reluctantly, highlighted by Komendant in his monograph on concrete structures published in 1972.[36] The logic behind the Vierendeel trusses in the Salk paralleled Kahn's use of them in Richards. Truss construction replaces a beam's solid vertical web with a network of axially loaded members, substituting simple compression and tension for shear. This enables the physical separation between tension and compression chords without the weight of a solid web. Again, as at Richards, Vierendeel trusses reversed the logic of simple trusses' diagonal arrangements, providing robust moment connections between the flange elements and the vertical posts separating them. These posts resist the internal shear in the trusses' web, which is transmitted by the moment connections into the tension and compression members at the bottom and top of the truss.[37] While trusses of traditional shape are familiar solutions to clear-span situations, their depth is greater than that of a simple beam, and the provision of services either underneath or above such a truss implies an increased floor-to-floor height. In service-intensive programs such as laboratories, the depth of the mechanical systems is often as great as the required structural depth. There is thus efficiency in combining structure and services in the same section, whether that section is a three-dimensional truss or a punched beam, as at Yale, or a planar truss with carefully thought-out voids, such as the Vierendeels at Richards and La Jolla. Pulling up the mechanical entrails of a building into these sectional harbors allows the structure to touch the space below. It can be exposed, showing off its dimension and patterns, making the integration of structure and services visible.

The Salk trusses consist of a 2'-0" compression chord along their top edge and a tension chord of varying depth at their base. These are separated by two end posts and

149

five intermediate posts on 10'-0" centers. This arrangement provides openings in the truss that vary from 5'-0" to 6'-0" in height and from 7'-9" to 8'-3" in width. The three trussed boxes that make up a typical laboratory block section are stacked atop 11'-0"-high columns that mark the only structural footprint on each laboratory floor. Komendant realized an additional sectional efficiency by using posttensioning cables in the lower, tension chord of each truss. Tightened against blockouts in the corridor walls, ¼" cables take the gravity loads from the vertical posts out to the exterior column lines, where they are cancelled by the compressive abilities of the truss's concrete. A minimal concrete enclosure protects the cables and provides a rigid connection between them and the shear columns. Each Vierendeel thus imparts only vertical loads to the columns below, allowing simple connections and eliminating bending in the columns and foundations.[38] The roughly catenary curve of the posttensioning cables places the largest truss openings in the center of the section, where Fred Dubin's mechanical engineering scheme suggested they would be the most effective.

The Vierendeel system thus provided porous, deep structural members that allowed uninterrupted space within the laboratories below and a sparse grid of shear columns within the intermediate floors. Komendant was satisfied with the performance of the scheme, though he continued to feel that the solution was not statically expressive.[39] The Salk's location in a well-known earthquake zone also required Komendant to work through its unique seismic characteristics. In February 1963, the City of San Diego responded to the submission of Komendant's structural calculations with concern about the ductility of the system during an earthquake.[40] Later that month, Komendant flew to the jobsite to explain the system to the city's building inspectors.[41] As originally conceived, the rigid concrete frame would have been brittle, with the potential to snap in a large earthquake, risking collapse. The city's engineers suggested steel, which would bend, not break, in a large earthquake. Concerned about the implications of such a change, Komendant proposed a modification to the original concrete scheme, taking advantage of the Vierendeel's simple connections to their support columns. These were redesigned as true roller joints, allowing the interstitial boxes to move relative to the columns above and below. To prevent the floors from completely decoupling, Komendant designed an additional posttensioning system, consisting of vertical cables running continuously through the columns. These relatively slack cables go into tension if the floors move, exerting a righting force while not permitting any damaging moments to transfer. As Komendant later reported, moderate earthquakes during and after construction proved the worthines of the scheme.[42] Thus, much like Richards, the Salk's structure was an assembly of

150

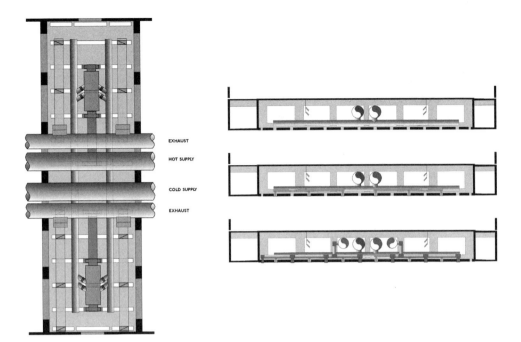

Diagrams of the laboratory block's mechanical systems as designed by Fred Dubin. Typical bay (left) and section (right) showing positions of hot and cold supply air and return air ducts

concrete parts—here poured in place rather than prefabricated—connected by tight steel cables and connections.

Services

Komendant's "breathing structure" harbored an intricate circulatory system designed by mechanical engineer Fred Dubin. Where the folded-plate scheme had relied on vertical towers with individual air handlers and transverse trunking, the Vierendeel structural scheme involved a more efficient, longitudinal approach. At the eastern end of each laboratory block, the two mechanical wings accommodated chillers, air handlers, and equipment. Major supply and exhaust ductwork for the laboratories was designed to enter interstitial levels at the center of each block, where the voids in the Vierendeel trusses were greatest. At 20'-0" intervals, branch ducts carried hot and cold air to the sides of the laboratories, where blending boxes mixed air to the required temperature. Woven between the supply system's outlets, exhaust ductwork simultaneously extracted air from the laboratories and returned it to the central trunk.[43] This arrangement placed the high-maintenance blending boxes closest to the outboard service corridors, while allowing access to pipe runs in the outer thirds of

151

Interior view of pipe space showing a Vierendeel truss

each interstitial space. The major ducts, measuring 4'-0" in diameter, were placed at the center of the floor plate to avoid restricting access to any pipes or boxes, allowing easier maintenance and reconfiguration than the folded-plate scheme's tight confines.

To connect the interstitial services to the laboratory spaces, Kahn, Dubin, and Komendant developed a simple but effective ceiling slot detail. Where the folded-plate scheme had assumed a relatively fixed starting configuration for pipes and ducts, the reality of the Salk was that laboratory groups and requirements would be in flux throughout the building's life. The laboratory's connections to its supply, exhaust, and piped services needed almost infinite flexibility, and the ceiling slab was thus conceived as a porous element. Based on the carrying patterns of the Vierendeels, the floor of each interstitial space included lines of 10"-wide slots placed 5'-0" apart, so that no point on the floor would ever be more than 2'-6" from potential access to the interstitial level.

Ordinary construction would have used a lightweight ceiling system with catwalks to provide access to the various ducts and pipes overhead. Instead, Kahn took Salk's suggestion that they "give the pipes a floor of their own" literally. The pipe level would

Interior view of a typical laboratory space showing the ceiling slot and lighting layouts

have a solid concrete floor slab, but the slots would be constructed using an ingenious, inexpensive method. The team developed a single aluminum extrusion, 8" deep, with a pair of continuous slots at the sides to accept connections for unistruts—lightweight rolled-steel channels with predrilled holes. During construction, the extruded sections were mitered and joined to form boxes that were temporarily fixed to the slab formwork with the slots facing inward. Electrical connections were then attached to each box, and as the 8" interstitial floor slab was poured, these boxes became mechanically fixed to the curing concrete, their mitered joints forming reliably dimensioned voids in the floor slab. The boxes were left in place as the formwork was removed, leaving continuous connections for unistruts, electric lighting, and services in the laboratory ceilings. The edging of the aluminum extrusions provided ledges for aluminum diffusers and registers; where required by Dubin's services plan, exhaust and supply boxes were simply bolted in place, gasketed, and connected to the ductwork above. Pipe drops of brake-shaped steel and aluminum could also be attached to the ceiling, allowing gas, air, and water services to connect with the benches below.

153

The light fixtures attached to these slots were 4'-0" linear fluorescent fixtures with parabolic louvers designed to spread light efficiently. Earl Walls's laboratory plans assumed that benches would be oriented perpendicular to the room's curtain-walled edges and thus perpendicular to the ceiling slots as well. In design meetings in 1962, Walls suggested that the light fixtures be oriented in the same direction as the slots, to most efficiently illuminate the benches below along their lengths—minimizing the amount of light that would miss the benches.[44] Kahn disagreed, believing that their orientation should provide a visual cross grain to the length of the laboratories. This issue was revisited in July 1963, while Edison Price, a manufacturer in New York, was fabricating the fixtures. Price agreed with Walls and informed Marshall Meyers that there was "absolutely no reason lighting-wise to turn the fixtures perpendicular to the slots."[45] Kahn, though, continued to insist on the perpendicular arrangement based on the visual cross grain of the laboratories. The light fixtures, by their linear arrangement and their bright apertures, provided a foil to the directionality of the ceiling slots, which to Kahn was as important as the efficiency of their illumination. But Kahn prevailed only after Price realized that parallel fixtures would cause harsh reflections in the laboratories' glass walls. As a result, the lights add the rhythm that Kahn desired to the ceiling of the otherwise chaotic laboratory spaces.[46]

While the slotted concrete ceiling allowed flexibility, the laboratory planning was remarkably traditional. Kahn's office had little to do with the laboratory layouts, leaving the technical and detailed design to Earl Walls, the Institute's in-house laboratory planner. Walls's planning was based on a racetrack model, in which core services are concentrated in the center of a floor plate. Actual laboratory bench spaces were placed at the perimeter, adjacent to daylight, with a service corridor and fume hood alcoves located between the two zones. Centralized functions, including glass washing and centrifuges, were located in the central bays of each wing, separating equal laboratory groups. This planning was an effective tool to deal with a fluctuating program; however, it did not take full advantage of the clear span provided by the Vierendeel spans and certainly did not exploit the slot layouts in the ceilings to their fullest potential. To this day the Salk has maintained the racetrack plan, which has proven functional and efficient, if architecturally disappointing. Nowhere in the complex has a full floor been opened up from one side to the other, and the result on the interior is a mazelike effect that is, unfortunately, remarkably similar to the experience of Richards. Yet again, the architectural implications of a truly free plan eluded Kahn, leaving only the lighting grid to organize and orient the open spaces that were quickly filled with equipment, partitions, and furniture.

154

Detailing and Construction

Writing in 1966, Komendant described Kahn's use of concrete:

> Buildings can tell wonderful stories of how they are made—from the
> gravel pit and cement factory to the final touch of the finisher—
> and also how they carry out their functions structurally. Only if the
> story is clear, pleasant, and exciting can the building be called true
> architecture.

> Of all Kahn's buildings, the most completely satisfying is the Salk
> Laboratories. A design is right in concrete when it could not have
> been built in any other material. When you look at Salk,
> you unhesitatingly answer that it could not have been built in any
> other material.[47]

Kahn's approach to the Salk's concrete detailing is perhaps best explained as a combination of logical execution with didactic expression. The Salk was Kahn's first major project to explore poured concrete as the primary element in a building's palette, and his approach and its results demonstrate clearly an empirical method and expressive intent. Yale had included board-formed concrete in its core elements and structural columns and had exposed the patterns of concrete construction in its ceiling. But these elements intentionally shied away from exposing large, uninterrupted planes of raw concrete, choosing instead to break up large surfaces with natural ornament in the case of the board forms and the high proportion of triangular voids in the Gallery ceiling.

155

Poured-in-place concrete is a risky material when exposed, as its surface appearance and finish are dependent on processes that are irreversible, hidden from view until complete, and sensitive to a range of variables. At Yale, its roughness had been part of a dialogue between contemporary finishes and an archaic quality that Kahn intentionally sought. The Salk's resolutely technical program, however, demanded a slightly different balance. Overall, the complex had to read as a place of scientific refinement. If Kahn continued to play with the idea of timeless forms and materials, it was evident that the distinction would have to be made between the archaic and the merely sloppy. Despite this, concrete remained the material of choice for Kahn, as it suited his desires for monolithic forms and the revelation of the processes by which they

Salk Institute for Biological Studies
San Diego, California
Louis I. Kahn, Architect
George A. Fuller Company, Building Construction
Date 2-28-64   Photo A /   NORTH LABORATORY FLOOR SLAB LOOKING WEST

Construction views showing Vierendeel trusses being poured (above)
and slots being formed in the floor slab of a typical pipe space (opposite)

were constructed. Komendant went so far as to suggest that Kahn inherently designed in concrete, that his "preliminaries" were inevitably "brilliant for concrete" because of their proportions, regularity, and mass.[48] The success of the Salk would assure concrete's status as Kahn's favored material, appearing as the primary element in the palettes of the Kimbell Art Museum, the Bangladesh Parliament, and the Yale Center for British Art.

156   To achieve concrete that would be satisfying to the eye and the touch, Kahn relied on expert advice from Komendant and Fuller, the contractor, both of whom, along with Kahn, went beyond conventional approaches and developed their own methods and techniques. As early as November 1962, both Jack MacAllister and Fred Langford, architects in Kahn's office, were on site full time, in part as coordinators of concrete and formwork. They eventually established an experimental workshop on site to explore the peculiarities of poured concrete.[49] Often, plain finished concrete is sandblasted or sacked with a light mortar after formwork is removed to deal with any imperfections. However, for Kahn, disguising the marks that showed how the wall came to be was a philosophical issue. Concrete was for Kahn at its most honest in its pure, unfinished state in which one could read the history of its making, a belief that prohibited any tampering with the appearance or condition of the walls after their

formation. This did not mean, of course, that Kahn had no standards or that he would have been satisfied with unsightly concrete. Rather, Kahn sought to understand concrete from its first principles and to devise ways in which the material could—naturally—be made to provide the highly refined surfaces appropriate for the building.

Kahn recognized that concrete, despite its liquid nature, possesses both pattern and texture because of the composition of the formwork surrounding it. At Yale, Kahn had specified a narrow board form, leaving vertical striations in the finished surface. This had enabled construction of the cylindrical stair; however, standard practice for large flat walls involved broad sheets of plywood to achieve a smooth surface, as Clark Macomber had suggested in his critique of the Gallery. The joints between plywood forms presented a problem, as liquid concrete can leach out of the formwork box and create projections in the finished wall. These joints can pull water out of the concrete mix through capillary action, leaving behind an area of weak concrete matrix that can crumble. Forms placed adjacent to one another can also bow out or even shift under the pressure of the liquid concrete, leaving discontinuities in the finished surface. Finally, multistory concrete frames must be formed in sequence based on the capacity of lower floors to support the liquid weight of new pours. Thus, floors are

157

Concrete courtyard wall showing its formwork pattern (above) and
a view of the cladding's teak infill panel (opposite)

often poured weeks after each other, and slight changes in humidity, temperature, or water quality between pours can result in different shades and curing patterns.

Given these factors, it seems almost reckless to design an exposed concrete building with no mitigation allowed after pouring. However Kahn, MacAllister, and Langford developed a formwork language that minimized the aesthetic risks and allowed the material's natural patterns to emerge. The major formwork panels consisted of ¾" plywood, in a stock size of 4' × 12', arranged vertically. To achieve a smooth finish, the contact surface of each plywood sheet was sanded and coated with resin, protecting the concrete from contamination and preventing water from seeping out of the matrix.[50] To avoid visible offsets, each plywood panel had its edge chamfered, so that any discontinuity between adjacent surfaces would be interrupted by a ¼" triangular projection, minimizing the appearance of potential errors. Between floors, where different pours met, a horizontal strip of wood was tacked onto the top of each form, creating a deep recess. This recess in the top of the pour was then used to align a tacking strip on the bottom of the next set of forms. The resulting shadowgap clearly transmitted the joint between the two pours while visually separating any differences in color or offsets between stories.[51]

To prevent forms from bowing under the hydrostatic pressure of liquid concrete, wire ties were used to connect shoring beams on the outside of the formwork. As at Yale, Kahn's specifications called for the resulting circular holes to be unfilled, except on exterior faces where they were to be plugged with hammered lead to seal the wire from the elements. The result throughout the concrete work is a rhythm of projecting ridges and indented tie holes and pour joints, presenting a constant order written across the exposed faces of concrete.[52] This natural ornament precisely fulfilled Kahn's idea of a building decorated only by the marks of its assembly and production. It would become one of his most reliable ordering devices, neatly combining an efficient construction process with a naturally occurring program of visual embellishment. The result of this effort is the Salk's most immediate quality—a monolithic concrete structure that, upon approach, reveals its structural and constructional modules through a pattern of raised and recessed marks left by the assembly processes of the building itself. The 4' × 12' module, about the size of two people standing atop one another with their arms outstretched, is a direct expression of human scale. This derives from the human component of its assembly—plywood is generally used in the largest size one worker can lift alone—and the result is a pattern that we perceive as an anthropomorphic measure, cast onto and into the material of the buildings' main masses. That this unique and subtle ordering system came about as the result of technical

159

View of a study tower with teak and glass infill panels (above)
and, opposite, a detailed section (left) and view of the Salk Institute's curtain wall (right)

considerations should by now be of no surprise—Kahn recognized the domain of
assembly as the most intimate of connections between the body and architecture in
drawing as well as construction.

Within the concrete frame, a family of infill panels provided a more finely grained
enclosure for the Salk's offices and studies. These areas, imagined by Kahn as the
"spaces of the carpet and oak table," demanded a warmer feel than the laboratories,
and Kahn therefore designed window panels of teak, a durable dark wood with excel-
lent resistance to salt air that required little finishing or maintenance. While these
frames occurred in different sizes depending on their location, the arrangement in
all cases is similar—a lower wall consisting of teak pieces with oak panels on the
interior and an upper panel containing a tall window with sliding interior shutters.
The four major components of the panels—stub wall, glass window, oak trim, and
shutter rails—come together on a sill that also serves as a chair rail and a support
for the shutter tracks. At the vertical edges of these assemblies, the infill panels meet
diagonal concrete shear walls with tall narrow windows that span the teak and
the concrete, slotted into each with no framing or substructure. Further emphasizing
the clip-on effect of the panels, teak panels connect to the concrete ceilings with a
simple shadowgap, yet the connection to the floor is a 2" x 2" drip edge, standing

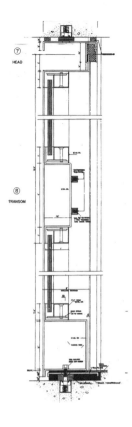

outside the line of the concrete face. The infill panels therefore rest visibly on the floor slab while their ceiling attachments appear tenuous, giving the sense that the panels have been set on their bases and rotated into position. From within, the teak panels fit into the concrete confines of the studies, offices, and library-like cabinets. Large panels of inlaid oak conceal pockets for sliding screens and windows, and contrast with the fine horizontals of the screens' jalousie-style louvers, echoing the lines of form and pour joints in the adjacent concrete.

161

The curtain walls surrounding the laboratory spaces further elaborate this clip-on approach. Daylight in the laboratory spaces had been a stated goal in the 1962 program, and the deep recesses offered by the exterior walkways on the service levels allowed floor-to-ceiling glass around the entire laboratory block while eliminating glare from direct sunlight, which had been a major problem at Richards. The laboratory cladding had to allow for a constantly changing layout, one that could require fire exits at various locations along the exterior walls of the blocks, depending on how groups planned to use the space. Larger laboratory equipment might also be moved in or out of the bench areas. The exterior wall, therefore, needed to be flexible, able to change quickly to accommodate alterations to the laboratory floors as groups moved in and out.

Coupled with these functional requirements, Kahn recognized the need to relate the cladding to the overall structural grain of the building. While the interstitial-level walkways included vertical slots to express the 20'-0" interior structural grid to the courtyard, the corridors outside the laboratories were adjacent to the columns themselves, a direct opportunity to convey the structural rhythm of the block. Kahn thus adapted the brake-shaped stainless-steel mullion system that he had developed for the American Federation of Labor (AFL) and Richards buildings to the peculiar requirements of the Salk. The laboratory wall is composed of large glass panels, held in place by bent steel elements similar to those used at AFL and Richards. It is panelized to span the 20'-0" column grid and to run the full 11'-0" clear height between floor and soffit, a "storefront" system that relies on structural support at all of its edges, rather than a true curtain wall clipped onto a structural frame only at key points. Shadowgaps at the top and bottom of each panel take up the tolerance dimension of the concrete floor and allow the lines of the storefronts to be precisely aligned along the length of the building. The metal door and frame are clearly set against the preexisting concrete structure, whose thickness compared to the insectlike metal again sets up a visual distinction between the high order of structure and the lower ones of passage and partitioning.

This steel glazing system stops at each column edge, its outer mullions overlapping the concrete by 2". A Z-shaped stainless-steel member accepts the end of the plate glass with a stop detail similar to those at the AFL and Richards buildings, then connects to a pair of nested stainless-steel clips that anchor directly to the concrete column. The face of the column is thereby exposed to the exterior, set back and between the edge mullions of each flanking glass panel. This reveals the storefront system as a set of clipped-on elements similar to the teak panels, while highlighting the regular rhythm and material of the concrete structural frame. These infill systems give the impression that they can easily be removed, while the massiveness of the surrounding concrete makes it clear that the structural frame is quite permanent.

The logical detailing of the curtain wall was matched by equally ingenious efforts at more intimate scales, including details at exterior doors, the office ceilings at the west end of each block, and mechanical chases throughout the complex. In each case, the detail was programmed by Kahn's office; the function of each component or assembly was radically reconsidered and designed based on what it was required to do and the methods by which it could be made. A small though ubiquitous detail neatly summarizes Kahn's concern for expressing the processes by, and the purposes for which,

162

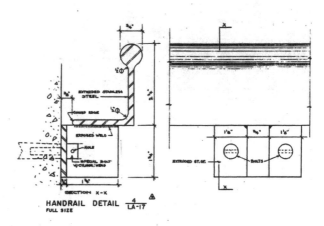

Handrail detail showing its extruded stainless-steel shape

the building was constructed. External handrails throughout the complex are fabricated of stainless steel, providing gripping surfaces and barriers along the edges of the cast-in-place stairs. Vertical elements of these rails are made of simple bars, assembled to form a code-required barrier. However, the gripping surface is a unique element, composed of what appears to be a steel angle attached to a small cylindrical top. This shape allows a broad connection surface for the vertical members below, critical to the welding process, while the round element provides a grip for the fingers, a comfortable dimension that invites the hand. While the rail at first appears to be two pieces welded together, the elements are actually monolithic, formed as a single stainless-steel extrusion. This is not a common process as extruded steel produces an irregular, striated surface due to its relatively low ductility and the resulting friction with extrusion dies. Here, however, the finish provides a texture that is both welcoming to the hand and more resistant to slipping. The resulting component saved the cost of welding two handrail elements together, but more importantly, it provides an almost subconscious invitation, through its texture, to the sense of touch.[53] The warm invitation of this cold surface and the surprisingly crude efficiency with which it was made reveal a mastery of material processes within Kahn's office that was formidable, if rarely noted.

163

A courtyard staircase

The Torrey Pines site was dedicated on 2 June 1962 in the midst of the change from the folded-plate scheme to the final, Vierendeel solution. Rabbi Morton J. Cohn delivered the address of consecration, describing the scientific quest as the analysis of "divine footprints" left for us to discover, paralleling Salk's and Kahn's notion that science and architecture explored both the measurable and the immeasurable, seeking transcendent meaning from the experimental process. Clearing of the site commenced on 25 June 1962 and was complete by mid-July.[54] Excavation proceeded after plan drawings were finalized in October, while concrete work followed the arrival of foundation drawings from Komendant's office in January 1963.[55]

While detail design work was being done in Philadelphia, MacAllister and Langford worked with Fuller on site to refine the color and finish of the concrete work. Friction between Kahn's office and the contractor emerged as the basement pours were used to test formwork configuration over layout and color. Both Komendant and Fuller saw Kahn's actions as meddling with a supposedly finished design, but these incidents highlight Kahn's empiricist leanings. He saw no reason to not improve the design as it was built, learning even from finished elements, while the contractor and Komendant maintained a more limited scope, being more concerned with the building schedule.[56] Despite his frustration with Kahn's process, Komendant volunteered to remain on site for an extended visit in fall 1963, assisting with formwork composition and concrete vibration. The effect on concrete quality following his tutorial for Fuller's workers is apparent in the building today, as there is a noticeable difference in walls poured subsequent to Komendant's visit.[57]

Work proceeded with the north wing one story ahead of the south. In both wings, the service and study towers were built slightly ahead of the laboratory floor construction, and by the end of January 1964, the north wing had been poured up to the level of the first interstitial space. As Fuller gained experience with the trusses and the tendons, work progressed rapidly, and by July 1964, the *San Diego Evening Tribune* reported that the Institute was "near the half-way mark."[58] Concrete work was completed in March 1965, and Komendant's design proved its structural capacity as metalwork on the curtain walls was completed only a few weeks later.[59] In July 1965, major construction work was finished, and the process of fitting out the laboratories and installing the mechanical systems began, a process that would take over a year.

The Courtyard

By late 1965, with construction on the laboratory blocks complete, the central space was still used as a construction staging area, and plans for its landscaping remained incomplete. In the 1962 program, the courtyard spaces were to have been lined with poplars, and drawings of this space show parallel ranks of trees recommended by a local landscape architect.[60] Unhappy with these preliminary schemes, Kahn did not pursue any of these options, and by 1965 the courtyard's design remained unsettled.

In 1964 a proposal by Kahn and sculptor Isamu Noguchi for the Adele Levy Memorial Playground on Riverside Drive in Manhattan was included in *Modern Gardens and the Landscape* (published by the Museum of Modern Art), alongside works by Mexican architect Luis Barragán. Kahn, sensing a kindred spirit, contacted Barragán shortly after the book's publication, and following initial correspondence in January 1965, Kahn visited Barragán in Mexico City. By the end of that year, Kahn asked him to advise on the still outstanding issue of the Salk's courtyard.[61] Barragán's visit to the site, from 23–25 February 1966, has passed into legend. Kahn recalled later: "He turned to us and said, 'I would not put a single tree in this area. I would make a plaza.... if you make a plaza, you will have another façade to the sky.' I was so jealous of this idea that I could not help adding to it by saying 'then we would get all those blue mosaics for nothing,' pointing to the Pacific Ocean."[62]

This moment is often claimed as a demonstration of Kahn's openness to inspiration, as his sudden acceptance of this apparently radical idea exposed the latent power in the elements of the site. However, Kahn might well have anticipated Barragán's reaction, as his exhibited projects included the remarkably austere Plaza de las Fuentes in Mexico City, among others. Kahn's visit to Barragán's house would have only reinforced the emotive qualities of the empty courtyard. While part of the house looked out on a controlled wilderness, its primary exterior space—doubtless the one in which Kahn saw a parallel to the Salk—was its roof terrace, an empty space bordered by high stucco walls whose only view was to the sky, with not a plant in sight.[63]

The Institute's reaction to the idea was mixed, and their agreement on the austerity of the courtyard did not come until ten months after Barragán's visit. Summarizing the debate a year later, Kahn wrote, "to those not present at the time…a totally paved Plaza seemed to be a harsh solution."[64] Salk charged Kahn with summarizing the status of the plaza suggestion in December 1966, to which Kahn responded with his now well-tuned balance of poetry and prose:

> The Plaza is entirely paved with San Miguel Stone which is laid tight without mortar joints. The center canal has constantly running water. The east planting encourages one to enter the Plaza from the arcades rather than to enter directly from the end. The system of narrow drainage slits tie into existing sub-surface drains and ensures positive runoff of rainwater. A broad area adjacent to the pool is surrounded by low, solid stone benches, a place to stop and enjoy the pool and the Plaza....
>
> I believe that this solution is good in bringing together the two Laboratory Wings, to encourage free circulation and to inspire use and activity within the Plaza. The sensitivity of the building and this space to the many moods of the sky and the atmosphere will make the Plaza a place always changing, never static, full of the never ending anticipation of the rising and the setting of the sun.[65]

Eventually, Italian travertine was agreed upon as a more affordable paving.[66] The resulting space is among the most iconic in all of modern architecture, but the source of its exquisite proportioning, its intensity of color, and its focus on the raw materials of site and construction emerged only as the result of the design processes surrounding it. Its walls were the logical results of discussions and exercises involving laboratory design, the detailing of the concrete, and the careful configuration of the study towers. The courtyard had, in fact, essentially designed itself, the space being the negative of the rigorously ordered buildings designed around it, ornamented only by the marks of process and assembly. Barragán's suggestion to leave it empty was really an acknowledgment of the inherently compelling visual order of the surrounding forms and materials, confirmation of Kahn's inherent belief that a properly conceived and executed architectural solution would, by its very adherence to principles of logic both timeless and contingent, have aesthetic value.

Assessment and Expansion

The Salk's opening occurred during a time of financial hardship for the Institute.[67] With polio long out of the headlines, donations anticipated by Salk and Basil O'Connor had failed to materialize, and the Institute moved laboratory groups into only the north wing, shelling out the south wing while occupying some of its floor space for meeting rooms and administration. Nevertheless, the Salk Institute began formal operations in the Kahn building with a staff of two hundred in fall 1966. While there were some reservations about the laboratories, involving ongoing mechanical issues and daylighting conflicts with microscope work, the complex quickly proved its worth in ways both measurable, for the technical tasks at hand, and immeasurable, as an inspirational place in which to work.

167

Over time, the most effective component of the laboratory blocks proved to be the interstitial spaces. While Dubin's mechanical and piped services were equal to the task at the opening, the service floors allowed groups to move in and out without disrupting neighboring spaces.[68] In 1972, when the south wing was finally fitted out, exploding energy costs forced the Institute to adopt a different mechanical strategy, eliminating hot-air ducts and instead providing constant cool air to laboratories with reheating coils at the supply boxes. This retrofit of the shelled interstitial space was accomplished easily because of the Vierendeel trusses' flexible layouts.[69]

The primary shortcoming of the scheme as built was its lack of administrative and meeting facilities. Plans for the Meeting House complex had been put on hold in early 1965 as financial pressure on the Institute deepened. While the Institute made do by carving these functions out of laboratory and office spaces for nearly twenty-five years, it became a serious problem by the late 1980s. By then, the Salk had established itself as one of the premier research centers for molecular biology and genetics, but the lack of meeting space made it impossible for the Institute to host conferences. Space for research was at a premium for the expanding Institute, and laboratories for computer-intensive work in genetics began to require a much different, less service-intensive approach than that offered by the Kahn blocks.[70]

In 1991, Jonas Salk announced plans for an expansion to the east of the existing laboratory blocks, following two years of study by former Kahn associates Jack MacAllister and David Rinehart, then with Anshen + Allen. Reinstating the original design for the Meeting House was rejected because of the need for additional laboratory space and the changed nature of scientific conferences. However, the site itself had also changed dramatically. No longer an oceanfront retreat, the Salk had been surrounded by the suburbanization of La Jolla and by development around the San Diego campus. MacAllister and Rinehart, who had advised Salk on issues of refitting and renovating the Kahn buildings, were asked by Salk to produce a design that would allow the expansion of the Institute while remaining true to Kahn's vision.

The architectural community met Salk's announcement with clamorous protest, highlighting the bivalent legacy of Kahn's work. On one side, the Institute—and Salk himself—believed that the correct way forward was to allow its work to continue at its accelerating rate. On the other side, a group of architects and critics expressed heartfelt concern that the emotional power of the original buildings would be lost. Despite the suburbanization of the site, the courtyard and its approaches presented a kernel of architectural space that for many demanded preservation, not capitulation to the density of its surroundings.

The new addition's program included conference facilities in addition to laboratories and office space. MacAllister and Rinehart's schemes proposed a strong closure to the eastern end of the courtyard axis, covering the area then occupied by a eucalyptus grove that, it emerged, had been planted after the building's opening to salvage land in a drainage plain. However, the "discovery" of the courtyard through these trees had become an integral part of the complex's architectural experience, and when

168

initial schemes replaced this grove with a formal courtyard, reaction in the architectural press was apoplectic.[71] Following colloquia with the architectural community, Kahn followers, and the City of San Diego, the scheme was revised to add distance between the new project and the old and to allow for an orchard to replace the original eucalyptus grove.

The east wing opened in 1996 to predictably mixed reviews. Although the transitional space between the new and old is not the serendipitously raw experience of the eucalyptus grove, the buildings themselves do expand in provocative ways upon tectonic themes in the older structures. The concrete work was based on the original Salk formwork, where reveals and projections were designed to add visual relief to the surface. Yet the original formula was transformed by intense experimentation by Rinehart and McAllister, and the results are remarkable, with glassy, marblelike surfaces and a thoroughly consistent color throughout. Other aspects, including structural glass curtain walls and the use of bead-blasted stainless-steel panels and perforated timber screens, suggest a translation of Kahn's principles into materials and systems unavailable in 1965.

Salk, who died while the east wing was being completed, was upset by the controversy that erupted over the addition. In a 1992 interview with Michael J. Crosbie of *Progressive Architecture*, Salk stated that the purpose of the Institute and of the additions was to ensure "continuity with change, as distinct from the idea that this is supposed to be a place where architectural genius is to be fostered."[72] Salk feared the fossilization of the Institute were it not allowed to expand on its own terms and summed up his attitude toward both critics and the Institute's architecture by pointing out that "Architecture is used here. Some people pursue science for human use, in contrast to science for the sake of science. This architecture is for human use, to serve a purpose."[73]

It is useful to compare this statement with *New York Times* critic Herbert Muschamp's plea that the original Salk courtyard—in his view the "most sublime landscape" ever produced by an American architect—be left untouched. Salk was no philistine, and his appreciation for the atmosphere of the Kahn buildings was boundless. Yet ultimately the Kahn buildings and those of the east wing were most valuable to him as vessels for the research of the Institute, and the quality of the complex stemmed in no small part from its flexibility and its functional solutions. Given that Kahn often credited Salk with being the true designer of the original complex and taking into

169

account, too, Kahn's reaction to Salk's rejection of the folded-plate scheme, Salk's opinion seems to demand attention.

Muschamp's use of the term "sublime" in assessing the Salk is particularly troubling. Defined as a mystery that "exceeds our perceptual and imaginative grasp," "sublime" fails to describe the Salk. In fact, the Salk seems to be anything but sublime. During the debate over the addition, Muschamp wrote of the courtyard's poetic qualities:

> First, sky; then, as you walk through the grove, the roof lines of the two laboratory buildings that rise up ahead on either side. The roof lines look saw-toothed.... and as you move closer [they] slice through the sky like two serrated blades, carving it into a solid block of space that descends to fill the central court.... The surroundings offer so little distraction.... There are the proportions of the laboratories, the thickness of their concrete walls, and a mottled bloom on the surface of the concrete that picks up the light and gives the walls a mirage like shimmer.[74]

As emotionally powerful as this experience is, each of its elements can be entirely explained as the result of Kahn's empirical process. This suggests that rather than being a consciously intended, sublime experience, the Salk's courtyard actually derives its power from the cumulative effects of decisions regarding the constructed and functional realities of the spaces and elements involved—not from any deific abilities or transcendental effort on Kahn's part. The "serrated blades" of the courtyard edges are the angled walls of the studies, configured in such a way as to give each room a view of the ocean. Their stagger is due to the eastward room in each block jutting out further, allowing inhabitants to see past the study in front of it. While this creates a syncopated perspectival effect, undoubtedly adding to the thrust of the space, it nevertheless stems from the requirement to provide each room with a west view. The proportions of the laboratories were derived not from isolated decisions regarding ideal shapes or mathematical harmonies, but rather from the reality of the height limits imposed by neighboring developments and the resulting need to balance the sectional requirements of the laboratories and their servant spaces. While adding to the complex's sense of permanence, the thickness of the concrete walls is due to the seismic requirements of the site and, in some cases, to the need to conceal posttensioning tendons. Certainly Kahn and his office can be given credit for the aesthetic effect of the concrete surface, yet this was again the result of constant experimentation with a common material and the orchestration of field knowledge, not merely the stroke of a master's brush. Indeed, rather than *veiling* the realities of the structure for perceptual effect, Kahn orchestrated a building that is constantly *conveying* both its function and its own fabricational processes. There is precious little in the Salk that is hidden from us; rather, its beauty may be ascribed precisely to its *revelation* of its own motive and final causation, its construction and function. There is nowhere an attempt to trick our visual or kinesthetic sense—the space has not been selfconsciously manipulated. Rather, the power of the building comes from the fact that it reveals the constructed order of the space simply and clearly, giving us a tangible link to both the intellectual effort of its conception and the labor of its construction.

It is worth remembering that this "sublime" space was not even intended by Kahn until late in the process, after he and Barragán noted the effects of the sun on the bare concrete walls. Not to plant the courtyard was a decision to reveal the existing logic at work in the Salk's buildings, which had emerged only as the design and building had progressed. Until Barragán's visit—or perhaps shortly before—Kahn's intent had been to mask the courtyard elevations with poplars and planting. The revelation of the buildings' natural ornament, enhanced by morning and afternoon sun, suggested that these elevations, though subconsciously executed and not originally intended to be the straightforward expressions they have become, contained within them the synthesized orders of the entire complex. Across the building's scales, from that of the Vierendeel trusses to that of the handrail, Kahn's empirical design process suggested that every element, every component, every space would find its own proper standing in the overall complex. Kahn had explored this at Yale and Richards, but it was in La Jolla that this constant attention to ordering first seems to have produced a building that wove these ideas into a tenacious whole. The Salk is a testament to the power of architectural prose. Its measurable aspects are so thoughtfully assembled that it stirs the immeasurable, a building-up of and beyond daily experience that appears transcendental but is firmly rooted—like the best of Kahn's work—in the daily minutiae of practice, construction, and performance.

1. Dorothy Ducas, "Jonas Salk," in *Heroes for Our Times*, ed. William Yolan and Kenneth Seeman Giniger (New York: Overseas Press Club, 1968), 70–71.

2. Ibid.

3. Sabin and Salk disagreed over the potential for the live-virus type, which was exacerbated by the Foundation's premature publication of Salk's findings in *Time* magazine in February 1953. Salk's subsequent broadcast on CBS radio in March further incensed Sabin, as well as others in the scientific community who felt that Salk had violated scientific protocol by reporting his results directly to the public.

4. A Salk Institute pamphlet, n.d., the California Room, San Diego Public Library, in a file marked "Salk Institute for Biological Studies."

5. Richard Saul Wurman, *What Will Be Has Always Been: The Words of Louis I. Kahn* (New York: AccessPress/Rizzoli, 1986), 296.

6. "Salk-UC Research Lands Explained," *San Diego Municipal News* 1, no. 3 (June 1960): 1.

7. *Louis I. Kahn: In the Realm of Architecture*, ed. David B. Brownlee and David G. De Long (New York: Rizzoli, 1991), 330.

8. This last element, as Brownlee and De Long point out, overlapped the boundary (agreed upon with the city) between lands deeded to the Salk and those left to the University of California.

9. Kahn to Basil O'Connor, 16 September 1960, Louis I. Kahn Collection, University of Pennsylvania and the Pennsylvania Historical and Museum Commission, Philadelphia (hereafter cited as Kahn Collection), LIK box 107.

10. Louis I. Kahn Office, "Abstract of Program for the Institute of Biology at Torry [*sic*] Pines, La Jolla, CA.," n.d., Kahn Collection, LIK box 27 ("Salk Institute for Biological Studies, La Jolla, California"), file marked "Salk—Program Notes, June 19." Although no date is provided, it is apparent from the scheme described that this document was written in late 1962.

11. Ibid.

12. Ibid.

13. Louis I. Kahn, "The Philadelphia School," *Progressive Architecture*, April 1961, 141–48.

14. Ibid. This arrangement suggests very nearly the eventual configuration of the 1993 additions by Anshen + Allen. Kahn's consistent inability to correctly assume the importance of the automobile would occur again—with more dramatic consequences—in Fort Worth. Here, the much larger parking lot required by the finished scheme suggested a reversal of the parking location and the expansion location.

15. Neither the Village nor the Meeting House were built, due to continuing budget problems during the design process. However, some conference elements were included in the 1993 additions, to the east of the original laboratory block. The Meeting House in particular has aroused generations of speculation, as it represents the most purely monastic form in Kahn's oeuvre. Neither of these elements were subjected to a detailed design process, and thus they remain outside the scope of this study.

16. Kahn Office, "Abstract of Program for the Institute," n.d. (but likely 1962). All dimensions are taken from the drawing marked "A-5, Upper Level Plan, $\frac{1}{16}$"=1'-0" VOID," n.d., Kahn Collection, LIK folder 030.1.C.540.

17. Kahn Office, "Abstract of Program for the Institute," n.d. (but likely 1962).

18. Drawing marked "A-13, Section North-South ¼"=1'-0"," n.d., Kahn Collection, LIK folder 030.1.C.540. An alternate configuration with an upper beam depth of 6'-9" is shown on drawing L-A16, "Section Through Typical Lab," 17 January 1962, Kahn Collection.

19. Ibid.

20. August Komendant, "Structural Calculations for the Salk Institute for Biological Studies," April 1962, 6–8 (bound originals), August Komendant Collection, Architectural Archives of the University of Pennsylvania, Philadelphia.

172

21. Kahn Office, drawing L-A16, "Section Through Typical Lab." See also Komendant, "Structural Calculations for the Salk," 6–8, for detailed dimensions of these beams.

22. Kahn Office, drawing marked "A-5, Upper Level Plan."

23. In the upper laboratory, the stagger between floor and ceiling beams allowed waste lines to run directly from sinks into the floor channels formed at beam junctions.

24. Bound copies of these calculations are in the Komendant Collection.

25. Kahn to Komendant, 25 July 1962, Komendant Collection, box 21 ("August Komendant Correspondence").

26. Ibid.

27. Jonas Salk, quoted in Wurman, *What Will Be*, 296.

28. Ibid.

29. Louis I. Kahn, "Remarks, 1965," in *Louis I. Kahn: Writings, Lectures, Interviews*, ed. Alessandra Latour (New York: Rizzoli, 1991), 207.

30. Ibid., 206–7.

31. Jack MacAllister, conversation with the author, June 2001.

32. Komendant, memorandum, 19 May 1962, Komendant Collection, box 21 ("August Komendant Correspondence").

33. Further evidence of this pressure can be seen in the fact that the revised scheme offered just over half the laboratory square footage included in the original. The built complex contained six laboratory floor plates, each approximately 62'-0" x 240'-0", with a surrounding exterior corridor. The original scheme would have built eight laboratory floor plates, each approximately 80'-0" x 245'-0".

34. Preliminary civil and architectural data reached La Jolla in mid-October. See box P-26 ("Salk Institute for Biological Studies, La Jolla, California") in the Kahn Collection.

35. August Komendant, *My 18 Years with Architect Louis I. Kahn* (Englewood, N.J.: Aloray, 1975), 51.

36. August Komendant, *Contemporary Concrete Structures* (New York: McGraw-Hill, 1972), 464–67. The final Salk arrangement is covered briefly, followed by a more extensive evaluation of the original, "structurally correct" scheme. Neither is credited to Kahn.

37. Explanations of the Vierendeel truss in contemporary literature can be found in Mario Salvadori and Robert Heller, *Structure in Architecture: The Building of Buildings* (1963; repr., Englewood Cliffs, N.J.: Prentice-Hall, 1975), 192.

38. Salk Institute for Biological Studies, construction drawing LS-31, 9 January 1963 (revised through 6 December 1963), stamped August Komendant, Kahn Collection, LIK folder 030.1.C.540.

39. Komendant, *My 18 Years*, 50.

40. R. C. Doland (City of San Diego Building Inspector) to Komendant, 14 February 1963, Komendant Collection, box 21.

41. Komendant, *My 18 Years*, 52.

42. Ibid., 53. Komendant's work elsewhere in the complex was also notable, if not as dramatic as his solutions for the laboratory section. On either side of the laboratory blocks, the sets of five study and service towers were designed as rigid frames, with large concrete shear panels providing lateral resistance in all directions. To avoid crushing by differential seismic movement from the comparatively "loose" laboratory blocks, these towers were not structurally connected to the laboratory blocks themselves. Rather, each tower stands independently from the main structure, separated by a ½" gap with a premolded neoprene filler in a visible red color that Kahn felt recalled the lead of medieval construction. Office and mechanical wings at the extreme ends of the laboratory blocks were likewise designed as rigid concrete frames, again with seismic separations from the main laboratory structure. The clarity of the scheme was apparent to San Diego's building inspectors, as the building permit for the concrete structure was issued on 28 May 1963—the same day Komendant submitted the final drawings.

43. This arrangement occurs only in the north wing, which was the first to be completed, as discussed below. The south wing, shelled for several years, was outfitted with a more energy-efficient VAV air system in the early 1970s, although the access strategy remains similar.

44. Minutes of meeting held in Louis I. Kahn offices, 8 August 1962, Kahn Collection, LIK box 21 ("August Komendant Correspondence").

45. Marshall D. Meyers to Jack MacAllister, 31 July 1963, Kahn Collection, LIK box 27 ("Salk Institute for Biological Studies, La Jolla, CA").

46. Meyers to MacAllister, 2 August 1963, Kahn Collection, LIK box 27 ("Salk Institute for Biological Studies, La Jolla, CA").

47. August Komendant, "Komendant on Concrete," *Progressive Architecture*, October 1966, 208.

48. Ibid.

49. Memo on expenses agreement, 21 November 1962, file marked "Galen Schlosser," Kahn Collection, LIK box 27 ("Salk Institute for Biological Studies, La Jolla, CA"). This memo indicates that the Institute provided a site office, a leased car, and an employee house at 9527 La Jolla Farms Road.

50. "Laboratory for Life Science Designed to Defy Time," *Engineering News-Record*, 27 January 1967, 80.

51. See Edward Ford, *The Details of Modern Architecture*, vol. 2 (1928–1988) (Cambridge: MIT Press, 1996), for a complete explanation of this formwork process.

52. Salk Institute for Biological Studies, Architectural Specifications, section 2-02, "Concrete—Special Requirements," Kahn Collection, LIK box 27.

53. In 1972, an OSHA inspection revealed that the handrails on the landings of the Salk's external stairs were not code compliant because they did not meet the 42" requirement for a guardrail. Kahn's office advised on the solution, which was essentially a second guardrail of the same construction set slightly inboard from the original. This fix did not include a new gripping surface, and while consistent in material and detailing, its position does slightly interfere with the hand's motion as it grips the first rail.

54. Photograph by Dick Whittington dated "7-15-62" and reprinted in Komendant, *My 18 Years*, 43.

55. Transmittal in LIK box P-26, Kahn Collection. A preliminary building permit issued in early 1963 allowed foundation work to proceed prior to the issuance of a full structural permit, and crews began to work immediately on retaining walls and basement shear walls. See Dick Whittington photograph dated "5-29-63," Kahn Collection, binder labeled "Kahn Archival Photography: Salk 540, vols. 1 and 2," reprinted in Komendant, *My 18 Years*, 59.

56. Ibid., 58–60.

57. The earliest pours visible to the public are the retaining walls of the courtyard-side garden courts on the north block, where visible staining, honeycombing, and pour lines are evident in the basement walls.

58. Mike Konon, "Biological Institute Nears Half Way Mark," *San Diego Evening Tribune*, 17 July 1964, C1:1.

59. George A. Fuller Co., "Monthly Report—March 31, 1965," Kahn Collection, LIK box P-26 ("Salk Institute for Biological Studies, La Jolla, California").

60. See file marked "Roland S. Hoyt" in the Kahn Collection, LIK box 27 ("Salk Institute for Biological Studies, La Jolla, CA"). Hoyt is credited as "Landscape Architect" for the project in "Laboratory for Life Science Designed to Defy Time," *Engineering News-Record*, 27 January 1967, 80.

61. Daniel Friedman, "Salk Institute for Biological Studies, La Jolla, California, 1959–65," in *Louis I. Kahn: In the Realm of Architecture*, ed. David B. Brownlee and David G. De Long (New York: Rizzoli, 1991), 334.

62. Kahn to James Britton (Editor, *Urban Design Review*), 12 June 1973, Kahn Collection, LIK box 27, file marked "Salk Correspondence—1972."

174

63. Emilio Ambasz, *The Architecture of Luis Barragán* (New York: The Museum of Modern Art, 1976), 33–43.

64. Kahn to Salk, 19 December 1966, Kahn Collection, LIK box P-26 ("Salk Institute for Biological Studies, La Jolla, California"), file marked "Salk—Garden." San Francisco-based Lawrence Halprin worked throughout the summer and fall of 1966 to develop alternative proposals, including the provision of orange trees in the plaza. Compromise schemes using ground cover to soften the suggested expanse of stone were also considered, and Fuller priced one option using low, flowering shrubs at the request of Kahn's office. Kahn continued to suggest a return to the empty courtyard; Halprin finally resigned the commission, recognizing Kahn's commitment.

65. Kahn to Salk, 19 December 1966, Kahn Collection, LIK box P-26 ("Salk Institute for Biological Studies, La Jolla, California").

66. "Budget Estimate—28 April 1967," Kahn Collection, LIK box P-26 ("Salk Institute for Biological Studies, La Jolla, California").

67. Scientists began moving into the laboratories in August 1966, when the exhaust system became operable. By 24 October, after complaints from scientists, the Institute realized there were major deficiencies in the laboratory exhaust and briefly considered the need to shut down the entire laboratory block for safety reasons. Exhaust velocity from the mechanical wing was less than half its design value and temporary nozzles were installed to ensure proper ventilation of noxious fumes from the site. The problem was eventually traced to a budget-led redesign of the exhaust treatment system, and meteorologists at New York University, who advised slight modifications to both the exhaust nozzles, devised a fix. The services were finally approved in April 1967.

68. Currently the Institute changes out thirty thousand square feet of laboratory space per year and can reconfigure an entire laboratory bay with a crew of only six. Robert Lizarraga (Facility Services, the Salk Institute), conversation with the author, June 2001.

69. *The Salk Institute: Architecture and Engineering* (La Jolla: The Salk Institute, n.d.), 11. Other elements have not proven themselves as well. The central courtyard, despite its profound architectural attractions, has not proven itself to be the social hub of the complex. Rather, the lower courtyard at the west end of the complex has taken on this function, due to its proximity to the cafeteria and to its shade trees, leaving the courtyard as more of an iconic, rather than functional, space. A fungus problem on the teak windows, which has required constant cleaning, and the corrosion of the copper-screen frames within these units have added an unintended blue-green highlight to the reddish brown of the infill panels. While Kahn had assumed that the teak panels would fade to a gray similar in tone to the concrete, the cleaning process constantly renews the strong color that he and Salk had hoped would fade with time.

70. Dr. Brian Henderson, "A Delicate Balance," *Architecture*, July 1993, 45.

71. Herbert Muschamp, "Critic's Notebook: Art and Science Politely Disagree On an Architectural Jewel's Fate," *New York Times*, 16 November 1992, C11:3.

72. Michael J. Crosbie, "Dissecting the Salk," *Progressive Architecture*, October 1993, 47.

73. Ibid., 47.

74. Herbert Muschamp, "The Wrong Prescription," *The New Republic*, 10 February 1992, 27.

175

> In the art gallery at Yale I only came to a very slight conclusion there
> about order.... If I were to build a gallery now, I would be more
> concerned about building spaces which are not used freely by the
> director as he wants. Rather I would give him spaces that were there
> and had certain inherent characteristics.... The director would be
> fitted out with such a variety of ways of getting light, from above,
> from below, from little slits, or from whatever he wanted, so that
> he felt that here was really a realm of spaces where one could show
> things in various aspects.
>
> —Louis I. Kahn

Thirteen years after the Yale Art Gallery was completed, Kahn was given a chance to continue his investigations into the balance of structure, function, and light required by a late twentieth-century museum. The Yale Gallery had begun with George Howe and Charles H. Sawyer suggesting an open plan with flexible loft space, but it ended for Kahn with Paul Rudolph's evisceration of that idea and the imposition of fixed gallery walls. Since it had to house a variety of different functions during its first few years, the completely undefined loft spaces were, perhaps, the only option available. But Kahn recognized that the Gallery's primary shortcoming was that its spaces

The Kimbell site (the vacant area in the center), west of downtown Fort Worth. Camp Bowie Boulevard runs along the left-hand side.

were ordered only on the minute scale of its triangular ceiling grid. The major structural modules at Yale, the 20' × 40' bays, were, if anything, underemphasized, and the galleries felt amorphous, lacking the spatial definition that Rudolph clumsily provided in 1958. Indeed, the Gallery's open plan had been a major source of the building's critical appeal, a response to the fixed, confined way art was experienced in typical museums. Faced with the opportunity to design a second major museum, Kahn actively sought a balance between the functional flexibility desired by curators and the spatial definition provided by the expressed structures of Richards and the Salk Institute.

The Kimbell Art Foundation had been founded in 1936 with the collection of Kay Kimbell, a local entrepreneur who made his fortune in grain milling, food processing, and oil concerns.[1] Kimbell was an enthusiastic amateur collector. His home had served as a space to display a rotating selection, but his will left instructions that half of his estate be used to build a permanent venue for the collection through his Foundation. After his death in 1964, his widow contributed the remaining half of the Kimbell fortune to house the Foundation and established an acquisitions program to bring high-quality artworks to Fort Worth.[2] Curator Richard F. Brown, then in the midst of resigning his position as director of the Los Angeles County Museum of Art, was retained to develop the collection and build a new, more public home for the fledgling museum.[3] Brown had left Los Angeles after disputes with the museum board regarding the design of its new building, claiming that the trustees had subordinated the need for a community institution to their own "desire for a monument."[4] Crucial to his conception of the new Kimbell Museum as a humanly scaled institution was the time Brown spent as a research scholar at The Frick Collection, which is housed in a large mansion in New York. Following his departure from LACMA, Brown embraced the opportunity to work with the Kimbell Foundation to create a museum that would welcome the community rather than monumentalize its founders.[5]

Fort Worth had two new museums in the 1960s. What is now the Fort Worth Museum of Modern Art had built new facilities west of the city at the edge of the Will Rogers Coliseum complex. The Amon Carter Museum, dedicated to Western and American Art and designed by Philip Johnson in 1957–61, occupied the summit of a large, sloping, triangular space; left as a forecourt to the Will Rogers buildings, the area designated for the Kimbell Foundation's new museum lay between Lancaster Avenue, Camp Bowie Boulevard, and Arch Adams Street. The city had owned the land since its purchase for the sesquicentennial and had intended it for a major public health complex that was eventually constructed a block further north. With the Carter Museum and the Museum of Modern Art at its western tip, the site became a de facto cultural center and a logical choice for a third arts institution. Fort Worth leased the block's eastern ten acres to the Kimbell Foundation with the agreement that the easternmost of the two Coliseum forecourt drives, Will Rogers Drive East, would be removed and landscaped, giving the museum a large contiguous site.[6]

180

Richard Brown had included Kahn on a shortlist of internationally renowned architects in 1966, along with Skidmore, Owings & Merrill, Mies van der Rohe, Ed Barnes, Marcel Breuer, and Paul Rudolph.[7] The choice of Kahn over the other architects on the shortlist was, at first glance, unusual. Mies van der Rohe had by 1966 completed the National Gallery in Berlin and Cullinan Hall in Houston, while Breuer was finishing work on the Whitney Museum of American Art in New York. Kahn had only the Yale Gallery to his credit, and that building, distinguished though it was, was by this point more than a dozen years old. Kahn's reputation for innovative building and beginning each project from first principles attracted Brown, however. Having considered Mies for the Los Angeles County Museum, Brown was well aware that he would come to a new project with preconceptions based on his own theory of materials and space and with less of an interest in designing for the Foundation's specific aspirations.[8]

The Kimbell's design and construction team. Seated, from left: Preston M. Geren, A. T. Seymour, A. L. Scott, and Louis I. Kahn; standing, from left: Benjamin Bird and Richard F. Brown

A self-professed admirer of Kahn's, Brown had also been a trustee of the La Jolla Museum of Art, which hosted a show on Kahn's work in winter 1965. Brown felt that Kahn was "younger" in spirit than any other architect on the shortlist, willing to "approach the problem like Adam," and to find solutions that would reflect the Kimbell's unique ambitions. Speaking as the building was completed in 1972, Brown noted that this intuition had proven true: "Kahn's attitude is much more all-embracing…. He's willing to let the specific situation posed by the creation of a building guide him and tell him what the structure, engineering and esthetics ought to be."[9]

After touring work by architects on the shortlist, Brown recommended Kahn to the Kimbell's board in October 1966; they immediately approved the choice.[10] Contractual arrangements for the Museum's design were made, giving the Kimbell Foundation the security of a local architect while giving Kahn the latitude he required to make design decisions. Preston M. Geren, a local architect with a track record of successful buildings, was made Associate Architect with Kahn. Geren had his own engineers, though they would eventually be replaced as structural issues proved, by their own admission, to be beyond their abilities. Cowan, Love, and Jackson, a local mechanical engineering firm, was hired based on their work with Geren in the past, and Richard

181

Kelly, who had assisted with lighting design at Yale and the Salk, was hired to help ensure the mix of daylight and artificial illumination desired by Brown.[11]

Richard Brown's Program

Whereas Kahn's work for the University of Pennsylvania and Jonas Salk had relied on a fairly abstract notion of those projects' requirements, Kahn found a client in Brown with very specific ideas about how the building should perform, how it should feel, and how it should define and expand a visitor's experience. In June 1966, Brown drafted and sent to Kahn a nineteen-page "Pre-Architectural Program," of which only eight pages were the expected floor areas and programmatic divisions.[12] The remainder of Brown's missive contained a wide-ranging "General Philosophy," details on the site's sociocultural, economic, physical, and climatic environments; a narrative describing activities anticipated in the new building; and seven pages of thoughts on lighting, installation, security, and acquisitions policy. This was a program document written with care and enthusiasm by a director who had seen these aspects of museums done well at the Frick and poorly, in his view, at the Los Angeles County Museum. Brown noted at the outset that, while it was expected that the building would "be a creative contribution to the history of the art of architecture," this was not to come at the expense of function or performance. "The building itself," his program demanded, "should play a supporting role to the reasons for its existence."[13] Brown emphasized that the typical museum attendee in Fort Worth would not be overly sophisticated; the Museum would need to respond by being "warm," supportive, never intimidating. Human proportion and experience were to be its key elements rather than pretense: simplicity, directness, clarity, and exquisite craftsmanship were all specifically required. Brown noted the unusual circumstances of the fledgling collection, asking for flexibility in layout and assurances that the building would not "yawn openly" at its first visitors, who might see a building only half-filled with artworks. Repeating a key constraint from the Salk project, Brown pointed out that the Museum had agreed not to restrict the Amon Carter Museum's view of Fort Worth's skyline across the park, capping the Kimbell's height at 40'.

Brown repeatedly emphasized the need to provide and to control lighting in the galleries. His program noted the "extremely intense" sunlight of north Texas, and it catalogued the issues this raised, including the visual and psychological effects of seeing a bright exterior from inside, concerns about glare, and, most ominously, the damaging effects of direct sunlight on art objects.[14] In a separate note, Brown returned to lighting requirements for the galleries in subjective terms, as a functional illuminant and as a psychological necessity:

> The creation of the ideal total visual situation, of course, involves the physics, physiology and psychology of it: i.e., all levels of perception. But, we are not after a measurable, physical quantity, or a physiological reaction; we are after a psychological effect through which the museum visitor feels that both he [*sic*] and the art he came to see are still a part of the real, rotating, changeable world.[15]

Kahn must have read these words with both recognition and anticipation. Here, he had a true fellow believer in the measurable and immeasurable aspects of light. The Kimbell's development would in part be the story of how this passage in Brown's program was interpreted by Kahn and his collaborators.

Reflecting in 1997 on the Kimbell's twenty-fifth anniversary, Kahn associate Marshall Meyers noted that Brown's program had recalled for Kahn the Kröller-Müller Gallery in Otterlo, Netherlands, designed by Henry van de Velde and completed in 1953. Kahn had seen this building—a small, modestly scaled museum in a park—during his attendance at CIAM's (Congrès Internationaux d'Architecture Moderne) nearby conference in 1959, and he evidently now appreciated the Kröller-Müller's programmatic similarity to the Kimbell, particularly in its park setting and its single-level distribution of gallery spaces.[16] Moreover, the Kröller-Müller galleries were built with precisely the emphasis on daylight requested by Brown. Painting galleries had skylights with operable louvers, permitting diffused, indirect illumination, while sculpture galleries also had large side windows that permitted more direct daylight and an opportunity for patrons to view the landscape.

183

Schematic Design

Through the winter of 1966–67, Kahn advanced design ideas at two scales. Drawings in Kahn's hand show a restless urban imagination, deploying galleries, auditorium, and ancillary areas throughout the eastern half of Will Rogers Park, surrounded by gardens and enclosing courtyards. These exercises verged on the grandiose, with little relation to the list of functional areas given in Brown's program, yet they set

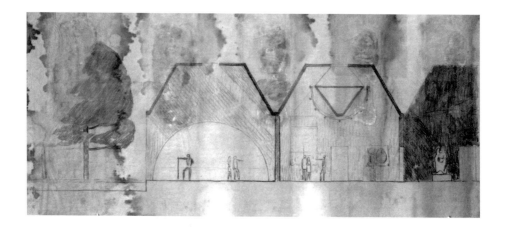

Section through the first folded-plate scheme

an ambitious goal for the Kimbell as a civic monument, suggesting ancient parallels in Fort Worth's new cultural district. The overall scheme presented to the Museum in March 1967 was mammoth: a square block six hundred feet on each side with two large, asymmetrically placed courtyards and smaller sculpture courts scattered throughout.

Parallel to this exercise in planning and urban scale, Kahn worked at finding a solution to Brown's lighting concerns. Given the height restriction on the site, a roof-light scheme was an obvious step. But Kahn's dissatisfaction with the bright ceiling planes of top-illuminated galleries led to alternate solutions, all based on extruded sections with various arrangements of slots and baffles designed to bounce a measured quantity of overhead light into the display spaces. This recipe led to over one hundred separately identifiable approaches, involving often-subtle variations on the basic theme.[17] These were woven into Kahn's site vision, forming spatial and formal building blocks for the overall planning, and were tested by crude ray-tracing that predicted where sunlight would be transmitted, reflected, and excluded in section. By spring 1967, Kahn and the office began to focus on an arrangement of trapezoidal roof plates with triangular beams carrying lighting and ductwork through their center, a distinct recapitulation of the Salk's folded-plate scheme.

CHAPTER FIVE

First folded-plate scheme, ca. 1967

This folded-plate section was presented to Brown and the Foundation in March 1967. While the plan and roof section would change dramatically during the next twelve months, this scheme was a key moment in the project's development. Kahn had produced an initial response at two intertwined scales—that of the site and that of the gallery. He used the evolving gallery section as a module, extruding it across the site and multiplying it as needed to logically deploy exhibition spaces, an auditorium, and administrative functions in relation to surrounding streets and pedestrian paths. Kahn remained intensely interested in the overall site massing, but it was the section that proved most critical to the problem posed by the single-story museum—a modular roof permitting natural illumination, offering controlled flexibility in planning, carrying air and electrical services, and—unlike Yale—providing a compelling definition to the spaces below. While no detailed structural design was undertaken at this point, it is clear that Kahn was grappling with the roof's static performance. The folded plates' depth made the modular sections efficient structurally, but their arrangement demonstrated some uncertainty on Kahn's part. The galleries and roofs in these plans show a regular column grid, indicating that Kahn thought of them as short vaults spanning the bays' width, not as the long members spanning the bays' lengths that they would become.

KIMBELL ART MUSEUM

If the process of linking module with site planning promised integration among urban scales, environmental systems, and architecture, it also addressed lessons in gallery design that Kahn had learned from Yale. The Kimbell's reliance on a gallery-sized module limited possibilities for rearranging gallery space, balancing the need for flexibility in floor layout with Kahn's desire to define architectural spaces. Walls for the display of paintings had obvious attachment points at the low ceilings under the folded plates, leaving linear galleries that would maintain the spatial definition that Kahn sought. This scheme permitted considerable flexibility, but the roof's metric would be difficult to violate; however the floor might be laid out, the overhead rhythm would visually organize the entire museum. In proposing the section module as the Kimbell's basis, Kahn addressed the conflict that he had recognized between a free plan and ordered space, providing an opportunity to define the Kimbell's galleries with an overhead roof without confining them inside fixed walls.

After his presentation to the Kimbell in March 1967, Kahn returned with a detailed site model in May. It maintained the folded-plate scheme, now deployed in a more nuanced version of the square-site layout that included plantings and gardens appropriate to the park setting. This second model showed a slot for toplighting at the peak of each folded plate, with the outermost modules devoted to a continuous arcade encircling the building. In this scheme, Kahn showed, for the first time, a detailed floor plan. The complex was divided into two pieces, separated again by a paired courtyard. To the west, temporary galleries flanked an asymmetrically placed axis that passed between the courtyards to form the circulation spine for the permanent collection along the site's east end. Belying the roof's linear module, these galleries were subdivided into rectangular rooms, arranged to conform with a regular cross grid, matching column lines along the outer edges of the four arcades. The main circulation spine included a grand, three-part staircase connecting a lower-level automotive entry at Arch Adams Street.

Much as Jonas Salk had expressed concerns about Kahn's early proposal for the laboratory sections, Brown wrote to Kahn of his growing concerns about the design in July 1967. He agreed in principle to the strategy that had been presented—a folded-plate roof slotted to permit daylight and interior lightcourts and a plan that was neither fixed nor entirely flexible—noting that it was "exciting" and "in perfect harmony with what we are envisioning."[18] However, he expressed two serious reservations about the proposed building's size and scale. Addressing size, Brown noted:

186

Four-hundred feet square is a hell of a big square, and it might seem, in the setting, the city, and in relation to neighboring institutions, etc., just plain ostentatious. Within that big square you wind up with an awful lot of cubic *space* that must be heated, air-conditioned, illuminated, etc.,...all of which costs money and labor to do, and I want as much money as possible saved from maintenance so I can buy more and more *art* as the years roll by, not just keep up the house.[19]

The 400' square had, three months before, been 600', but it was still too big. Kahn had at his disposal the program issued by Brown for only 67,000 square feet of space, less than half of the footprint being proposed. These presentations showed the Foundation the potential for the Museum as a monument with grand civic ambitions, but it would be the budgetary discipline asked for by Brown that would distill this ideal into the condensed final building. Kahn's ambition, combined with the constraints imposed by Brown and the budget, were allied with the focus on the roof as the design's essential problem. Together, these factors would lead to a museum that maintained the formality and dignity of Kahn's large early plans, brought down to a reasonable size while adding the functional rigor of the sectional solution.

The gallery section at this point was the source of Brown's second concern, that of scale. In developing tall, monumentally scaled sections, Brown was worried that Kahn had ignored the program's desire for "harmonious simplicity and human proportion." The folded-plate roof, and subsequent options showing a semicircular vault nearly thirty feet high, seemed likely to intimidate and alienate the typical patron. Brown again wrote passionately but firmly: "The average size picture on the walls of the KAM will be about 2½ feet in one direction and 3 or 4 feet in the other.... I'm worried about how a little old lady from Abilene is going to *feel* looking at our 15 inch Giovanni di Paolo on a wall 15 feet vertical, with a vault above that which goes up to 30 feet."[20]

187

Kahn, again, must have felt the frustration of an ambitious scheme being brought down to earth. But between July and September 1967, he worked to refine the square plan to its essentials, relying on the extruded gallery module while adjusting it to meet Brown's desire for "warmth and charm" within the scheme's "direct, simple, spare shell of structural validity and integrity."[21]

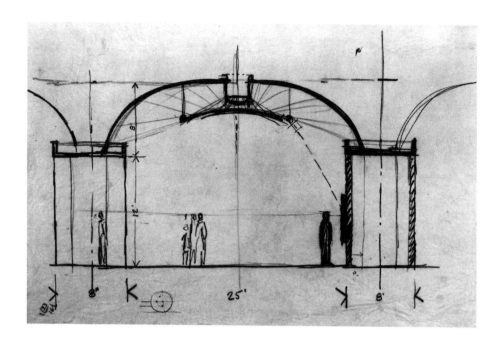

Sketch of a transitional scheme showing curved roof forms and mechanical trays

Shells and Slots: The Final Roof Scheme

In late summer 1967, Marshall Meyers returned to Kahn's office after a two-year sojourn with another Philadelphia architect. Meyers had trained as an industrial designer at Pratt Institute and received his M.Arch. from Yale in 1957, as one of the first graduates to have studied under the fourth-floor drafting studios' tetrahedral grid. His position as editor of *Perspecta*, Yale's architectural journal, put Meyers in contact with Kahn; he joined the office immediately after receiving his degree. His background in industrial design had left him with great abilities as a detailer, and his work on Richards in particular had been deeply valued by Kahn. Upon his return, Meyers was put to work on the Kimbell's section. Kahn had agreed to present a revised scheme on 22 September, and the input of Meyers is evident in the drawings presented. In addition to perspectives showing a long, low building with vaulted roofs, a single section showing a gently curved roof form, slotted at the top with a curved light reflector, was included. This parallel exercise by Meyers made sense of Brown's concern for intimacy and natural lighting. The shape was a flattened arc, with the same functional disposition as the July semicircular scheme and brought down in scale to nearly half its original height. By this point Kahn had recognized the need to align services with the structural scheme, and this sectional drawing showed trays

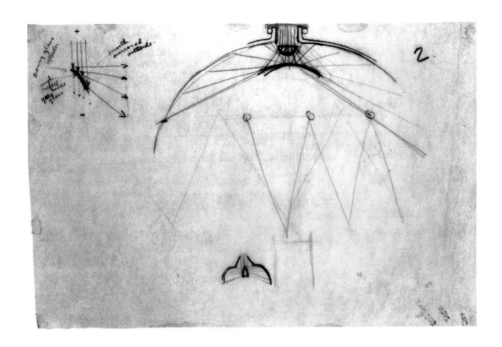

Section study of a reflector and roof shape

suspended from the roof's springing points, carrying ductwork and concealed lighting. These mechanical trays formed flat ceilings between the spaces defined by the curved roofs, low interstitial zones that were spatial foils to the main galleries. Services were thus contained within secondary spaces, but here they were woven into the building's fabric. No longer—as at Richards—did they stand outside the pristine volume of a served space. Rather, they became an intimate part of the building's spatial narrative. These low interstitial zones were contiguous with the free-plan galleries, enabling curators to display works in spaces of varying heights and providing an overhead rhythm that strengthened the galleries' major axes while defining a powerful set of cross-axial directions.

Between 22 September and 30 November 1967, Meyers made two great strides in his work on the Kimbell's roof. The first was his conception of a reflector that both transmitted and diffused light, a "beam splitter" similar to the partially silvered mirrors used in film cameras.[22] This device would separate light coming through the top slot of the roof shells into two paths, reflecting some light onto the curved roof shells and thereby washing the major display surfaces with diffused light. Additionally, Meyers hoped to find a material that would also transmit a small percentage of light from the slot, adding diffused daylight as background illumination in the gallery spaces.

189

Sketches of various roof-lighting options

By adjusting the beam splitter's reflectance, the mix of wall and room light could be fine-tuned, and diffused light could be transmitted throughout the main level without introducing damaging direct rays or a bright ceiling.

The second advance made by Meyers was the solution to the roof module's curvature. Kahn's presentation in June had proposed a semicircular ceiling, which Brown had found ostentatious and thus, dictated by its geometry, too high. Kahn's response in September had been a flattened arch, which met Brown's requirements but was not particularly graceful. Meyers had explored the possibilities of a flat roof with quarter-round edges, ellipses, and segmented circles, none of which proved up to the task. The problem was therefore to find a continuous, aesthetically pleasing curve that would provide the low ceiling Brown desired.

Meyers recalled later that the solution to the roof's curvature presented itself in early November 1967 while he was reading Fred Angerer's 1961 book, *Surface Structures in Building*. The book documented surface, or shell, structures in engineering and architecture. Angerer explained shell behavior in contrast to skeleton construction. Whereas office and residential construction use columns, walls, and beams to stack floors atop one another, surface structures span large spaces by distributing

Zarzuela Racecourse, Madrid. Eduardo Torroja, 1935.
Cantilevered gullwing shells over the main stand

loads across a two-dimensional surface rather than along the single axis of a beam
or column.

Flat slabs without beams, supported only by columns, were the first surface structures
to be designed as such by pioneers Robert Maillart and Albert Kahn from 1910–15.
However, Maillart's 1939 pavilion for the Swiss National Exhibition, an arching concrete slab only 2½" thick that spanned more than 45', suggested new possibilities for
shaped or folded surfaces acting like hollow beams. A fold or curve in the cross section of a surface structure has the same effect as the separation of flanges by a steel
beam's web; the physical separation allows material at the cross section's top and
bottom to develop a resisting moment that can carry bending loads. Such a structure's efficiency, measured by the average distance of a section's area from its center
of gravity, may be lower than that of a simple beam with the same dimensions. But
the advantage of a folded or curved surface is that it also covers space and thus can
serve as its own environmental enclosure. In Eduardo Torroja's cantilevered roof for
the Zarzuela Racetrack (1935), for example, the material at the shell's top is in tension, while the material at the shell's bottom is in compression. This surface structure works exactly like a cantilevered beam, but it combines the covering function
of a slab with a beam's carrying action. While the eye may perceive a structure like

191

Test shell for the roof of Torroja's Zarzuela Racecourse with tensile reinforcement

the Zarzuela roof as a series of shallow arches, the view of a single unit being poured reveals otherwise. In fact, each "arch" is composed of two opposite halves of a gull-wing-shaped unit. From the reinforcing pattern it is apparent that the curved cross section is incidental to the shell's basic performance—that of a cantilevered beam. The structural behavior of a simply supported shell, such as Maillart's pavilion or Torroja's Madrid Pelota Court (1935), is analogous to that of a simple beam, with tension at the shell's top and compression below. But in shells, the beam's "web" is typically stretched out to act as a roof, in addition to its structural purpose, vertically separating the shell's flange areas at its top and bottom in order to resist bending. Shell structures typically consist of two orders of structural members: the shell itself, shaped to an ideal form, and a secondary structure, often internal but also frequently visible, whose task it is to maintain the shell's shape. In Maillart's pavilion, for example, a pedestrian bridge and lateral beams at the structure's base held the edges together, maintaining the arch's curve and preventing it from flattening out.

Angerer's book contained a section on barrel shells: long beamlike structures composed of curved extruded plates. As Meyers recalled, among the illustrations of various curves was a cycloid (see figure 62 in Angerer's book). This curve, the line that results from tracing the position of one point on a moving wheel, solved the

192

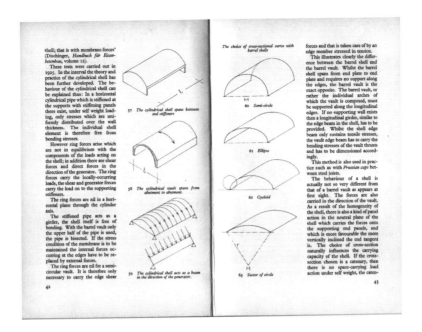

Pages from Angerer's *Surface Structures in Building* with cycloid shape
(right-hand page, third from top)

aesthetic problem of the roof shape. Lower than a semicircle and an ellipse, yet offering the chance to be visually unified with the side walls, the cycloid was also a naturally intriguing shape, a mathematical and geometrical curiosity with Renaissance precedents.[23] There is, however, no particular structural magic about the cycloid, and while Meyers would later say that the curve had "long span possibilities," its performance as a shell section is actually no better or worse than a singly curved arc of the same height. Coincidentally, on the page opposite the cycloid curve in Angerer's book, there are drawings showing the difference in behavior between a cylindrical vault and a cylindrical shell. The first, according to Angerer, spanned "from abutment to abutment," with its main structural action occurring along its cross axis. The cylindrical shell, however, spanned "between end stiffeners," acting "as a beam in the direction of the generator." In the first case, the load carried by the shape is transmitted to walls at the vault's edges, imparting a horizontal thrust. In the second, however, the load is carried along the shell's top and bottom fibers and is only transmitted to the ground at the columns or walls at the ends. There are, as Angerer showed, secondary stresses within the shape that basically try to flatten out the shell, reducing its structural depth and imparting some outward thrusts to the shell edges, in particular at its corners. Such shells do require secondary structures to maintain their

 193

shape; however, these may be much smaller than buttresses, as the major carrying action of long cylindrical shells is along—not across—their main axis.

Such subtle static behavior eluded Meyers and Kahn who, believing the cycloid would act more like a vault, asked Philadelphia engineer Nicholas Gianopulos for advice. Apparently confirming Meyers's misconception, Gianopulos was troubled by the daylight slot at the top of the Kimbell's roofs. If the cycloid were a true vault, this slot would have occurred at the section's area of greatest stress. To his credit, Gianopulos confessed that the behavior was beyond his abilities to calculate, and he suggested that Meyers discuss the design with August Komendant, who calmly pronounced that the shell would work as drawn, but with three modifications. First, curbs at the skylights' edges would be needed to stiffen the thin edge along its top fiber and to add cross-sectional area at the point of greatest compression. Second, diaphragms at the shells' ends would be required to hold its edges in place and keep it from flattening out. While these diaphragms would need to be relatively big—1' deep by 2' thick in Komendant's initial estimate—they would guarantee the performance of a thin roof shell, which in the end could measure only 4" thick. The third modification was that the roof shells would need to be posttensioned, with cables draped through their lower halves to absorb the considerable tensile forces that would develop in beams 150' in length. While Komendant's first two modifications involved secondary structures to hold the shells' shapes, posttensioning was to be a major element in the structural performance of these roofs, making them, again, hybrids of steel and concrete. But whereas Yale's ceiling and Richards's structures were both seen as steel systems rendered in concrete, the Kimbell shells would be more ambiguous, deploying the two materials in a more balanced way and leading to a structural form that defied the limitations of both.

Meyers described Komendant's approval of the cycloid as "abrupt," almost casual. Yet the shell Komendant was approving was not radically different from shells built in Germany over the previous ten years. While the cycloid drawing in Angerer's book achieved some measure of fame due to the Kimbell, other drawings by Angerer bear a remarkable resemblance to the Kimbell's shells as described by Komendant in his book *My 18 Years with Architect Louis I. Kahn.* While the roofs are spatially vault-like, Komendant preferred to describe the structure as a series of gullwing shapes, much like the cross section of Torroja's racecourse grandstand, with a deep zone in the middle and curbed skylights at the edges. Angerer showed two examples of this gullwing shell, one for a proposed rail-station roof, the other a "cantilevered cylindrical shell with interspaced roof lights" that bears a remarkable resemblance to the Kimbell scheme. Here again, while the space is surmounted by what appears to be a split cylindrical vault, the structural section reads as V-shaped, or as gullwing shells supported on columns.[24]

In addition to his proposed structural modifications, Komendant objected to Kahn's scheme for carrying ductwork under the cycloids. In the September 1967 drawings, trays extended across the full dimension of the intermediate "service zones." These trays were shown wider than the gap between the actual roof shapes above, meaning that the tray's edge extended beyond the curves' springing points. While this provided space for uplighting the shells and air supply, Komendant noted that it concealed the junctions between the shells and the low, service-zone ceilings. More importantly, he argued against the metal trays' single, central connections to the roof structure, suggesting instead that two small "marginal" beams be located at each springing point, with the mechanical system concealed between them. Nonetheless, he was overruled for the moment, and drawings taken to Fort Worth for meetings at the end of November 1967 showed the cycloid shells with wide metal trays slung beneath them.

Planning: "H" and "C" Schemes

The November 1967 floor plan was smaller than the one shown in September, with no exterior arcades and considerably tightened internal planning. Known as the "H-plan" for its footprint, it consisted of two separate pavilions linked by a three-bay concourse. The west end of the "H" still contained temporary galleries, a shop, and the auditorium, while the east pavilion contained service and administrative areas in the basement. Linking the two, the grand axis was reduced, with a stair at its east end linking to the covered auto drop-off. The roof shells were to be supported on a forest of columns, demonstrating that if Kahn and Meyers understood the shells' carrying action, their long-span potential remained elusive. While this plan was approved as presented, Brown wrote Kahn in December with another set of concerns, in particular, that an initial estimate of construction costs had to be submitted to the Museum's board before any formal approvals could be given.[25]

Cost and schedule concerns, along with growing tension between Kahn and Geren, shadowed the Kimbell design from this point forward. While Kahn had worked with associate architects before, he found this a difficult match from the beginning. Preston

195

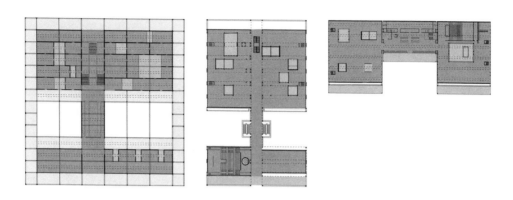

The Kimbell's three planning stages: the "square," "H-plan," and "C-plan" schemes

Geren's reputation had been built on predictability in cost and schedule. His buildings were competent and invariably within budget, but by his own admission they were conservative and not particularly innovative. While Geren was involved as an advisor in the early stages of the Kimbell's design, his office did not play a role in the scheme's basic conception. As the project moved forward, Geren's responses to the challenges of Kahn's design—in particular the cycloid vaults and details—demonstrated a greater concern over costs and responsibility for its radical construction. Kahn was forced to defend his process and the design at every turn. This began with estimates based on Kahn's plans and Komendant's preliminary design for the roof shells. Kahn and Geren both had estimators prepare costs, and both architects emerged from the process believing the project would cost around $6.2 million. Brown had, by this point, firmed up a budget of $5.9 million, and he asked Kahn to continue looking at possible cost savings. Kahn, by Meyers's account, welcomed the opportunity to subject the design to such pressures, but after spending from January to August 1968 cutting costs, Kahn and Brown became convinced that the team had been pursuing a flawed scheme. Some reductions were obvious and acceptable; the number of light fixtures, for example, was reduced, and the basement service level was redesigned several times. Geren, however, pointed out that both time and fees were being diluted by the ongoing redesigns, suggesting to Kahn that a radical move was required to develop a scheme that would meet the budget and allow the project to progress.

In August 1968, Kahn and Meyers held a discussion with Richard Brown that led to a complete redesign, albeit one based on what had been learned in previous iterations. Brown had identified a major flaw in the H-scheme: the plan's western portion, containing the lecture hall and temporary exhibit gallery, was also the main entrance. Visitors on their way to the main gallery space would often see these two major spaces empty when exhibitions were being changed—not exactly the warm welcome that Brown sought. On 20 August, Kahn responded to Brown's concerns by reorganizing the Museum's gallery level into a long rectangle, extending west to east from an entry garden off Will Rogers Drive to Arch Adams, adding a lounge across from the temporary gallery and burying the auditorium underneath. This solution, which squeezed the H-scheme's "legs" into a single form, was quickly abandoned, however. Instead, one month later, Kahn sent drawings to Brown in which the Kimbell's ultimate concept was apparent, if not finalized. Dubbed the C-scheme, it reversed the logic of the previous attempt, stretching the program along the site's eastern edge and pulling back its entry from the park's western edge. What had been an entry pavilion was now recessed within the plan's depth, articulated by a long notch in the western elevation. Temporary and permanent galleries were shown in the resulting north and south lobes, respectively, separated by the indented lobby. This removed the entry even farther from Will Rogers West, but it provided a formal forecourt, a clear division of temporary and permanent collections that allowed the former to be shut off from the latter during reinstallation, and a clear service plan in the basement. The north–south roof module thus ran across the Museum's primary division in three lobes, emphasizing the interweaving of program, site response, and structure. While this scheme would undergo major alterations before its completion—notably a reduction from seven parallel bays to five—the Kimbell's form was absolutely apparent here. Like the Salk, the Kimbell's final scheme crystallized on the basis of empirically gained knowledge from the wreckage of previous schemes.

This final plan—three groups of parallel cycloid vaults, with public functions in the center, galleries to either side, and an undercroft containing offices, service and conservation areas, and a loading dock—was the result of a complex building-up of programmatic, structural, and performance concepts. Here again, the *esquisse* did not come immediately; instead, Kahn and his team arrived at this point after a year of testing, development, and iterative redesign demanded by the pressure exerted by the

197

Foundation's budget and Brown's tenacious insistence on human scale. Komendant was dismissive of this process: the client's objections to the original scheme's size and scale "were welcome to Kahn because he himself did not like the design and layout any more. A quite normal process with him; if there was a three- to six-months [*sic*] time lapse, radical changes could always be expected. And so the entire preliminary design found its way to the wastebasket."[26]

Kahn's structural engineer, again, had not been in favor of change. Yet Komendant's understandable frustration does not do justice to Kahn's process. It was not simply that Kahn had become bored with the earlier design. Instead, the first designs had tested the limits of the project's economy and the Museum's taste for bold architectural statement. Subsequent work had refined the essence of these early overscaled schemes—a formal plan made up of a linear gallery module that admitted light while ensuring flexibility in layout—into a design that fit the Kimbell's budget and aspirations. This occurred both gradually and in occasional bold leaps, a process that accepted ideas both evolutionary and revolutionary but that in each case relied on iteration to explore the implications of Brown's complex requirements and their execution. The inherent logic of the final scheme and its almost perfect fit with its internal program is a testament to two years of tireless experimentation.

From this point forward, however, once the vital requirements had been established, this final scheme held on tenaciously throughout the development process to even Komendant's satisfaction. If the Kimbell—like Richards, like the Salk, even like Yale—had bubbled up from the wealth of programmatic, economic, and performance particulars, it would percolate back down through these levels of detail. But now the *esquisse* controlled the design of these smaller scales. Having nurtured a scheme suited to Brown's program, the development of this concept through the contingencies of site, materials, and configuration would prove to be a constant challenge. Each detail would be measured against its support of the *esquisse*—now set as a C-shaped building composed of cycloid-sectioned gallery modules running north–south. Still further reductions to this scheme through one last round of budget discussions—frustrating though they must have been—were described by Kahn as "wringing the water out of the design," suggesting that in hindsight he respected the pressure that budget issues brought to bear on the creative process.

Design Development and Crisis

The first few months of 1969 were supposed to have been devoted to transferring the design to Geren's construction drawings and commencing construction. Thomas Byrne, a local contractor, was brought on board in late 1968, which allowed a full cost analysis prior to the completion of construction documents. The cost analysis was still not encouraging—the construction estimate by the beginning of the year was still over budget, but in a climate of rising construction prices, the Museum agreed to begin preliminary sitework in July, before Geren could complete construction drawings. Kahn, meanwhile, was directed to reduce costs further. By March 1969, the galleries and undercroft had been compacted in both directions. One whole line of shells was removed, and the program was compressed into the resulting space—five shells in each gallery bay and four in the central piece. At the same time, the building was shortened, with the length of each wing now measuring only 100'. Also in this scheme, the auditorium was moved from the south wing to a single bay and service zone in the north. By the end of March 1969, Kahn and his office cut nearly 25 percent of the Museum's cost, a prodigious feat in light of the fact that the impact of the initial conception was retained.

As the design went through this final cost cutting, a crisis emerged in the production of construction drawings. Geren's office, already pressed for time, complained about Kahn's deliberative approach in redesigning to reduce costs. Worse, to Komendant's surprise, Geren had quietly assumed contractual responsibility for the project's engineering and proposed radical changes to the gallery floor structure and the cycloid shells, which he claimed were unsound. When Geren suggested eliminating the shells in favor of a flat concrete roof in June, Kahn, Meyers, and Komendant flew to Fort Worth. Meyers had warned in November that Geren lacked the expertise to design the shells, and they were preserved only after Komendant's insistence that they were structurally viable and that he should be retained to supervise their development.[27] Tensions increased in July. Brown, growing frustrated with the job's progress, contacted Kahn by telegram and urged that he "straighten out Geren immediately."[28] After discussions among Kahn, Brown, and Komendant, Kahn urged the Museum to insist on Komendant's being engaged as production designer, taking over the responsibility for structural drawings that Byrne could use to commence work.

Komendant recalls this episode in his memoir, *My 18 Years with Architect Louis I. Kahn*. Documents show that he might have single-handedly rescued Kahn's design and reputation. Geren, by now desperate and implicated in the problem, wrote Komendant on 19 July asking him to design and prepare construction drawings for the structure from the gallery floor up.[29] Geren insisted that his office maintain control over the lower level; concerned by recent requests from Kahn that the main gallery floor be posttensioned to allow for longer spans and thus fewer columns, Geren was adamant that this level, the first to be poured, should not be subject to changes. Komendant, however, insisted that if he were being brought on board to save the project, he must have complete control over the design.[30] Desperate for someone else to share responsibility, Geren relented. Komendant again flew to Fort Worth, taking both Kahn's design drawings and Geren's preliminary construction drawings and signed an agreement on 29 July. Just two weeks later, on 15 August, Komendant returned a set of preliminary structural drawings and calculations, a feat that eclipsed even his legendary performance on the Salk. Geren suggested some minor adjustments, but the structural drawings were released on 29 August, exactly one month after they had been commissioned.

Given absolute authority, Komendant mandated major changes involving the cycloid's detailing and the gallery floor's construction. Of these, the design of the cycloid shells' stabilizing arches led to a critical debate with Kahn. During the design's early stages, when Komendant was simply Kahn's consultant, he had shown a 1'-0" constant depth arch at the end of each cycloid to stiffen the thin roof shells. Kahn and Meyers developed a detail that demonstrated the structural independence of this element from the wall below, showing a glass lunette separating the two elements. Now, having calculated the stresses within the roof, Komendant altered the arch shape and with good reason. The arches needed a certain cross section to transfer the shells' weight to the columns below. However, their secondary function was to maintain the shells' shape at their corners, preventing them from flattening out and losing their structural depth. Here it is useful to imagine each end arch as a pair of arms gripping the corners, holding the ends inward to maintain the shells' shape. As such, their most efficient shape would be two cantilevered beams that sprang from each shell's crown, wrapping around the cycloid and diminishing in cross section as they approached the corners.

The diminishing shape, of course, belied the gullwing section as described by Komendant and reinforced the misreading of the roofs as vaults. Komendant was unconcerned with this emphasis, instead urging Kahn to accept the purely structural validity of these elements. The Kimbell's roof may thus be read as the series of gullwing elements mentioned previously, knitted together at their ends by a "stitching" of cycloid arches, whose primary module aligned with the galleries, offset by one-half bay from the main gullwing rhythm.[31] Kahn did not approve of the change in shape, believing that it confused the shell's reading. Under duress from the schedule, however, he agreed to Komendant's design, changing the glass lunette to a variable depth, from 4" at the top to 9" at the base, revealing the column's dimension and emphasizing the depth of these end arches at their centers. Kahn's agreement to this change was also intended to "honor the engineering" as a show of respect for Komendant's remarkable efforts.

Komendant's second major change to the roof structure was to demand that his scheme for the shells' base, with doubled marginal beams, be implemented in place of the concealing metal trays. This would more clearly express the shells' geometry and function and, not coincidentally, add more cross-sectional area in the location of greatest tensile stress.[32] Komendant additionally argued for a clear exposition of the junction between shell and beam; it should be made obvious that the shells do the carrying and that the beams are supported by the curved shapes above. Between the downstand beams, Komendant allowed "just the space we have, not a square inch more" for ductwork, with grilles running under the beams' bottom to allow for supply.

Komendant finally expressed concern about the gallery floor's performance. Geren had redesigned the floor as a waffle slab, eliminating the dead load of a flat plate and, in his view, making the basement's long spans more efficient. Komendant, in reviewing the plans, noted that the combination of widely spaced columns in the basement and upstand concrete walls at the gallery level could all be used to lengthen the spans. In response to information from Brown that the galleries might carry heavy sculptural objects, Komendant also redesigned the floor system as a two-skinned hollow slab with intermediate vertical fins connecting top and bottom and posttensioning cables following lines of maximum stress. This section bears a resemblance to the Vierendeel floor trusses of Richards; however, it was achieved by much simpler methods. As the floor was poured, lightweight polystyrene blocks, 30" wide, were placed in a grid pattern, and the slab was poured around and over these. The result was a 14"-thick concrete slab with most of its weight replaced by the foam pockets, providing an additional permissible floor loading, not to mention a savings in concrete of more than 1.5 million pounds. This ingenious solution, while hidden from view, was a great source of pride for Komendant, who had himself photographed victoriously hoisting a foam block over his head as the slab was poured around him.[33]

August Komendant hoisting one of the foam blocks used to lighten the weight of the gallery floor slab. Looking on are Richard Brown (left) and Virgil Earp (right)

Final Design

The Kimbell's final scheme was a distillation of the original 600'-square design's themes and strategies. It had been refined by constant budget pressures, a gradual reconciliation of the Kimbell's ambitions with its resources, and the development of an ideal section module, itself the product of constant negotiation among functional, material, and aesthetic needs. As with Kahn's other major projects, the plan's apparent simplicity and effortlessness belied its complex knitting together of structure, space, and service into a coherent, easily read whole. The final design broke down the Museum's functions into three wings, each composed of parallel cycloid shells and their related service zones. To the north and south, the main galleries were organized around courtyards—two in the south wing, one in the north—that induced a sense of progression, while providing the glimpses of nature that Brown had requested in the program. In the plan's center the intentionally compressed volume contained the entry, along with an associated lobby and shop, across the width of two cycloid bays. The library was housed in the center wing's eastern vault on the main floor and mezzanine. The basement was devoted to art handling in the north wing; offices, conservation, and storage were in the south wing, illuminated where necessary by light slots slipped between the front "porches" and the building itself. A lower lobby that opened up to the parking lot along the site's east edge took its place in the basement plan's center, connected to the main lobby above by two travertine-framed staircases.

The service zones running parallel to the cycloids were complemented by two major slots running perpendicular through the building's depth, slicing between the three main gallery volumes. At the intersections of these slots with the roofs' service zones, air handlers in the subbasement fed conditioned air through vertical risers. From here, supply air was run through two ducts in the underbelly of the gullwings' centers, feeding out through grilles located just below the concrete structure's lowest edge. Return air, ingeniously, was to be dumped through floor-level slots at the galleries' edges into the basement, where negative pressure ensured a constant flow of low-level air from the galleries. While the mechanical system of an art gallery is considerably less complex than that of a laboratory, Kahn nonetheless gave it a respectful place in the design's overall order, weaving ductwork and grillage into the building fabric. Primary circulation was aligned along and across the cycloids, while secondary and service circulation elements such as fire stairs, connections to the lower lobby, passenger elevators, and even an aisle of the auditorium were contained by the service zones' positions and directions. The Kimbell thus carried the Trenton Bath House's gridded logic into a more complex and legible spatial system, as its service zones were threaded throughout the galleries' spaces and defined major circulation paths, not merely the intersections of a grid.

This legibility of the design's conception was paralleled by a frank exposition of the processes involved in its execution. The building's three front porches of one roof shell each were designed to explain the cycloid's construction and structural performance. While the center pavilion's porch is contiguous with the building's curtain wall, narrow light slots separate the two flanking porches from the building enclosure. The shells' end arches rest on four corner columns, and they reveal patched areas where posttensioning cables were tightened. There is no doubt that these are shells—not vaults—as the light slot to the basement on one side and the void of the park on the other offer no longitudinal support. However, on both sides of the cycloid, a continuous gutter was included, one that is overscaled and, curiously, made of concrete, not metal. This could easily have been hidden or detailed as an attached metal element. A clue to its conception, however, lies in the linear reveal on the shell's inside, located at precisely the point where the thin concrete roof would intersect the marginal beam on a typical interior shell. The gutter occurs where the roof slab would be on the interior shells. It is, in fact, not only wicking rainwater away from the building but also stiffening the shell's edge, preventing it from flattening out, just as the end arches and slot curbs maintain each shell's structural shape. Explained in this way, we find a consistent explanation of the porches' structure, including a subtle but statically correct distinction between the edge shells and the interior shells. Kahn, in an interview given as the building was nearing completion in June 1972, remarked: "The porch…we wanted to have [it] as a kind of—the sense of how a building is made on the exterior, that's what it is. The sense of how a building is made is done like a presentation[,] like a piece of sculpture outside of the building."[34]

Construction

By the end of 1969, contractor Thomas Byrne had excavated the Museum's site, but work slowed while the drawings caught up, following the delays involved with redesigning in the spring and summer. Relations between Geren's office and Kahn were set back further by Geren's death in September 1969, after which the project was run by his son, Preston Geren Jr. One of the most contentious issues in the transition from the drawing board to the jobsite was concrete quality. After Komendant's suggestion to use some of the upper levels' exterior walls as spanning beams, Kahn employed Fred Langford, who had opened his own consulting office after working on the Salk's concrete, to develop the Kimbell's formwork. In November 1969, Langford met with Meyers; Byrne's project manager, A. T. Seymour; and one of Langford's job captains onsite in La Jolla to review the concrete work at the Salk. By that point, Byrne had spent much of the downtime after excavation preparing sample walls for Kahn's review, a process that lasted into 1970. Before Byrne could begin work on the superstructure, one key piece of information was required: the pattern of form joints on the concrete surfaces, which was needed before any formwork could be assembled. Langford's drawings, which had been scheduled for delivery in August, did not arrive until December, despite threats from Seymour to shut down the job if they were late. When they were finally transmitted, Seymour wrote to Geren Jr. complaining about the "very detailed systems indicated for forming this concrete."[35] In response, Kahn described the rationale of what, on a typical project, would have been left to the contractor's discretion:

> Fred Langford's reasoning in arriving at the markings is based on
> conveying to the eye the record of events of forming and pouring. He
> believes as I do that every building should have a logical system in

View of the formwork being stripped from
the foundation wall. Note the position of
the tie wires and chamfers

keeping with the material, aesthetic, and *operational conditions.* I
hope Mr. Seymour sees these advantages technically which would be
from the architectural point of view more expressive of an order.[36]

Kahn visited the jobsite in early February and convinced Brown, Geren Jr., and
Seymour to accept a compromise. Byrne would be allowed to use formwork of their own
design based on Kahn's aesthetic intentions as outlined by Langford, and Seymour
himself would later admit to being pleased with the "consistent, harmonizing effect"
of Langford's formwork details on the finished walls.[37] The specifications issued by
Kahn were based on the Salk's, but they were updated to include the results of lessons learned on that job, with a mix that would guarantee both a "warmer tone" and
material strength. In the initial pours, fortunately confined to the basement, Byrne
did not properly vibrate the liquid concrete, which caused water to collect against
the wood formwork's surface as the concrete cured. The result was a stained, blotchy
surface that Kahn rejected.

Langford and Komendant traveled to Fort Worth in early May, joining Meyers
for a review of concrete poured since the first wall and found it acceptable. Seymour
and Byrne had, as they progressed, become more adept at achieving the high

KIMBELL ART MUSEUM

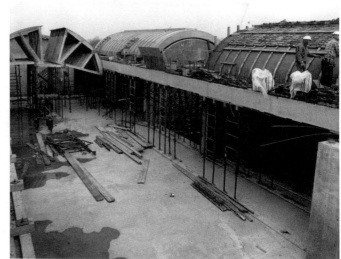

Construction views of concrete formwork for the Kimbell's roof shells.
Mockup (left) and progress of shells on site (right)

finish demanded by the specifications. Komendant continued to advise on technique, particularly the need to hammer and vibrate forms to dissipate air and water in the concrete slurry. He became a regular presence on the site, becoming well acquainted with Byrne and Geren employees and enjoying his status as design authority in Kahn's absence. As work progressed to the gallery slab, Komendant's presence became invaluable as the posttensioning required to limit the floor's deflection required expert advice and scrutiny. Throughout construction, he became a calming presence as the job moved upward through the structure and approached the challenge of constructing the cycloid shells.

The roof, of course, presented unusual construction problems. With little experience in thin-shell design, the contractors asked Komendant for help as they examined ways of fabricating the cycloids. Project superintendents Virgil Earp and L. G. Shaw finally devised an ingenious scaffolding system and a unique process of pouring to achieve the shells' complex curvature. Earp and Shaw built formwork sections of simple two-by-six lumber, cutting the cycloids' curvature out of marine plywood and supporting it with wood braces. The formwork sections were each composed of two 19'-0"-long halves, hinged at the top and braced with a 1'-0" plywood strip at the base. The pouring surfaces were made of layered ⅜" sheets of plywood bent to

Roof formwork being assembled over a steel reinforcing cage

the required curve and covered with an oily coating to ensure a smooth finish and easy removal.

At the beginning of a roof pour, simple flat formwork was used to build the low marginal beams. Once these had cured to working strength, the hinged formwork was raised and unfolded into place. A steel reinforcing mesh was then laid over the curved forms, held apart from the plywood by metal "chairs," and posttensioning ducts were laid out and connected to the reinforcing cage. Curved blocking elements made out of two-by-fours were then attached to this reinforcing cage, running from the cycloid's base to its top, and these were used to attach the outer skin of the formwork mold, made of short two-by-sixes nailed to the curved blocking. These horizontal pieces were placed in layers, and concrete was then poured one foot at a time to limit the fluid's pressure between the two layers of formwork, leaving a thin shell of 4"-thick concrete surrounding the metal reinforcing and posttensioning ducts.

After the shells had cured to working strength, the internal steel tendons were stressed, and the lower formwork, no longer bearing the shell's weight, was removed by folding the cycloid truss in on itself. On the shells' top, the horizontal two-by-sixes were removed, but the curved blocking was left in place. The result was a smooth,

Views of the construction site in January 1971 (above)
and of the interior finishes being applied (opposite)

finished concrete surface on the inside and a top surface that included generous
strips of nailable timber to attach the roof skin, as well as a 1½" zone, the depth of
the removed horizontal wood strips, for fiberglass insulation.[38] Atop the shells, Kahn
specified hammered lead for the roof surface to protect the vulnerable concrete
beneath. Due in large part to the construction of a mock-up panel that allowed
experimentation in placement, the shells were completed in only nineteen months,
from March 1970 to October 1971.

During this time, major elements of the building were still being designed, intensify-
ing the friction between Geren Jr., who was concerned about the contractual obligation
to stay on schedule, and Kahn, who continued to search for solutions that were consistent with the design's conception and not mere expedients. As construction continued
through 1971, details became increasingly important. Kahn's responses to requests
for information on the site reveal that he was actively engaged in designing through
to the end of construction. Of particular note are the storefront windows in the main
entry, which represent a further refinement in Kahn's exploration of brake-shaped
stainless-steel framing, and the handrails on the two main staircases, fabricated out
of bent and curved stainless steel to match the radius of a human hand's grip.

More prominently, the reflectors used to illuminate the roof shells' interior surfaces provided Marshall Meyers with the opportunity to design a component that restated in a single assembly the vault's geometric logic. Working with lighting engineer Richard Kelly and manufacturer Edison Price, Meyers set to work as early as 1968, refining the "beam splitter" to diffuse light throughout the gallery and wash the gallery walls with gentle, natural daylight. The three experimented at first with partially silvered Plexiglas. Kelly, however, realized that the ideal shape for casting the vertical rays offered by the skylight onto the cycloid shells would be a complex, multiradius curve, difficult to maintain in a plastic material. Kelly instead suggested making the reflector out of thin-sheet aluminum polished only on one side, offering a matte finish to the galleries and a reflective surface to the skylight. This material, commonly used in lighting fixtures, could be perforated to permit diffused light into the galleries, and as a sheet, it could be bent to any curve necessary. Kelly commissioned Edison Price to determine the proper profile using a rudimentary computer program, and the resulting shape—a gentle curve with cutoffs at top and bottom to prevent direct light from reaching the gallery walls—matched Kelly's original sketches. To hold the specular aluminum sheet in place, aluminum "yokes" were placed at 10'-0" intervals along the reflector. These were rectangular in section, with vertical elements made from cut aluminum plate to match the reflector curve and horizontal elements

Interior views and details of the completed galleries showing
reflectors (above) and downstand service zones (opposite)

from thin-gauge aluminum sheet, which could be bent to the reflector's shape. When
attached to one another, these pieces formed a robust arm to which the lightweight
perforated sheet could be attached.[39]

The yokes were attached by solid aluminum rods to minor concrete beams crossing
the skylight. Because the point of connection was obscured by the reflector, the locations of these hangars were detailed using large, 2"-diameter "buttons" on the bottom face of the yokes, revealing the pin connection to the spaces below. At the reflector's top, an extruded Y-shape blocked raking light from passing directly to the gallery
walls, while the reflectors' bases terminated with continuous triangular extrusions
that joined the bases to the yokes. These bottom elements also supported continuous
light tracks that allowed easy refocusing or reconfiguration of spot lighting, providing Brown with the flexibility in illumination his program had requested. Overall,
the effect of the reflectors suggested both their assembly sequence—obviously following the concrete shell construction—and their rigorous functional conception.
As one of the earliest architectural elements to be designed using digital methods—however crude—it was only appropriate that these be detailed using materials
that connoted mathematical precision. The custom extrusion process was an ideal
choice, permitting very tight tolerances, guaranteed repetition, and sharp corners.

The extraordinary lighting effect that the reflectors created, however, is anything but mechanistic; its diffuse, silvery qualities are as immeasurable and poetic as the fixture is measurable and precise.[40]

Similar care was taken with detailing the cycloids' bases, where supply air entered the galleries. The cycloids' springing lines were located 12'-6" above the gallery-floor level, while the service zones were given a 10'-0" ceiling height, limiting the required height of temporary exhibition walls while providing a low foil to the galleries' expansive spaces. Komendant's marginal beams were only 1'-8" deep, leaving room for a detail of 10" between them and the ceiling below. The bottom planes of all ducts were set beneath the marginal beams' lower edges, allowing them to push air out into the galleries through a 5" horizontal grille. Dropped aluminum soffits were hung below this assembly, at the 10'-0" height above gallery-floor level, with a steel angle placed to take up the remaining 5" between the ceiling and the air grille above. Aluminum button details similar to those used on the reflectors called out the positions of otherwise hidden metal struts, which supported these components from the concrete above. The resulting detail very clearly distinguishes between zones of structure and service, in both horizontal and vertical planes. The vertical surface of the marginal beam is visually continued by the angle's leading edge; however,

211

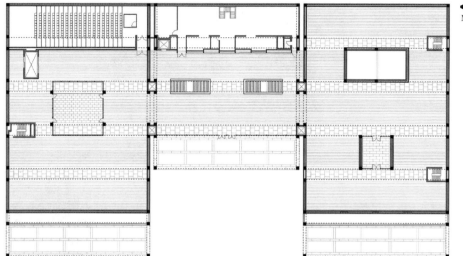

Gallery plan showing structure and grain of floor finishes

the supply grille is recessed between these. Thus there is no illusion that the angle is supporting anything, and the relatively minor role of air supply in the overall scheme is emphasized by the grille's subordinate, recessed position.

Through these and other, less apparent details, Kahn expressed the propositions of the *esquisse*—the use of a single-direction, folded-plate roof to shelter galleries whose layout ranks somewhere between *raumplan* and free plan, organized, if not delimited and serviced by, subsidiary equipment within the structural section's hollows. The galleries' end walls, for instance, alternate travertine with exposed concrete to reveal the supporting columns; the gallery floors use the directional grains of wood and travertine to contrast the axes of the galleries and the service zones. This collection of details reveals the logic of the building's careful interweaving of structure, space, and services. At every moment, from the first experience of the roof to the realization that the floor patterns, too, have been arrayed to tell the story of the building's conception, the intertwined logics of design and construction are presented as integral elements of the Kimbell's expression and experience.

For all of Kahn's innovation and despite the Kimbell's rich, complex solution, Richard Brown's comments following the Kimbell's opening suggest that we not view the design

212

as completely original. Brown pointed out that, along with its "fresh approach," the Kimbell actually bore a complex relationship to Kahn's earlier work. On the one hand, it represented a new solution to classic gallery problems and was thus a departure from other Kahn buildings:

> It's different from any of the others, not because Kahn simply tried to do something novel. He faced the problems posed by this new project with a ruthless honesty and objectivity about its demands. Out of trying to solve those demands, obviously a different building had to emerge.[41]

Yet in the same interview, when asked when in the design process the image of the "barrel series" emerged, Brown responded with a frank description of Kahn's working method:

> The basic structural and space-creating idea did not emerge from our discussions at all. That was already in Lou Kahn's mind and had been for a long time, I think. And when he was commissioned to do this particular job, he reached for that structural idea as ideal for it.... After he'd thrashed the problem out enough he reached for the cycloid vault because it would enable him to get this marvelous strong light in from the top and because it would free him to create a space that would be totally flexible, standing as it does on only its four two-foot square piers on either end...a floor uninterrupted by piers, columns or windows, and perfect lighting, giving total freedom and flexibility to use the space and install art exactly the way you want. That freedom is grand, but it imposes a discipline immeasurably [sic] great.[42]

213

While Kahn's Beaux-Arts's leanings may incline us to see the galleries as vaults, here it is useful to emphasize again that they are shells, operating as one-way beams, permitting this "disciplined freedom" in the space below. Additionally, it is noteworthy that each of these shell-beams carries in its underbelly the mechanical entrails of lighting and conditioned air, permitting servicing on a very fine linear grid. In fact, if we accept Komendant's description of the shells as gullwing shapes and fill in his section with the ductwork required to supply the galleries, a startling parallel emerges—this section is topologically and functionally similar to the early, folded-plate scheme

Comparison of the Salk Institute's folded-plate scheme (left)
and the final, gullwing shape of the Kimbell's roof shells (right)

for the Salk Institute's laboratories. Both sections rely on an extruded concrete beam, folded around a pair of voids. The top void in the early Salk scheme was to be occupied by pipes and catwalks, functions that were not required at the Kimbell. However, the lower void in each was sized for ductwork—supply and return at the Salk, supply only at the Kimbell. In each case, these ducts were fitted between downstand beams that played a structural role secondary to the folded shape above. Both systems terminated at a skylight slot that brought daylight into the space, a detail that revealed in both cases the structural schemes' linear nature; the "bailiwick" that Kahn regretted losing in the final Salk scheme reemerged as the Kimbell's "vaulted" gallery space. The integrated structural idea and space-creating conception that Brown spoke of was not simply the cycloid's shape, which itself had emerged from discussions about the character of the Museum's spaces. It was, rather, the notion of long-span, one-way folded shells, hollowed out to provide horizontal runs of services, that Kahn had been forced to abandon on the Salk project a few years earlier. They were deployed here for a less service-intensive program and reconfigured based on the Kimbell's particular needs, but their ability to define space and express the building's dense weavings of service and structure fulfilled the lost promise of the early Salk scheme.

Assessment

The Kimbell opened in October 1972, though it had been occupied since at least June of that year. "Fort Worth," Meyers would recall, "really knew how to throw a party," and the celebrations that greeted this new civic work were fueled by the ecstatic reception given to the building by the national press. *Newsweek* hailed the Kimbell as the crowning achievement in an "outburst" of American museum building that had included structures by Mies van der Rohe in Houston, Gio Ponti in Denver, and I. M. Pei in Washington.[43] *Progressive Architecture* described the building as a "definitive work," and Kahn unaccountably made the pages of *Vogue* for the second time, with the Kimbell serving as notice of a "New Texas Boom."[44] The building put Fort Worth on the map in terms of both culture and architecture, and it remains a destination for pilgrimages by students and architects alike.[45]

Critical reaction was similarly effusive. William Jordy wrote one of the first major critiques of the project in June 1974, juxtaposing the Museum with the contemporaneous Exeter Library in New Hampshire and finding in both a restoration of "right perspective and good sense after an orgy of tragic disillusion."[46] For Jordy, the Kimbell represented a step forward from limpid functionalism, in that Kahn's design had "reconstitut[ed] the programme in the light of what the institution primarily *is*," rather than simply what its list of spaces denoted.[47] Recalling Banham's critique of Richards, Jordy acknowledged "skepticism about the retrospective ring of Kahn's statements and…the tendency toward an archaic monumentality" that seemed perhaps misplaced against the work of a younger generation. Despite finding fault with the fit of the library and auditorium into the section, Jordy recognized the multivalence of the Kimbell's forms and spaces, noting that the distinction between the Kimbell and Exeter was that the Kimbell negotiated levels of "functional use…structural syntax…. and ceremonial extrapolation of this syntax."[48] Of course, Jordy's analysis also referred to Kahn's Beaux-Arts training. While this article appeared a year prior to the Museum of Modern Art's exhibition of Beaux-Arts drawings, a growing interest in classically derived composition during the mid-1970s was an obvious point of critical reference for a building that so seamlessly wove together historical allusions and technical artistry. The Kimbell was viewed by many as a revival of formalist composition, in opposition to the perceived sterility of much postwar modernism; it became associated with the flowering of historicist imagery being promoted by, among others, erstwhile Kahn employee and student Robert Venturi. For all the richness of the cycloid shells, their immediate critical impact was as an *architecture parlante* in which a rising generation saw an expressive, visual excess beyond the dry functionalism that had driven museum design in the 1960s. The Kimbell was also noted for its domestic scale, its disciplined flexibility, and its landscape design. Richard Brown continually praised its unintimidating, comfortable spaces, comparing it to a fourteenth-century palazzo that allowed him to arrange works so that "they have conversations with one another."[49]

The Kimbell has become one of the most praised and beloved examples of postwar American architecture, and its influence on museum, landscape, and civic design has resonated in numerous projects. It was awarded the American Institute of Architect's prestigious Twenty-Five Year Award in 1998, and it regularly receives praise as one of the finest examples of American architecture—postwar or otherwise.[50] Likewise, it has been phenomenally successful as a museum, setting records in its opening years for annual attendance by a Texas museum while hosting blockbuster shows ranging from Chinese decorative arts to a cold-war exhibition of Impressionist paintings in Russian collections. It drew more than a million visitors in its first five years and proved its versatility by playing host to more than four hundred thousand museumgoers in 1994.[51]

Praise for Kahn's design reached a fever pitch when the Kimbell was the subject of expansion plans by Edmund Pillsbury, who was named director after Richard Brown's death in 1979. Plans presented in 1989 by architect Romaldo Giurgola, a colleague of Kahn's at the University of Pennsylvania, were sharply rebuked by many of Kahn's collaborators. Giurgola proposed maintaining the cycloid module but extending the galleries to the north and south, essentially extruding the plan to the site's edges. In fairness to Giurgola, Kahn's original plans called for an even larger complex based on the single gallery module that would have extended to the site's four corners. Giurgola's scheme was modest in comparison, yet Paul Goldberger, among others, noted that the distillation Kahn had effected in developing the final scheme had not created a "slimmed-down" version of the original, but rather a "fully realized work in itself."[52] The Kimbell's floor plan had not been truncated by the project's budget pressure; it had been entirely redesigned. Tinkering with this layout, adding galleries, for instance, on the auditorium's far side or changing the courtyards' relationships to the new gallery plan would inevitably throw off the Museum's careful grain and rhythm. Architects and critics including Richard Meier, Kenneth Frampton, Frank Gehry, and James Stirling wrote a spirited protest to the *New York Times*, not-

View from the south garden

ing that Brown's program had clearly stated that "the form of the building should be so complete in its beauty that additions would spoil that form."[53] While some critics bristled at this, noting that the Museum's success made some form of expansion necessary, and others noted that the signatories to the letter had themselves executed additions to sensitive precedents, an unanswerable objection was raised by George Patton, the project's landscape architect.[54] Patton noted that the extension would alter the sense of the Museum being in the park, not next to it, and that "crowding the Kahn building between pseudo-Kahn wings" would "spoil both building and site."[55] The sense of the building within the park had only gradually emerged during the design. Yet one of the classic views of the building remains its southern approach from Lancaster Avenue, where the cycloids' march over the sunken garden reveals the section, cross grain, and rhythm of the galleries inside. This, in addition to the spirited defense of the building by Kahn's widow, Esther, and his daughter Sue Ann, led Pillsbury to withdraw the proposal in February 1990, to the relief of an architectural community that would quickly reconvene in response to Jonas Salk's expansion plans a few months later.[56]

The Kimbell's legacy is twofold. As a museum it has been profoundly influential, inspiring intimately scaled, technically advanced museum design by Norman Foster

Renzo Piano's *hommage à* Kimbell: The Nasher Sculpture Center, Dallas, 2003

(the Sackler Galleries in London and the Joslyn Art Museum in Omaha, Nebraska) and Renzo Piano (the Menil Collection in Houston; the Fondation Beyeler in Basel, Switzerland; and the Nasher Sculpture Center in Dallas, among others). Each of these buildings has picked up the theme of the integrated ceiling, carrying on Kahn's dialogue of structure, daylight, and disciplined flexibility of gallery layout. The Kimbell's subtle monumentality—initially brought about by height restrictions but then conscientiously developed—has likewise influenced the design of museums by James Stirling and Charles Moore, who have sought to replicate its combination of formality and domestic scale.

Another major legacy of the Kimbell has been its technically enigmatic structure, as the nature and "correctness" of its roof shells have been debated since its opening. Komendant, of course, used the story of its roof development to point out Kahn's confusion about its refined structural design. More recently, probing essays by Peter McCleary and Guy Nordenson have extended a more sophisticated discussion of these shells. McCleary was the first to point out the staggered modules of structure and gallery, noting that the gaps of the skylights define the structure on the gull-wing module and proposing that the "unity of structure, light and room" is left incomplete by this offset of the structural grid.[57] Nordenson, on the other hand, has

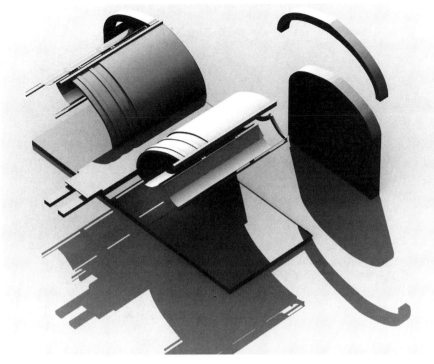

Exploded view of the Kimbell's module as built showing
reflector, ductwork, concrete shells, end arches, and walls

offered a more sympathetic reading, noting Kahn's knowledge of advances in shell structures and quoting Kahn's 1959 statement regarding the need to integrate lighting with structure:

> Suppose you got the right engineer, let's say Candela or Nervi to do the building for you—and then you said "Now, how shall we light it?" then you're wrong. Or if you then said, "How shall we breathe in this place?" you are also wrong. In the very fabric of making it must already be the servants that serve the very thing I've talked about— its timbre, its light, and its temperature control; the fabric of the construction must already be the container of these servants.[58]

219

The complexity of the Kimbell's roof is thus neatly aligned with the sophistication of its program. Brown had asked for regularity with flexibility, a monument with modesty, light with shade. Komendant and McCleary were correct in pointing out that the roofs are not statically "pure," that their shapes are compromised by mechanical, lighting, and compositional factors. But the Kimbell's shells do appear more rigorous if a wider horizon is adopted in considering these performance requirements. This requires seeing the shells as the product of a lengthy, evolutionary process, beginning

Front entry porch

from the particularities of Brown's program, instead of an intent to produce structural purity divorced from the contingencies of a program.

Reading the rich weaving of functional, constructive, and spatial factors from the "immeasurable" spaces of the galleries is particularly rewarding. The structure is staggered from the main galleries' metric and, indeed, from its own stabilizing arches at the building's ends. Much of the structure's carrying and holding action is concealed from view. But the Kimbell offers us several keys to decoding its constructed logic. The lunette windows at the galleries' ends tell us that the end walls play no supporting role, that the columns alone support the cycloids. If we arrive at the building's front, we are shown the porch vaults, the "excess" structure whose narrow-edge beams reveal the minor outthrusts of the cycloid shapes. As we move through the Museum's galleries, the plan's A:B:A:B nature is constantly reinforced; a one-way servicing strategy is made clear as we cross the building's main grain and pass under the rhythm of low, mechanical zones between galleries. A walk through the galleries is thus an invitation to reconstruct the interwoven logics of span, rigidity, lighting, and servicing in our own experience. Not all visitors will be so inclined, and Kahn has provided for them as well, in that the architectural program's summary logic—rectangular rooms arranged in parallel with a curved, toplit ceiling—is lucidly expressed throughout, in particular on the elevations. Additional layers of meaning, dialogue, and integration in the various systems that make the building work are continuously expressed by Kahn's detailing, which reveals the building's assembly process and its function at even the most intimate scale.

In failing to find a simple answer to the problem of the roof, McCleary in particular seemed disappointed. However, his analysis did not account for the richness of the holistic solution, nor for the pleasures inherent in the experience of the intricate knitting together of the Kimbell's aspirations, the raw stuff of its construction, and the mechanisms of its daily performance. The Kimbell is often referred to as the best constructed expression of Kahn's philosophy regarding materials, assembly, and performance. That it is, in the end, such a complex fabric is not its greatest failing, but its greatest strength. Immersed in a new milieu of technically conceived cultural buildings—in particular Tadao Ando's new building for the Fort Worth Museum of Modern Art across the street—the balance struck by the Kimbell in its scale, materials, and detailing is all the more apparent. It would come to be recognized as the greatest of Kahn's works, a building that provides a summary of his philosophy and a collection of spaces that shares the same genesis as those of the Yale Art Gallery. Bathed in sunlight manipulated by a master experimentalist, moving under a hovering set of richly conceived and endlessly allusive concrete roof forms, both architects and patrons have found repose and inspiration in the Kimbell's conceptual and physical weavings.

221

Endnotes

1. Richard F. Brown, "The Kimbell's Dream—Now a Shared Vision," *Fort Worth Star-Telegram*, 1 October 1972, special section on the Kimbell Art Museum, 7. The definitive history of the Kimbell's foundation, design, and construction remains that of Patricia Cummings Loud, *In Pursuit of Quality: The Kimbell Art Museum* (Fort Worth: Kimbell Art Museum, 1987).

2. Richard Brown described much of the collection as "optimistically attributed" when he took over as director of the Museum. "Kahn's Museum: An Interview with Richard F. Brown," *Art in America* 60, no. 5 (September–October 1972): 44.

3. Anne Miller Tinsley, "Kimbell Art Director Is Nationally Known," *Fort Worth Star-Telegram*, 8 November 1965, 1.

4. "Los Angeles Art Museum Head Quits After Denouncing Trustees," *New York Times*, 8 November 1965, sec. 1, 42.

5. "Director Chosen for Kimbell Art," *Fort Worth Star-Telegram*, 8 November 1965.

6. John Ohendalski, "Kimbell Art Museum on Carter Square Given 'Go,'" *Fort Worth Press*, 9 November 1964, 1. The location of Will Rogers Drive East is still plainly visible, along the allée of trees immediately to the west of the Museum's main entrance and on axis with the main Coliseum building. When the Museum was scaled down in the late design stages, there was apparently never any thought given to reinstating this drive, although it would have alleviated substantially the underuse of the main entrance.

7. Loud, *In Pursuit of Quality*, 10.

8. "Kahn's Museum," 44.

9. Ibid.

10. "Philadelphian Picked to Design Art Museum," *Fort Worth Star-Telegram*, 30 October 1966, 1–3.

11. Full project credits are included in *Architectural Forum*, July–August 1972.

12. "Kimbell Art Museum: Pre-Architectural Program," Louis I. Kahn Collection, University of Pennsylvania and the Pennsylvania Historical and Museum Commission, Philadelphia (hereafter cited as Kahn Collection), LIK box 37. Brown's program is reprinted in Loud, *In Pursuit of Quality*.

13. Loud, *In Pursuit of Quality*, 1. Here, one cannot resist a comparison with Mies van der Rohe's National Gallery, in which the artwork was essentially banished to the basement while the primary architectural space was reserved for the above-ground long-span lobby.

14. Ibid., 3.

15. Ibid., 14.

16. Marshall D. Meyers, "Remarks on the Occasion of the Twenty-Fifth Anniversary of the Kimbell Art Museum at the Accademia di Architettura in Lugano, Switzerland," 6 December 1997.

17. These sketches are contained in LIK folder 730-4 of the Kahn Collection.

18. Brown to Kahn, 12 July 1967, Kahn Collection, LIK box 37. The description of Kahn's approach is borrowed from Meyers, "Remarks on the Occasion."

19. Brown to Kahn, 12 July 1967, Kahn Collection, LIK box 37.

20. Ibid.

21. Ibid.

22. Meyers was inspired by a 16mm Bolex camera he owned to try this principle as a solution to the toplighting requirement. See Marshall D. Meyers, "Making the Kimbell: A Brief Memoir," in *Louis I. Kahn: The Construction of the Kimbell Art Museum*, ed. Luca Bellinelli (Milan: Skira, 1997), 21.

23. *Scientific American* had published a column on the cycloid's bizarre properties, along with a method to construct it using a coffee can and a pencil. According to Meyers, this method was used to make the initial drawings. The cycloid had at one point been called the "student's

curve" because of the calculations of its simple area (three times the area of its generating circle) and circumference (four times the diameter of its generating circle), neither of which rely on π. It is also found in the physics of falling objects; for example, as marbles placed anywhere on a cycloid will, due to differential acceleration, reach the center at the same time.

24. Likewise, Jurgen Joedicke shows examples of industrial buildings that used parallel shells of cylindrical section, occasionally split by central skylights into gullwing shapes. See Jurgen Joedicke, *Shell Architecture* (New York: Reinhold, 1963); Leonard Michaels included examples of cylindrical concrete shells in his book *Contemporary Structure in Architecture* (New York: Reinhold, 1950).

25. Brown to Kahn, 11 December 1967, Kahn Collection, LIK box 37.

26. August Komendant, *My 18 Years with Architect Louis I. Kahn* (Englewood, N.J.: Aloray, 1975), 117.

27. Meyers to Komendant, 27 November 1968, Kahn Collection, LIK box 37 ("Kimbell Art Museum"), in the file marked "Dr. Komendant, Kimbell Art Museum." Geren's office had, apparently, sought help from other engineering consultants, all of whom—unaware of his prior involvement—had suggested Komendant as the only engineer who had the expertise to ensure their performance.

28. Brown to Kahn, telegram, 4 June 1969, Kahn Collection, LIK box 37.

29. Geren to Komendant, 19 July 1969, ibid.

30. "Considering the existing conditions, general state of design, time lost since contract was signed with Thos. S. Byrne Inc, and my rather tight time schedule, I believe the structural work...can be carried out qualitatively and economically with only one person in charge, whose decisions should be honored by the Architects and Contractor.... There is no time to carry out special studies about the main floor structural system.... I will make prompt decision at the site [about] what would be the most qualitative, economical and practical solution at the given conditions." Komendant to Geren, 24 July 1969, August Komendant Archives, Architectural Archives of the University of Pennsylvania, Philadelphia, box 7.

31. As Aurelio Muttoni has pointed out, even this structural shape was not quite adequate and needed to be reinforced—at first with a horizontal tie rod and, in the end, with a cage of steel bars.

32. Meyers to T. E. Harden and Geren, 19 February 1969, Kahn Collection, LIK box 37.

33. A. T. Seymour, "The Immeasurable Made Measurable: Building the Kimbell Art Museum," *Via* 7 (1984): 81. Komendant was shown with the foam block, surrounded by A. T. Seymour, Director Richard Brown, and Project Superintendent Virgil Earp in "Construction 'First': Art Museum to Use Styrofoam in Floor," *Fort Worth Star-Telegram*, 7 August 1970, A-4.

34. Kahn, interview by M. Marlin, 24 June 1972, Kahn Collection, LIK box 37.

35. Seymour to Preston Geren Jr., 19 January 1970, ibid.

36. Kahn to Geren Jr., 1 February 1970, ibid.

37. Seymour, "The Immeasurable Made Measurable," 81.

38. In addition see Seymour, "Break-Away Forms Cast Arching Roof," *Construction Methods and Engineering*, April 1972, 90–92.

39. Geren's drawing describes this element as an "Alum. Yoke Folded Plate" and shows the cover plate attached with screws. This description has been erroneously relied upon by some studies to suggest that the yokes are, in fact, folded to achieve their cross section—a geometric impossibility. It is likely that the aluminum elements were brazed, a type of aluminum welding that was common by the early 1960s, particularly where fine finishes were required and where different thicknesses were being attached.

223

40. In June 1971 a mock-up of the skylight revealed that, while the reflector bounced adequate light in both directions, the north–south orientation of the skylight slots allowed noon light to strike the end walls of galleries directly through the reflector's perforations. Meyers credited Geren's job captain, Frank Sherwood, with suggesting that these two issues—direct sunlight and the available width of perforated aluminum—be solved with a single detail, an expressed "hinge" about two-thirds of the way up the reflector that would allow the material to change. In galleries, the top portion would be solid aluminum sheet, blocking noontime rays and casting more light onto the concrete shells. In public areas, this top portion could remain perforated, allowing a view of the sky through the scrim of the reflector.

41. "Kahn's Museum," 45.

42. Ibid., 48.

43. Douglas Davis, "The Museum Explosion," *Newsweek*, 17 September 1973, 88–89.

44. "Fort Worth's Kimbell: Art Housing Art," *Progressive Architecture*, November 1972, 25, 29. Also see Barbara Rose, "New Texas Boom," *Vogue*, 15 October 1972, 118–21, 130.

45. "This will put Fort Worth on the map in more ways than one. Culturally, the world will know about Fort Worth. There's no doubt about it." Charles Cowles (Publisher, *Artforum*), quoted by Jim Marrs, "You Can Be Art Critic Tomorrow," *Fort Worth Star-Telegram*, 3 October 1972. For a local assessment, see Jan Butterfield, "Kimbell Building among Kahn Best," *Fort Worth Star-Telegram*, 1 October 1972, G-1.

46. William Jordy, "The Span of Kahn," *Architectural Review* 155, no. 928 (June 1974): 320.

47. William Jordy, "Kimbell Art Museum," *Architectural Review* 155, no. 928 (June 1974): 330.

48. Ibid., 335.

49. "Fort Worth's Kimbell," 29. Reaction to the Museum's park setting and its landscaping, however, were mixed. While George Patton's designs were effusively praised, the front entry's relationship to the park proved problematic. Visitors arriving by car invariably enter the complex to the east, off Arch Adams Street, from which there is no direct access to the front lawn. The secondary entrance, from the lower level up the paired staircases to the main lobby, has become—by default in an autocentric city—the main entrance, and the approach from the park is only possible at the end of a long walk from the parking lot. Had the eastern half of Will Rogers Drive not been removed at the project's conception, it is possible that this would have served as a convenient drop-off to the front entry. During the numerous cost-driven redesigns, though, the building shrank from the western edge of its site, leaving no good automotive access to the main floor's entry. The resulting landscaped areas, in particular the south garden, however, have become important set pieces, providing a field across which the building's elevations can express the roof shells' sectional logic. Likewise, the major pedestrian approaches from the north and south under the porches add a welcoming connection from the other institutions around the park and introduce the building through these didactic elements, as Kahn intended.

50. In 1973 Byrne & Co. won an annual "Build America" award for the Kimbell, recognizing its innovative construction process. "Local International," *Fort Worth Magazine*, May 1973, 42. Other awards included the National General Contractors Association's "Best Building" award in 1972, the Illuminating Engineering Society's 1973 Lumen award, and the 1975 Honor award from the American Institute of Architects. "Kimbell Art Museum to Get Architect's Honor," *Fort Worth Star-Telegram*, 27 April 1975, E-1.

51. Janet Kutner, "Kimbell Celebrating," *Dallas Morning News*, 9 October 1977, C-2.

52. Paul Goldberger, "Architecture View: Sincerest Flattery or the Subtlest Form of Dishonor?" *New York Times*, 24 September 1989, sec. 2, 33.

53. Philip Johnson et al., "Kimbell Museum: In Praise of the Status Quo," *New York Times*, 24 December 1989, sec. 2, 2.

54. Benjamin Forgey, "The Delicate Art of Expansion: In Fort Worth, the Kimbell Museum Furor," *Washington Post*, 13 January 1990, C1. See also Mark Stankard, "Kimbell Museum: Wielding Names Like Weapons," *New York Times*, 7 January 1990, sec. 2, 3.

55. George Patton, "The Kimbell Museum: Preserve the Classic Balance...and Setting," *New York Times*, 19 November 1989, sec. 2, 3.

56. "Lou rarely spoke of his finished work, but he truly loved the Kimbell, for he felt he had created something that was perfect in itself." Esther I. Kahn, "The Kimbell Museum," *New York Times*, 26 November 1989, 2-3-4. For the denouement of the expansion affair, see Paul Goldberger, "The Kimbell Decides Its Building Is a Treasure to Be Cherished," *New York Times*, 28 February 1990, C-13, 1.

57. Peter McCleary, "The Kimbell Art Museum: Between Building and Architecture," *Design Book Review* 11 (Winter 1987): 35–55.

58. Kahn quoted in Guy Nordenson, "The Lineage of Structure and the Kimbell Art Museum," *Lotus* 98 (1998): 28–48.

6
CONCLUSIONS

Louis I. Kahn died on 17 March 1974 while returning to Philadelphia from Ahmedabad, India. His
death seemed premature for his seventy-three years.
The office was as busy as it had ever been, building
on the worldwide acclaim granted to the Salk and
Kimbell buildings. Over the course of his later career,
since the completion of the Yale Art Gallery, Kahn
had built three dozen projects, of which several have
come to be recognized as some of the finest works of
American architecture. Yet it seemed as if his career
were picking up momentum at the time of his death,
with his fluency in the formal, spatial, functional,
and constructed grammars of architecture reaching
their peak.

Among the projects in the office during the last
few years of Kahn's life, several done with August
Komendant pushed dramatically technical agendas.
In Venice, Kahn and Komendant proposed a suspended
conference hall, using steel cables and posttensioned
concrete to raise a twenty-five-hundred-seat auditorium above the city. For Olivetti's American production
lines outside Harrisburg, Pennsylvania, Komendant
and Kahn developed a field of concrete parasol structures, each balanced against the others with openings
at the internal connections to allow daylight through
to the factory floor. While the factory's mechanical
system was simply hung beneath the shells of the parasols, and thus not clearly integrated with the structural grid, the module's relentlessness and its definition of the space inside make it one of Komendant's
purest structures.

From 1966 until 1973, the two men worked on a unique
structural and constructional system for a thirty-story
office tower in Kansas City. The project involved a traveling formwork system that would gradually make a
central concrete core that the formwork would then

Olivetti-Underwood Factory,
Harrisburg, Pennsylvania.
Louis I. Kahn with
August Komendant,
1966–70.
Aerial view of concrete
parasol structure

228

climb. After reaching the core's top, a new formwork system for the floors would slide back down the core, leaving the office floors in its wake. Structurally, the tower was designed to suspend the outer edges of all levels, enabling the slipforming to progress downward, eliminating all interior columns.[1] The project was halted when financial backers nervously refused to fund the radical construction, and in 1973 the commission was dropped, although Skidmore, Owings & Merrill eventually built a tower of conventional construction on the site.

Kahn's untimely death matched a financial crisis in the office that belied its busy pace. The premature termination of the Kansas City project added to the near-simultaneous loss of a large urban project in Baltimore. Meanwhile, active projects in southern Asia for the Indian Institute of Management and Sher-e-Bangla Nagar, the new Bangladeshi capitol, had been lavished with attention by Kahn despite their lower fees. Kahn's office was bankrupt, with nearly one-half million dollars of debt, resolved only by the State of Pennsylvania's purchase of the office's drawings and letters in 1976. The absence of Kahn's leadership led to the cancellation or recommissioning of about ten projects, but many of the office staff resolved to complete work on three buildings: the Yale Center for British Art, completed by Marshall Meyers and Anthony Pellecchia; the Family Planning Clinic in Katmandu; and the Sher-e-Bangla Nagar capitol in Bangladesh, the latter two completed by David Wisdom and Associates. The office's dissolution had the effect of spreading Kahn's influence widely. While many associates and collaborators remained in Philadelphia, others found themselves in New York, New Haven, and as far afield as California, creating a diaspora of acolytes who faced the challenge of implementing Kahn's

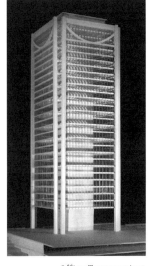

Office Tower project, Kansas City, Missouri. Louis I. Kahn with August Komendant, 1966–73

229

principles in surroundings that were not always welcoming to his thoughtful process.

What to make of Kahn's career and wide-ranging architectural philosophy has been a constant challenge to critics, historians, and practitioners. The fact that his career paralleled that of Philip Johnson and other late modernists made his emphasis on language a key pillar of the postmodernist movement. Robert Venturi's work in Kahn's office in the mid-1950s, in particular on the City Tower project, inspired key tenets of Venturi's work set forth in his *Complexity and Contradiction* (1966). Venturi's celebration of "richness and ambiguity" cites a half-dozen Kahn projects, though it is tempting to speculate that Venturi himself brought much of this attitude with him to Kahn's practice, rather than vice versa.[2] In any event, the Kimbell Art Museum's subtly inflected symmetry in 1972 came at an opportune time for Beaux-Arts revivalists, who were interested in challenging modernist orthodoxy by returning to formal composition and rigorous planometric order. Arthur Drexler's exhibition of Beaux-Arts drawings from the nineteenth century at the Museum of Modern Art in 1975–76 provided a radicalizing position from which to view Kahn as a prophet of a new classicism. A generation subsequently claimed Kahn as a legitimizing influence in a largely stylistic battle between the "old new" of prismatic, abstract modernism and the "new old" of more exuberant, classically inspired postmodernism.

This interpretation of Kahn's work, encouraged by Vincent Scully's continued comparison of Kahn's buildings to archaic precedents, lasted only as long as the popularity of born-again classicism itself. In more recent years, interpretations of Kahn have tended toward more phenomenological positions on the experiential power of such basic architectural elements as light, mass, and order. Here, another aspect of Kahn's lectures—his metaphysical pronouncements on the transcendental nature of daylight and materials—has provided fuel for a wholesale adoption of Kahn as an architectural shaman. Seeking a reconnection to architecture's primal meanings in an age of surface effect has been seen as a powerful act of cultural resistance, and Kahn's resolutely intense approach has met the desire for a spiritual progenitor quite neatly. John Lobell's *Between Silence and Light* has been the primary source for interpreting Kahn's emphasis—whether intentional or not—on mandalic geometry, ideal proportions, and the immeasurable visual effects of sun and shade.

A more considered interpretation of Kahn's interest in the ontological consequences of building has been inspired by Kenneth Frampton's landmark *Studies in Tectonic Culture*, which posits Kahn as a key figure in the sacralizing of the act of construction. By understanding Kahn's acceptance of the "brute" facts of building as the basis for meaningful architectural expression, Frampton's book has largely rescued Kahn's interpretation from the merely stylistic or metaphysical, seeing such buildings as the Kimbell as "a meeting between the essence of things and the existence of beings."[3]

Kahn and the Expression of Technology

Parallel to these interpretations, however, is another demonstrable influence on a generation of architects interested in the roles played by expressive building technology itself—a very different interpretation than the ineffable, phenomenological, or existential approaches suggested by Lobell and others. Architects such as Norman Foster, Renzo Piano, and

Richard Rogers have sought to deploy technological solutions in buildings in ways that express directly the logic of their assembly and performance. Rather than creating a transcendental experience, these designers have instead found meaning in the architectural explanation of fundamental construction and performance principles, revealing how and why a building was made and thus finding a method of relating designer, maker, and observer in a rich conversation. Kahn's interest in expressing these principles was, to be sure, only a part of his philosophy, but it is palpable in his writing and to a greater extent in the experience of his buildings. More provocatively, there is evidence that Kahn's constructed language relied on the clear explanation of these principles to forge connections between the measurable world of construction and structure and the immeasurable realm of architecture's emotional and spiritual potential. It may be going too far to claim Kahn as a "high-tech" architect, but the principles of this admittedly loose school—the quest for a building's proper order, a balance between rationalist and empiricist methods, a hierarchy of details that communicate how and why a building was made, and a belief that beauty can arise from a proper understanding of prosaic materials and assemblies—link this latter generation directly to Kahn's process.

Such a claim is evidenced by the connections between Kahn and technically inclined designers such as Richard Rogers, Norman Foster, and Renzo Piano. Of the group, Piano had the most direct contact with Kahn's office, spending several months there in 1966–67 working on the Olivetti factory's roof system. While brief, Piano's tenure in Philadelphia was important; he had sought out Kahn and gained the equivalent of an internship there through connections with the Olivetti company. Piano had a practice

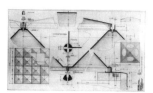

Olivetti-Underwood Factory, Harrisburg, Pennsylvania. Louis I. Kahn with August Komendant, 1966–70. Drawing of early roof system by Renzo Piano

in Genoa at the time, so such a pilgrimage reflects a determined effort to work under Kahn. Piano would go on to interpret Olivetti's structural field in lighter-weight materials, notably in his design for the Italian Industry Pavilion at the 1970 Osaka Expo, where reinforced polyester panels took the place of the concrete parasols.[4] More directly related to Kahn's oeuvre was Piano's building for the Menil Collection in Houston, designed between 1981 and 1986. The de Menil family had in fact commissioned Kahn in 1973 to design a museum that would display their collection to the public using natural light, an obvious reference to the success of the recently opened Kimbell Museum. Prior to his death, Kahn drew up a scheme that involved a toplit, linear module with an extruded, triangular roof that could be deployed in two directions. This project was abandoned in 1974; however, Dominique de Menil continued to work out a program for the museum, and the commission was finally awarded to Piano in 1981. Piano's scheme evolved quickly, from a version of Kahn's centralized gallery sections to one that acknowledged the site's directionality and the desire to bring in only indirect, generally northern daylight. The result was a roof made of parallel *ferro-cemento* light scoops created by bending wire mesh over a mold and then coating it with a light layer of cement. Deployed, as at the Kimbell, over a formal plan with internal asymmetries, this rooflight system provided a subtle order to the Menil space, eschewing the hierarchy of Kahn's curved roof shells and instead offering a grain more akin to the Yale ceiling.

Foster and Rogers's links to Kahn were more amorphous than Piano's, but nevertheless important. Both traveled from their native Britain to New Haven in 1961–62 to earn their master's degrees from Yale. The School of Architecture was by then firmly under the control of Paul Rudolph. Kahn had long since

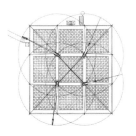

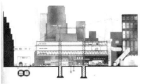

Standardized Hospital Module. Renzo Piano and Richard Rogers, 1970. Plan (top) and section (bottom)

233

departed for the University of Pennsylvania; however, the drafting studios were still on the Art Gallery's top floor, and Kahn's presence was still deeply felt in the "instructive challenge to young architects" of that building's ceiling. Vincent Scully's lectures in architectural history brought up Kahn's work on a regular basis, and Kahn's practice was newly ascendant with the completion of the Richards complex. Foster and Rogers worked together on projects while in New Haven, and their thesis project for a new Yale Science Campus clearly shows an affinity for Kahn's definition of service elements as key parts of an overall architectural expression.[5] This scheme borrowed directly Kahn's early treatment of the Richards's exhaust towers, using them to demarcate clusters of laboratories along a generally linear scheme. Foster's work during his time at Yale was perhaps the more deeply Kahnian of the two.[6] A notable project in 1961 for a city office tower proposed cantilevered studios of open plan office space, which stepped out between vertical piers as the building rose. This showed a remarkable affinity to Kahn's earlier scheme for the Richards's duct towers. While Mies van der Rohe, Paul Rudolph, and even Frank Lloyd Wright were all palpable influences on Foster and Rogers, the two visited Kahn's office on their summer journey west to California, seeing the just-completed Richards building. Kahn's influence was made manifest by their subsequent work.

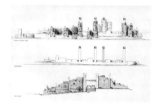

Science Campus for Yale University. Thesis project by Norman Foster and Richard Rogers, 1961

234

Foster and Rogers formed Team 4 with Su Rogers and Wendy Cheesman on returning from New Haven, and the work of this group from 1963–67 suggests lessons learned from the Art Gallery and Richards. Daylight played an important role in all of their schemes for housing. The Murray Mews houses in London displayed a clear hierarchy between servant and served spaces, along with a stainless-steel window assembly that recalled Kahn's detailing. Team 4's masterwork, the Reliance Controls Factory in Swindon completed in 1967 is usually interpreted as Miesian, yet the steel detailing of its expressed structure is remarkably unpretentious. Whereas Mies had worked over and folded steel shapes for visual effects such as reentrant corners, at Reliance steel fixtures and W-shapes were used "as found" (in Banham's words), as the Smithsons had at Hunstanton and as Kahn had at Yale and Richards. Reliance Controls garnered an aesthetic from the deployment of basic materials in an expressive and coherent manner, with layers of steel-work indicating both the performance of the structure and the process of its assembly.

Rogers would go on to explore a highly expressive version of Kahn's dialogues between servant and served, most notably in the Centre Georges Pompidou, designed with Renzo Piano and Ove Arup from 1971 to 1977, and in the Richards-like Lloyd's of London building, designed from 1978 to 1986. Pompidou's circulatory and mechanical functions are arranged in two distinct ranks on the long sides of a rectangular gallery block, with a structural cross grain woven into the exhibition spaces and the two service strips. Lloyd's is a more direct interpretation of Richards, with a prismatic office block surrounded by service towers that appear to have been clipped on. Lloyd's exposed ducts are themselves a significant departure from Kahn's quest for a visual ordering of these unruly elements, and the complex's appearance from the outside contradicts the rigorous mechanical logic of the Lloyd's block. However, the building's structural fabric is, again, a clear continuation of Kahn's principles and elements, a dialogue between precast framing and in situ floors, an allusion to the pairing of systems at Richards. The floors themselves are essentially an updated version of the Yale Art Gallery's system, here on a rectilinear grid and with a three-dimensional

Reliance Controls, Swindon, England. Team 4, 1967. Isometric of a typical structural bay

Reliance Controls. Detail of structural connection

Centre Georges Pompidou, Paris. Renzo Piano and Richard Rogers, 1971–77

Vierendeel system that efficiently carries floor loading while permitting space for integrated lights, ductwork, and electrical cabling. Rogers's use of shadowgaps at all scales reveals the building's assembled
nature and creates the distinctions between materials
and components that Kahn sought to achieve throughout his later work.

Foster's continuation of Kahn's principles has been
more nuanced but equally pertinent, focusing on
clear hierarchies of structure, cladding, and services
as well as a desire to modulate otherwise free-plan
space in architecturally distinct ways. Early work
such as Foster Associates's design for the IBM Pilot
Head Office in Cosham, England (1970–71), carried through the themes of structural and mechanical integration learned in part from the Art Gallery.
These weavings were now clad in a developing system of glass skins that borrowed its corner detailing
from Richards but nonetheless moved in a new direction, toward a daring, precise expression of the glass
pane as glass itself, with its framing pulled into the
building. At the Sainsbury Center for Visual Arts in
Norwich, England (1974–78), Foster's parallel interests in structure, services, and cladding were combined
in a direct manifestation of Kahn's servant/served dialogue, with an open truss structure wrapped around a
central volume of display space. The open trusswork
contains mechanical systems and lighting in its horizontal plane, while the walls hold both risers and
ancillary facilities such as toilet rooms. Shadowgaps
throughout show how the building was put together,
in particular the exterior skin, where prefabricated
aluminum panels were zipped into place with neoprene gaskets. The Hong Kong and Shanghai Bank,
designed between 1978 and 1986, has been Foster's
clearest expression of a pure servant/served dialogue
in plan, providing a clear distinction between office

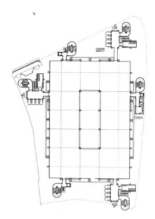

Lloyd's of London.
From top: plan, exterior
view, and view of the
atrium. Richard Rogers
Partnership, 1978–86

floors and the circulatory and mechanical spaces that provide for them. The Bank also weaves these spaces within a structural cage that provides the overall project's elevational grain, expressed in a set of Vierendeel ladder-truss columns. It is tempting to note that the Bank's construction, whether knowingly or not, was a neat restatement of the Kansas City tower's proposed process, in that the Bank's floors were suspended from bridging elements between the main columns, growing downward as the structure grew up.

Sainsbury Center for Visual Arts, University of East Anglia, England. Foster Associates, 1974–78

Later work by Piano, Rogers, and Foster has elaborated on formal and expressive principles fundamental to Kahn's philosophy. Rogers has taken the expression of servant spaces and elements to extraordinary lengths, notably in his headquarters building for Channel 4, London, finished in 1994. This structure takes Kahn's interest in distinguishing components and systems through all levels of planning, from the site scheme itself down to the overly articulate details of curtain walls and handrails.

Channel 4 headquarters, London. Richard Rogers Partnership, 1994

Foster's clearest debts to Kahn have been twofold. On the one hand, dialogues between heavy and light construction in such projects as the Canary Wharf Underground Station (1999) have continued Kahn's quest for a constructed order based on assembly, with the demonstration of the sequence of construction as a primary element in the building's aesthetic. On the other hand, Kahn's emphasis on clarity of form resulting from an empirical building up of programmatic, environmental, and structural issues has been strikingly illustrated by buildings such as Stansted Airport in Essex (1991) and the Swiss Re headquarters in London (2004). Stansted is ultimately an heir to Olivetti, where a single repeatable module combines structure, cladding, and mechanical services legibly deployed throughout a grid. Swiss Re

237

Canary Wharf Underground Station, London. Foster and Partners, 1999

represents a unique form based on the simultaneous considerations of floor-plate arrangement and structural performance, and its diamond-shaped pattern can be seen, though again perhaps not intentionally, as an updated version of Kahn's wind-braced Kansas City tower. Piano, meanwhile, has notably continued a dialogue with Kahn's lighting principles first seen in the Menil building. This has occurred most recently in his design for the Nasher Sculpture Center in nearby Dallas (2003), where the Kimbell's perforated aluminum skylight has been stretched and flattened into a ceiling whose cells are angled to bring in only diffuse, northern light. The Nasher can be read as a direct tribute to the Kimbell on other levels, notably in its employment of expressed curved ceiling modules and its use of travertine throughout. Other projects by Piano, especially the Jean-Marie Tjibaou Cultural Center in New Caledonia (1999), have sought a Kahnian balance between structure and passive environmental performance.

Swiss Re Tower, London. Foster and Partners, 2004

All of these projects suggest a continuation of Kahn's basic principles: that buildings should honestly reflect both their aspirations and the struggles to realize them, that design concepts should be built up from constructive and performative requirements, and that a design's order should be assessed against its objective performance and its ability to speak through its form and materials. The work of Foster, Rogers, and Piano can be read as adopting these Kahnian principles while replacing his preference for the heavy and the antique with a preference for the lightweight and the prospective. This technically progressive attitude has proven itself to be at times remarkably in touch with Kahn's humanist leanings.

238

The Menil Collection, Houston, Texas. Renzo Piano Building Workshop, 1986. View of interior

Five Points: Kahn's Architectural Philosophy and the Role of Building Technology

It may, therefore, be productive to parse Kahn's philosophy regarding the technical aspects of building, with the goal of subtly recasting his work and at the same time proposing a theoretical underpinning of latter developments in the expressive use of building technology based on Kahn's practices. The formal similarities between Kahn's work and that of his technically inclined heirs are paralleled by a consistent, thorough philosophy regarding the resolution and expression of buildings' formative and performative aspects. These can be laid out as five major themes. First, architecture as a discipline relies in part on distilling a global sense of Order out of an understanding of the contingencies and orders of individual sites, programs, and systems. Kahn's extensive discourse on Order, Design, and Form provides this scaffold, noted in chapter one. Second, these orders arise primarily from two realms, construction and function. Third, competing, reinforcing, and contradictory orders can be best organized and related to each other by means of a constructed language that distinguishes, balances, and interweaves. Fourth, through this process of ordering, designing, and expressing we can in fact arrive at an experience that transcends the often-mundane circumstances of its origins. Fifth and finally, this constructed language only makes sense as far as it is expressed to us visually, formally, and spatially. While this fivefold structure does not fully account for Kahn's entire philosophy, it does provide a consistent explanation of Kahn's written and spoken thought that parallels the foregoing histories of the buildings under study and goes part of the way toward establishing Kahn as a progenitor of the more recent experiments cited earlier.

239

Order, Design, and Form

Kahn's most fertile statements regarding his process and buildings have to do with his notions of Order, Design, and Form. Particularly during his later career, his statements on these ideas were messy and occasionally self-contradictory. Yet there is a fundamental logic to the overall structure of this trilogy that suggests the aspirations inherent in Kahn's work. "Order," noted Kahn in 1953, "is what we discover the aspects of."[7] It is, again, preexisting, inherent in nature, and something to which the mind constantly aspires. It is not, therefore, something that is manifest in the everyday. Rather, it is touched or revealed only by extraordinary effort, a distillation and intensification of the everyday that is approached by operating as closely as we can to the nature of the world around us. How we approach this ideal harmony of ourselves with our world is, Kahn posits, through Design, "a battle with the nature of man, with the nature of nature, with the laws of nature, with the rules of man, and with principles."[8] Design is what architects deal with on a daily basis, the process of reconciling the various circumstantial aspects of a given program and site with one another and with aspirations—both functional and aesthetic. The relation between Design and Order is thus the struggle between the material world's imperfections and the Ideal's aspirations. "Order includes all the designs of construction—mechanical and spiritual—and Design is merely the process of fitting them into conditions and coming up with a certain experience which strengthens and even enriches the order."[9]

Left to mediate between these spheres—the ideal and the material, the abstract and the concrete, perhaps even the mind and the body—Kahn suggests Form as the real-world manifestation of Design's meditations.

240

Defined most succinctly as characterizing "a harmony of spaces good for a certain activity of man" produced by Design in the quest for Order, Form approached for Kahn another expression of type. As humans build continually for one program or another, various themes emerge that define a type, whether for an office tower, a railway station, a house, a laboratory, or a museum. In each case, fundamental spatial and performative requirements indicate or prescribe a given set of formal particularities. For Kahn, the Form of a museum, for example, emerges out of the universal requirement for lighting with the peculiarities of exhibition, while the Form of a laboratory has more to do with resolving the requirements of air handling. To some extent, every museum and laboratory, no matter from what era, no matter in what location, no matter out of what construction, balance these two fundamental charges. To make his point clear, Kahn defined Form using an everyday type: "In form you might say the spoon has to have a container and an arm. You bring it into existence by designing it as deep or shallow, or long or short, or made of gold, silver or wood."[10]

"Spoon" is the more abstract, typological entity that each individual instance aspires toward, whereas "a spoon" is a particular object, "something prescribed by circumstances."[11] While architects deal in this latter, everyday realm, for Kahn it was architecture's fundamental goal to realize as nearly as possible the ideal Form rather than simply being content with the efficient arrangement of the circumstantial. This process of transcending the vagaries of a given situation implies an ordering of the material world on however small a scale through the application of intelligence through Design, and is thus a metaphysical step up toward the ideal of Order. Design, it turns out, is thus a fairly exalted activity as it links the body's material world with the mind's ideal realm.

The aspiration toward Form in a given project is really part of a broader aspiration toward Order, and the more carefully thought out and wholly conceived a given design is, the better it expresses Order's elusive quality.

This aspiration toward Order, an ultimate logic, drives our design work, but Form and Order are also only understood through their manifestations in nature and in human work. They are, in fact, otherwise unknowable. We cannot understand them without illustration, and thus the process, the "scaffold," operates in two directions. The closer our material interventions in the world approach Order, the greater our understanding, and thus the more likely that our future work will spiral ever closer. This is a progressive, evolutionary process, yet Kahn had no illusions about an ultimate end. He recognized that we are, mostly for the good, forever caught between the two worlds of the Ideal and the Real. The architectural act for Kahn was necessarily one of constant negotiation between these worlds, rather than a quest for perfection.

How this negotiation played out during the design process involved a search on Kahn's part for the proper hierarchy with which to arrange a building's various systems, materials, spaces, and components. This hierarchy had partly to do with the order of construction—what constituted a permanent frame, for example, versus a less robust infill—and partly to do with the ranking of functional importance accorded to each individual part. Form was thus an expression of a building's program and assembly, arrayed so that the "struggle" to realize the building's truths or aspirations through construction could be read and so that this constructed order could be aligned with ordering both internal and external forces to the specific circumstances of each project.

Construction and Performance

The apparent constant conflict between a building's ideal form and its material realization stemmed not only from the contingencies of external factors such as site, program, and budget. Kahn also recognized the inherent dichotomy in design between function and construction. Invariably, architects are faced with a gap between solutions that represent the best functional or aesthetic result and those that represent the most expedient or efficient way to build. To a great extent, this conflict is what makes up an architect's daily routine, and Kahn, as has been shown, was no exception. No matter how lofty his reputation, Kahn was inevitably tied to the realities of performance and assembly; his aspirations and those of his clients were set within the absolute and often opposing realities of the resources available.

This dichotomy has been recognized since at least the time of Aristotle, whose treatise on causation included an architectural parable intended to illustrate the distinction between two types of "cause." "The house is there," he wrote, "that people may live in it, but it is also there because the builders have placed one brick on top of another."[12] These two realms, which Aristotle termed final and motive causation—or what might more glibly be called the why and how of construction—were precisely the arenas in which Kahn felt the struggle to approach Form and Order through Design were to be played out. "How it was done, how it works should filter through the entire process of building," Kahn wrote, a neat description of this fundamental duality. "How something is done" relates to construction, while "how it works" describes performance and function.[13] The ultimate story of any building, Kahn believed, was told in the realms of final and motive causation, performance, and construction.

Kahn often said that it was more important to know "what to do than how to do it," suggesting that he prioritized a building's function over its assembly, Guadet over Viollet-le-Duc. But in fact his buildings are a careful balancing of the two. His interest in performance went beyond a mere functional disposition of spaces. Kahn notoriously derided program statements and the mathematical approaches of program analysis popular during his late career, "reprogramming" his clients' missives in light of their higher aspirations and suggesting that this realm of final causation could also involve the performance of individual components or assemblies. Kahn's associates recall him suggesting that they discover the "program" for a door handle, for instance, alongside his search for the program of the Ideal (in the Platonic sense) Museum instead of simply the contingent space plans for the museum under consideration. Thus, for Kahn, "what to do" included structural form, mechanical systems, and lighting in addition to the spatial layout of a plan or section. Discovering the order inherent in the performance of a building took on a primary role in Kahn's design process, aligning structural, mechanical, and functional concerns into holistically conceived schemes. At Richards, this occurred almost instantaneously, as the 45'-0" studio space proved to be a form that provided a functional layout and disposition for the laboratory planning based on a synthesis of plumbing, structure, and mechanical systems. By contrast, the Kimbell and Salk evolved quite slowly, as their proper functional orders proved more complex and less prone to such a simple solution. The Kimbell's vaults, for

244

example, were complex in their conception, and their ultimate logic is only apparent when the full range of their performance aspects—structural, daylighting, environmental, and planning—are considered. The Salk, on the other hand, took on the same basic task as Richards—that "the air to breathe should be away from the air to throw away"—but it did so within a bolder statement of the complex's ultimate "performance," based on the aspiration that contemplative space be woven into the fabric of daily routines, and thus into the fabric of the building itself.

Kahn's ultimate statements regarding the role of performance in architectural conception are his elaborations on his buildings and his comments on the servant/served hierarchy. This aphoristic description was too neat to describe the richness that Kahn managed to tease out of its basic premise—that buildings have a finely grained hierarchy of performance and that their spatial disposition should reflect and support this. Kahn's dismissal of bubble diagrams and other tools of program analysis stemmed from his belief that these did not address the more fundamental issues of architectural performance: how do we make spaces good for the activity required, and what do those spaces need to support that activity? In nearly all cases, this involved integrating environmental performance as well as storage, circulation, and plumbing into the very fabric of building. This was a key break with the elemental tenets of first-generation modernism, which had assumed the structural grid as the ultimate generator of architectural space. Such a singular approach to building technology led to an imperfect expression of a true architectural order, as a full accounting of a building's performance would not have permitted the squirreling away of ducts, pipes, and toilet rooms in search of structural purity that was, for example, Mies's modus operandi. Kahn's struggle at the Yale Gallery, his breaking away from the pure structural grid to demand proper space and articulation for the core elements, was a revelatory moment in this development of a more inclusive, integrated approach. Structural elements in Kahn's work after 1951 were almost universally hybrids, designed to fulfill both the performative requirements of bearing and transferring loads and the harboring of subsidiary systems, in particular the often-ignored demands of machinery, plumbing, and ductwork.

If Kahn's designs were typically built up from a concern for understanding the ultimate forms appropriate to a building's *performance*, they were realized through a parallel concern for expressing the building's *construction*. While this was balanced by his understanding of performance, it nevertheless became a tenet of great importance. In his detailing and interest in the jobsite's activities, there was a keen recognition that the recording of a building's physical manifestation was key to interpreting and presenting the "struggle of its realization" on site as well as at the drawing table. Two of Kahn's best-known statements reflect the importance he ascribed to expressing the marks and textures of construction. Writing in 1954, he defended his use of board-formed concrete at Yale while setting the stage for the more sophisticated approach to formwork as ornament that would occur at Richards and Salk:

> The feeling that our present-day
> architecture needs embellishment
> stems in part from our tendency to
> fair joints out of existence—in other
> words, to conceal how parts are put
> together. If we were to train ourselves
> to draw as we build, from the bottom

up, stopping our pencils at the joints
of pouring or erecting, ornament
would evolve out of our love for the
perfection of construction and
we would develop new methods
of construction.[14]

This sense of an ornament evolving from the process
of assembly is quoted almost directly from Viollet-le-
Duc, and is an entirely empirical idea of the building's appearance arising from the understanding and
expression of the processes that would form it.[15] While
the "perfection of construction" would prove an elusive goal, it is remarkable how thoroughly Kahn was
able to carry out this notion in his later work. This is
particularly notable at the Salk, where every element
is engaged in the process of self-revelation, from the
formwork patterns on its concrete to the teak panels' base details. Kahn compared his attitude toward
detailing to a carpenter who "never wants to cover
his work," noting that in cabinetry, dovetail joints
are left exposed as an indication of the craftsmanship involved, a piece of naturally occurring ornament that arises out of "how it was done."[16] For Kahn,
this sense of craftsmanship was key to establishing a
visual record of the level of attention and care inherent in a building, whether exposing joints in cabinetry, as at the Kimbell or Salk, or more expansively
insisting on the exposure of raw concrete as it came
out of its forms.

Beyond detailing, Kahn's famous dialogue with the
brick, that most humble of building materials, reveals
both a Shinto-like belief in an animating constructive
spirit and a remarkable parable regarding the desire
to express the Order of construction while constrained
by the realities of building:

> If you talk to a brick and ask what it
> likes, it'll say it likes an arch. And you
> say to it, look, arches are expensive
> and you can always use a concrete
> lintel to take the place of an arch. And
> the brick says, I know it's expensive
> and I'm afraid it probably can't be
> built these days, but if you ask me
> what I *like* it's still an arch.[17]

Again, there is a performance aspect to the brick's desire—that it "likes" to be in pure compression and that an arch enables it to do this without recourse to a new material or compromising the "purity" of its internal logic. But note that, as in most of Kahn's brick buildings, *the brick does not win.* Its proper order is subsumed by the overall construction's logic, and in the larger picture it proves, invariably, more efficient to actually install the concrete lintel. The ultimate message behind this parable is a radically empiricist one: in building up a rigorously tested logical structure, the inherent qualities of even the most basic element of construction must be sought out and the proper position of each element in relation to the larger order must be discovered. This process extended not only to brick, but also to concrete, which "wants to be granite but can't quite manage" without reinforcing, and steel, "an insect in strength."[18] The inherent qualities of the particular could, therefore, best be expressed by their relation to the whole. While such a wider horizon might compromise the smaller scale's "pure" expression, this sensibility allows a dialogue between each element and the proposition of a coherent, overall order. The brick may *want* to be an arch, but it *must* be part of a building, with all the pressures—budget and otherwise—that the larger order exerts on lower orders of construction and material.

248

Distinguishing, Balancing, and Weaving

Once established, the proper ordering of a building was to be laid out using a system of details and techniques that would visually record and express how various elements related to one another. This language adopted three primary modes: distinguishing elements by introducing shadowgaps and likeminded details, balancing the needs of competing systems to find forms that would accommodate them all, and weaving systems and materials together into inseparable wholes. These strategies were deployed to express the struggles of performance and construction within their own spheres of logic and in relation to one another in the final design.

The shadowgap was perhaps Kahn's most famous detail, a "distinction between things" in Anne Tyng's words that clearly demonstrates sequence or independence of function, an idea first explored in the Weiss House of 1947. Most notably, this detail occurred between structural frames and infill panels, for example at the Salk, but it can also be found where other systems or elements come together. In all of Kahn's concrete detailing, for example, shadowgaps reveal the junction between pours, while Yale's brick façade is clearly separated from the exposed columns on its end bays by a significant gap, demonstrating the distinction between the structure and its cladding. In Kahn's buildings, however, the shadowgap also appears on larger scales—between the Kimbell's three wings, for example, where deep recesses in the building's fabric point out the vaults' structural separation and the parallel distinction between gallery wings and the center volume's more administrative functions. The shadowgap in Kahn's work operates by essentially "insulating" one system or material from another, forcing each to come to logical constructed conclusions, which were often detailed as a subframe or a containing angle. This detail typically required extra space to permit the negative statement of the gap itself to read clearly, and it thus added "breathing room" to each component, forcing the design to allow systems and materials to conclude within the confines of their assigned module.

Such distinctions were often set in contrast to elements that fused, or balanced, more than one function or component into more complex, often ambiguous wholes. While critiqued by his engineers for producing "impure" structural elements in particular, Kahn incorporated more than one system or function into the form of an element, typically gaining spatial or economic efficiency while creating rich, provocative forms. Compromising the "integrity" of the Kimbell's roof shells, for example, by shaping them to simultaneously carry mechanical systems, introduce daylight, and define gallery spaces often drove Kahn's structural engineers to fits of despair. However, when seen within the building's complete order, the introduction of these additional functions necessarily modulated the structural element's shape in light of the building's overall order. The Kimbell's shells, for example, may have "liked" one shape or another, but when taking on the added programmatic imperatives of harboring ductwork and lighting, these forms were meaningfully inflected, not just expediently compromised. The result, when seen from any one system's perspective, may be imperfect, but the ambiguities of such a result fade when they are seen from the perspective of the building as a whole. Even in the case of Yale, the visual order lent by the ceilings is so pronounced that, depending on one's inclination, its structural inefficiencies seem to be either forgivable or part of a grand dialogue on the role of structure and service in the definition of space.

Balancing, or shaping members to accommodate more than one function, was most fully expressed in Kahn's notion of harboring structures. In all of the buildings under study, major structural elements—whether the Yale Gallery's floor system, Richards's spanning structure, the Salk's Vierendeels, or the Kimbell's roof shells—were conceived with hybrid functions in mind from very early in their design process. Kahn's belief that mechanical systems must be brought into the ordering of a building meant that other systems had to make space for the ducts and pipes that these programs inevitably required. Fusing bearing and spanning elements into a "container" for these serving functions meant an expansion of the very definition of structure, and enabled Kahn to use the structural grid of each building to more fully encompass the patterns of each building's use; air distribution, plumbing, and circulation were all thus organized on a grid that they themselves had partially conceived.

At its most accomplished, such harboring led beyond a simple balancing or formal compromise in the shaping of major structural members. Where solutions arose that were truly holistic, where the iterative process that Kahn adhered to and that so often upset his collaborators and clients produced truly evolutionary schemes, the results of this integration can be described as a full-scale weaving of systems, functions, and elements. Kahn hinted at this in various lectures, referring to the "fabric of construction" and to integration as "the way of nature." The process of correctly weaving the warp of ductwork, pipes, and circulation through the weft of structural members and systems could, in Kahn's view, lead to a truly "organic" building in which a "closer knowledge of nature" would complement perfectly our "constant search for order."[19] Certainly the mechanical plans of Richards or the Salk show this knitting together

251

of systems, with the structural and mechanical grain of each building being both subtly inflected by and ultimately tied to one another. At Yale this is literally true—the sheet-metal ductwork is embedded in the concrete slab. Invariably, Kahn's buildings reveal a rich hierarchy of patterning and graining, with circulation, structural, mechanical, and lighting systems all possessing their own logic but also pulled together into a single, legible "fabric." This is perhaps most striking at Richards, where the nine-square structural grid is shot through with mechanical ductwork on a basically radial plan and with plumbing on an orbital layout. However, the same claim can be made for the Kimbell, whose plan likewise shows threads of circulation, ductwork, and lighting parallel and perpendicular to the major pattern of structural shells. Most dramatic, perhaps, is the Salk, where the site plan, structural grid, major mechanical trunks, minor mechanical ductwork, ceiling slots, and lights alternate their orientation as they step down in scale, leading to a pervasive cross graining that ultimately ties the scheme together in both performance and experience. These physical weavings are, of course, themselves woven into the broad fabric of Kahn's sense of historical continuity.

252

The perception of these strategies—distinguishing, balancing, and weaving—gives observers an architectural language by which the designed and constructed orders of Kahn's buildings can be understood. Our eyes see the junction between concrete and wood at the Salk, for instance, as a kind of punctuation—one thing stops and another begins. Frame is distinguished from infill, structure from cladding, stone from wood, and we gain insight into where systems begin and end. Balancing is invariably something of a puzzle—why is it, for example, that there is no support under what appear to be vaulted porch roofs in front of the Kimbell? In presenting us with the slightly unsettling view of a vault floating in space, Kahn is preparing us for the spatial and structural balancings inside. This is how it works, the porches tell us. Watch for this long span inside, and note the patches on the ends of each shell, where the steel that holds the concrete's shape is announcing itself. Finally, the patterns of weaving that we can see—for instance, the ceilings of Richards—point out through their incredible complexity the lengths to which the design has gone in order to organize these elements. We may see a tapestry of sheet metal and concrete, but the complexity of these fabrics is carefully framed—the ducts never "get loose" in the space—and they possess an order of their own, not entirely apparent at first glance, but nevertheless explanatory in addition to being visually provocative.

Measurable and Immeasurable

The result of this devotion to teasing out, strengthening, and ultimately expressing the proper order of a given program through a carefully worked out visual language is ultimately the experience of lifting the base materiality of architecture to a higher intellectual realm. Kahn's buildings present the brute facts of their performance and assembly in fabrics so rigorously conceived that our experience of them transcends the ordinary experience of coarse concrete or sheet-metal ducts. It is through our experiential discovery of the order inherent in building and in buildings that Kahn suggests a link to something greater than the sum of the rough materials of which his buildings are composed.

Kahn spoke often of the process of building as beginning with the immeasurable, passing through measurable means as it is designed and built, and

253

then ultimately ending up in the immeasurable, back in the spirit of architecture. All of our work as architects is inspired not only by the objective data of the program at hand, but by greater expectations. The hope is that the end result will transcend normal experience for those who pass through the buildings we have designed. Yet the actual design and construction histories of Kahn's buildings suggest that, in fact, the immeasurable and the measurable were constantly woven into one another as he himself worked. In fact, all of his buildings began, in some fashion, in the realm of the measurable, as he generally started with a very practical attempt to divine the program in terms of uses. At Yale, for example, he spent five months immersed in the all-too-measurable aspects of bay sizes and site constraints. However, at some point in all of his designs—at the very beginning, it appears, in the case of Richards, but only after two years in the case of the Salk and the Kimbell— immeasurable moments led to the sudden crystallization of extraordinary, compelling designs synthesizing layers of competing orders. The subsequent design and construction processes on each of these projects substantiated these *esquisses* in material form, suggesting a parallel arc to his process that began and ended in the measurable—from a program to a physical object on the site—but that passed through the immeasurable—the moment of inspiration that saw, for example, the possibilities inherent in a concrete space frame or a harboring shell.

While Kahn's remarks are often interpreted as an endorsement of the immeasurable as the proper realm for architecture, they actually recognized the measurable as an equally valid territory. Gold, recall, belongs to the sculptor, not to architecture, and while the "spirit of existence" might be the ultimate goal for any individual architectural act, it is

254

the "quantities of brick, method of construction, engineering" that architects must deal with to approach that higher realm.[20] In Kahn's words,

> a building really aspires to be
> something, and it answers very
> much a way of life. But, this
> aspiration has to be constantly
> renewed and reborn and what is
> presented by the art of building or the
> art of painting or sculpture is in light
> of new techniques. The new techniques
> will help you....[They bring] before
> you new measurable means of doing
> that which your aspiration calls for
> and that's how you view technique:
> as a measurable means of expressing
> closer and closer the desire and the
> existence will of aspirations.[21]

Kahn's daily office routine, of course, was wholly, joyfully devoted to the measurable, with associates constantly working out details, exploring materials, and consulting with engineers regarding the brute facts of building necessary to achieve a particular design. In fact, Kahn's associates tended to be technically gifted, and Kahn understood that he needed a staff of materially minded architects and consultants to realize his more esoteric aspirations. Komendant was only the most notable example of a collaborator whose measurable process was almost entirely at odds with Kahn's—and thus indispensable to him. But the entire office spent the majority of their efforts in the material realm, researching construction methods, material fabrication, structural technique, and cost plans. They came to see Kahn's more visionary pronouncements as a speculative supplement to the office's work, not as the raison d'être for the work itself.[22]

255

This realization that we reach toward our highest aspirations with worldly materials properly considered and deployed was for Kahn a knitting together of the "Two Cultures" of C. P. Snow's 1959 Rede Lecture, which bemoaned the growing separation of science and the humanities. Architecture, in Kahn's view, was the natural meeting ground between these two, seen, however, in proper order: "All of science is a servant of art. Science deals with what is; art deals with what is not. But rich in every way, science wants to be expressed and inspired by the feelings of nobility, feelings of integrity, and love."[23]

If science is the servant of art—the measurable the servant of the immeasurable—then it is no great leap to see Kahn's dialogue of servant and served as the constructed ordering of these aspirations. Kahn's servant spaces are inevitably informed by science— ductwork, circulation, and structure occur within this realm. The served spaces are, in contrast, devoted to a higher aesthetic aspiration. Servant spaces, however, are throughout Kahn's work "expressed and inspired by the feelings of nobility, feelings of integrity, and love," given their own proper space in an architectural hierarchy discovered through empirical process but directed toward artistic realization. Architecture was, for Kahn, the *interweaving of science with art*, that which accommodates our bodies with that which lifts our minds. This was expressed through further layers of dialogue: what carries with what contains, what we move along with what we move across, what is woven with what is distinguished. And ultimately, perhaps, this weaving of science with art was Kahn's most overriding theme, pervading all other dialogues and suggesting why Kahn's buildings remain such provocative statements about architecture, experience, and technique even five decades after their

256

realization. It is also, one suspects, no coincidence that the greatest of these dialogues occurs in buildings devoted to the practice of science on the one hand (Richards and the Salk) and to the pursuit of art on the other (Yale and Kimbell). In the first pair, Kahn struggled to dignify the measurable work of laboratories with the aspirations of expression to create laboratories in which Picasso might feel welcome. In the latter, Kahn sought to determine the ultimate technical requirements of spaces suited to the display of art and to weave those requirements into a fabric of evocative spaces.

Expression and the Aesthetic Experience

If Kahn's conceptions stemmed from his continuously developing understanding of building science, the way in which these were made manifest focused on pure expression and on connecting with our minds and sensibilities as observers. It was not enough for Kahn to simply find an efficient solution; rather, it was paramount that a solution communicate itself visually or tactilely. Throughout Kahn's work, this connection of a building's assembly, its performance, and our perception of these were, again, woven together, solutions inseparable from expressions, details integrated with ornament. Kahn's approach lay somewhere between Buckminster Fuller, whose complex structures were well beyond the intuitive abilities of most observers, and Mies van der Rohe, whose apparently straightforward expressions of structure and function usually belied or concealed crucial aspects of both. Kahn believed that the ways in which a building's systems, structures, and materials were presented—through some combination of distinguishing, balancing, and weaving—must ulti-

257

mately be aimed at, and tested against, the built work's experience itself.

In his critique of Mies's Seagram Building in New York, often repeated in lectures and discussions, Kahn's passion for a frank but careful balance among systems, structures, and materials was most apparent:

> Take the beautiful tower made of
> bronze that was erected in New York.
> It is a bronze lady, incomparable in
> beauty, but you know she has corsets
> for fifteen stories because the wind
> bracing is not seen. That which makes
> it an object against the wind can be
> beautifully expressed, just like nature
> expresses the difference between the
> moss and the reed. The base of this
> building should be wider than the top,
> and the columns which are on top
> dancing like fairies, and the columns
> below growing like mad, don't have
> the same dimensions because they are
> not the same thing. This story if told
> from realization of form would make
> a tower more expressive of the forces.
> Even if it begins in its first attempts
> in design to be ugly it would be led to
> beauty by the statement of form.[24]

Kahn, writing this in 1961, had not yet had the full pressures of a commercial skyscraper applied to his methodology. When the opportunity arose in Kansas City, the negotiation between a full expression of wind forces and financial expediency was perhaps made more clear to him. But there is in this critique of Seagram a voice that is uniquely Kahn's. First, he recognized the beauty of the Seagram tower, and this was not simply politeness—Kahn understood the aesthetic achievement here. What bothered him was that the tower's beauty was so easily compromised by the inevitable revelation of the "corsets," shear walls hidden behind marble panels in the building's bronze skin that provided stability against wind forces. Once this becomes apparent, the tower's slim proportions seem contrived, out of balance when one considers the extreme measures required to sustain a slender tower against a force as fundamental as wind. A fully organic conception (note Kahn's biological reference) would have treated the building's lateral stability as a fundamental need, one that demanded a place not only in its structure, but in its visual expression as well. We deserve, Kahn seems to be saying, to know the whole story. Furthermore, Kahn suggests that Mies's purely rationalist approach—an abstract conception forced onto the systems and materials required to build it—cannot benefit from the evolutionary, iterative process that Kahn so rigorously employed. The "statement of form," drawn from structural performance, could have instead brought us to beauty *through* logic, immersing us in the world and not in an abstract realm of geometry, from and toward an *understanding* of how structures carry loads and how they resist wind. This could have been expressed in physical, visual terms, not in mere abstractions, much as the search for a clear, legible knitting together of function and technique led the designs for Yale, Richards, the Salk, and Kimbell toward a more complex, richer aesthetic than Mies's finely honed prisms offered.

Expression was, for Kahn, the opportunity to record both the jobsite's activity and that of the drawing studio. "I think that a building should show how it was made," he wrote shortly before his death, "and should give some idea of the struggle involved in building it."[25] The very purpose of his quest for order was to make a clear, legible statement *to us*, eliminating everything that would "blur the statement of how a space is made" and confuse our understanding.[26] This recording of the design and construction processes was not simply to be shouted into the void, nor was its intended audience limited to fellow practitioners. In all of Kahn's work, the intention was to provide a road map to the processes of design and to that of the jobsite, to record the inherently meaningful activities of design and construction. The details and finishes that Kahn insisted upon were designed to communicate these struggles to all, to enable the Kimbell's patron, for example, or the undergraduate at Yale to share the excitement and passion that Kahn himself felt for the universal and contingent truths of each project. What is perhaps most unique about Kahn's work is that however complex the structural, environmental, or constructional solution, its expression was always designed to communicate some fundamental principle of its conception as legibly and comprehensibly as possible. It may be that Richard Brown's "little old lady from Abilene" would not fully appreciate the mathematics of Komendant's posttensioning cables at the Kimbell, for example. But any of the Kimbell's visitors can surely recognize the shells' enormous spans, the constant rhythm of the roofs, and the exquisite quality of the silver light flowing off the raw concrete overhead. Architects and historians may develop allegedly deeper thoughts about the Kimbell's various elements and spaces. But these hardly invalidate the simpler, more direct communication that Kahn was keen to establish with a far larger population.

Architecture, Experience, and Dacca

Indeed, Kahn's buildings are so compelling in part because they have such a strong relationship to the everyday, both in their materials, which were the most basic available, and in the daily life of a building and its inhabitants. It was, Kahn felt, too easy to impress with finer stuff, in particular the marble, brass, and gold that his former colleagues at Yale, Edward Durrell Stone and Philip Johnson, had employed. Kahn's buildings and projects arose from the commonplace—even the more exalted programs, a theater and embassy among them. While they aspired to something transcendent, it is their rich connections to and among unadorned experiences—ours, that of the builders, and of Kahn himself—that gives his designs their enormous communicative power. Anyone, not just architects, can see in the imprints of the Salk's formwork, its folded steel curtain walls, and its carefully set cabinetry the hands of its designers and constructors. That these materials provide so rich an experience is a testament to Kahn's belief in the intensification of the everyday, in his spaces as concentrated precincts in which the inherent emotional and intellectual possibilities in even the simplest programs or materials could be clearly celebrated. These are not simple, declarative statements, but are instead constant provocations, with layers of alliteration, rich integration, and, ultimately, weavings of daily life with the universal. They integrate our experience with that of Kahn, his collaborators, and those who with their hands constructed these buildings. The labors of each are recorded in the fabric of Kahn's buildings not to be memorialized, but to be recalled and reread.

Kahn's life, of course, was devoted to the practice of architecture at its most intense and most searching, and thus the experiences of his struggles are perhaps particularly rich. Yet he also felt strongly that architecture was a human endeavor, and his collaborations and relationships with those around him were vital to his life and work as well. Thirty years after his death, associates and collaborators remain connected to one another through the intensity of their work with Kahn. His ability to gently coax engineers, contractors, fabricators, and clients along with him on his explorations and struggles may well have been his greatest asset. Kahn practiced architecture as an ultimately human endeavor, whose purpose was to bring us into his process and philosophy through our experience of the buildings whose designs he led. He aimed to show the inherent greatness in architecture and the architectural act, its unique potential to connect the basic stuff of life—physical and temporal—with our highest thoughts, beliefs, and aspirations. Walking through his spaces we discern not only the relationships between architectural, functional, and structural truths, but also the grandeur inherent in the struggles to pour concrete, assemble glass and steel curtain walls, and hang ductwork, until distinctions between built prose and architectural poetry dissolve.

This connection with the humanity of design and construction is nowhere more apparent than at Dacca, where the Bangladeshi capitol was constructed almost entirely by hand, bearing all the marks not only of manual labor but also of cyclones, flooding, and civil war. Dacca was certainly Kahn's lengthiest struggle, completed ten years after his death despite having been in the office since 1962. It is, too, one of his least "technical" buildings, in that its materials and systems were, of necessity, extremely simple. The building's foundations are built up from thousands of simple piers, stuck into the wet earth of Dacca's plain until the friction of the mud below provided enough resistance to support the forthcoming weight of the building. Its walls are of pure, poured concrete, with simple grace notes of stone

Sher-e-Bangla Nagar, Dacca.
Capitol of Bangladesh.
Louis I. Kahn, 1962–83,
completed by David
Wisdom Associates

262

communicating the pattern of its pours on the elevations. These walls are punched regularly with geometric shapes, none of which are really structural in any way but which bring diffused light into the parliament's ambulatories and then into the chamber itself. The concrete is as rough as any in Kahn's work and the interiors are spare. Dacca, however, is undeniably Kahn's most powerful creation, an achievement in the basest of materials for one of the most impoverished countries in the world, yet a work of such emotional resonance that it renders any academic argument regarding the true "meaning" or "importance" of his work unnecessary.

Kahn's buildings are saturated in experience, whether of the labors of Dacca or the industrial processes of Richards. A favored companion of poets and taxi drivers alike, he saw his work connecting to the entire spectrum of human activity, and the joy that he brought to his meetings with clients, contractors, and employees remains appreciable in the joy with which these discussions are recalled years later. Such a conception of practice, as an ultimately collaborative endeavor aimed at touching the minds and hearts of the widest population, was fundamental to the extraordinary human experiences that his spaces continue to provide, largely because the intensity of Kahn's experience in conceiving and executing these designs was so faithfully transcribed, so keenly presented to the legions of minds that would come to stand, for instance, in the courtyard of the Salk. Kahn called his buildings "offerings to architecture," but ultimately they are offerings to us, weavings of material and space, structure and service, poetry and prose, building science and building art.

263

Endnotes

1. Sara Esser, while a student at Iowa State University, prepared a history of this project as well as an analytical model explaining the building's structure.

2. Nicholas Gianopulos expressed this view to the author in an interview in June 2004.

3. Kenneth Frampton, *Studies in Tectonic Culture: The Poetics of Construction in Nineteenth- and Twentieth-Century Architecture* (Cambridge: MIT Press, 1995), 246.

4. Peter Buchanan, ed., *Renzo Piano Building Workshop: Complete Works*, vol. 1 (London: Phaidon, 1997), 49.

5. Kenneth Powell, ed., *Richard Rogers: Complete Works*, vol. 1 (London: Phaidon, 1999), 14–15, 20–21.

6. David Jenkins, ed., *Norman Foster: Works 1* (New York: Prestel Verlag, 2002), 28.

7. Louis I. Kahn, "Architecture and the University," in *Louis I. Kahn: Writings, Lectures, Interviews*, ed. Alessandra Latour (New York: Rizzoli, 1991), 54–55.

8. Louis I. Kahn, "The Nature of Nature," in *Writings, Lectures, Interviews*, ed. Latour, 141–42.

9. Kahn, "Architecture and the University," 55.

10. Louis I. Kahn, "On Philosophical Horizons, 1960," in *Writings, Lectures, Interviews*, ed. Latour, 101.

11. Louis I. Kahn, "Not for the Fainthearted, 1971," in *Writings, Lectures, Interviews*, ed. Latour, 261.

12. This parable is quoted in the introduction to D'Arcy Thompson's *On Growth and Form* (Cambridge: Cambridge University Press, 1961), 5. Kahn alternately recommended this literary work on biological morphology and swore he had never read it. However, this quotation near the beginning of the introduction suggests that even a casual browsing might have brought Aristotle's architectural metaphor to Kahn's attention.

13. Louis I. Kahn, "How to Develop New Methods of Construction," in *Writings, Lectures, Interviews*, ed. Latour, 57.

14. Ibid.

15. In one of Kahn's rare discussions of the Yale construction process, he noted the specifically heuristic nature of its formwork: "We accentuated the struggle of building; of building from floor to floor, because that joint is a critical thing in the construction. When you take the forms off, something always happens in a very ugly soupy way. Whereas, if you actually know that, and you place in there something which is very positive, you put this in it (pointing to form joint) so you can really see it, then it sets up its own pattern." Louis I. Kahn, "This Business of Architecture, 1955," in *Writings, Lectures, Interviews*, ed. Latour, 63.

16. Kahn, "How to Develop New Methods," 57.

17. Louis I. Kahn, "An Architect Speaks His Mind, 1972," in *Writings, Lectures, Interviews*, ed. Latour, 296.

18. Louis I. Kahn, "I Love Beginnings, 1972," in *Writings, Lectures, Interviews*, ed. Latour, 288.

19. Louis I. Kahn, "Toward a Plan for Midtown Philadelphia," in *Writings, Lectures, Interviews*, ed. Latour, 45. Compare this description with George Howe's view of the "organic" in chapter 1.

20. Ibid., 117.

21. Louis I. Kahn, "A discussion recorded in Louis I. Kahn's Philadelphia office in February, 1961," in *Writings, Lectures, Interviews*, ed. Latour, 125.

22. This sentiment has been expressed to me in interviews and conversations with Jack MacAllister, Nicholas Gianopulos, and Anne Tyng.

23. Louis I. Kahn, "Address, 1965," in *Writings, Lectures, Interviews*, ed. Latour, 208.

24. Louis I. Kahn, "Form and Design, 1961," in *Writings, Lectures, Interviews*, ed. Latour, 117.

25. Louis I. Kahn, "Harmony between Man and Architecture, 1974," in *Writings, Lectures, Interviews*, ed. Latour, 333.

26. Louis I. Kahn, "Order in Architecture," in *Writings, Lectures, Interviews*, ed. Latour, 79.

SELECTED BIBLIOGRAPHY

In addition to the sources listed below, numerous shorter articles and mentions of buildings discussed in this book can be found in the California Room of the San Diego Public Library (concerning the Salk Institute) and the local history department of the Fort Worth Public Library (concerning the Kimbell). Letters and documents relating to the Yale University Art Gallery exist in the Douglas Orr and A. Whitney Griswold Collections of the Manuscripts and Archives Department of Yale's Stirling Library. By far the most comprehensive collection of books, articles, and ephemera relating to Kahn's work can be found in the Architectural Archives of the University of Pennsylvania in the Louis I. Kahn, August E. Komendant, and Marshall D. Meyers collections, which also hold most of the drawings and sketches consulted. Additional drawings and photographs of the buildings under study are contained in the collections of the Kimbell Art Museum and the Yale University Art Gallery. A full set of Preston M. Geren's construction drawings for the Kimbell is in the Architectural Archives of the University of Texas at Austin.

Angerer, Fred. *Surface Structures in Building: Structure and Form.* London: Alec Tiranti, 1961.

"Art Serves Science: Alfred Newton Richards Medical Research Building, University of Pennsylvania." *Architectural Record*, August 1960, 149–56.

"Avant-garde Anachronist." *Time*, 10 June 1966, 70–71.

Banham, Reyner. *The Architecture of the Well-Tempered Environment.* Chicago: University of Chicago Press, 1969.

——— . *A Critic Writes: Essays by Reyner Banham.* Edited by Mary Banham, Paul Barker, Sutherland Lyall, and Cedric Price. Berkeley: University of California Press, 1996.

——— . "The New Brutalism." *Architectural Review* 118, no. 708 (December 1955): 355–61.

————. "On Trial 2: Louis Kahn and the Buttery-Hatch Aesthetic." *Architectural Review* 131, no. 781 (March 1962): 203–6.

Bellinelli, Luca, ed. *Louis I. Kahn: The Construction of the Kimbell Art Museum.* Milan: Skira, 1997.

Blake, Peter. "Are You Illiterate about Modern Architecture?" *Vogue,* 15 September 1961, 180–81, 214, 218.

Blaser, Werner, ed. *Norman Foster: Sketches.* Boston: Birkhauser Verlag, 1992.

Boyd, Robin. "The New Vision in Architecture." *Harper's Magazine,* July 1961, 72–81.

Brawne, Michael. *Architecture in Detail: Kimbell Art Museum.* London: Phaidon, 1993.

Brown, Jack Perry. *Louis I. Kahn: A Bibliography.* New York: Garland, 1987.

Brownlee, David B., and David G. De Long, eds. *Louis I. Kahn: In the Realm of Architecture.* New York: Rizzoli, 1991.

Buchanan, Peter, ed. *Renzo Piano Building Workshop: Complete Works.* 4 vols. London: Phaidon, 1993–2002.

Buttiker, Urs. *Louis I. Kahn: Light and Space.* New York: Whitney Library of Design, 1994.

"Carver Court, Coatesville, PA." *Architectural Forum,* December 1944, 109–16.

Davies, Colin. *High-Tech Architecture.* New York: Rizzoli, 1988.

"Defense Housing at Middletown, PA." *Architectural Forum,* October 1941, 216–17.

Dini, Massimo. *Architectural Documents: Renzo Piano, Projects and Buildings, 1964–1983.* New York: Electa/Rizzoli, 1984.

Dixon, John Morris, and James T. Burns Jr. "Kahn's Second Phase at Pennsylvania." *Progressive Architecture,* September 1964, 208–13.

Donohoe, V. "Downtown Philadelphia Loses its Only Kahn Building [*sic*]." *Progressive Architecture,* November 1973, 23, 26.

Fitch, James Marston. "A Building of Rugged Fundamentals." *Architectural Forum,* July 1960, 82–87, 185.

"Five Hospitals: A Critique." *Progressive Architecture,* November 1946, 81–88.

Ford, Edward R. *The Details of Modern Architecture.* Vol. 2, *1928–88.* Cambridge: MIT Press, 1996.

"Form Evokes Function." *Time,* 6 June 1960, 76.

"Fort Worth's Kimbell: Art Housing Art." *Progressive Architecture*, November 1972, 25, 29.

"Fortresses for Science." *Life*, 16 April 1971, 74–79.

Frampton, Kenneth. "Louis I. Kahn and the French Connection." *Oppositions*, Fall 1980, 21–53.

————. *Modern Architecture: A Critical History*. London: Thames & Hudson, 1980.

————. *Studies in Tectonic Culture: The Poetics of Construction in Nineteenth- and Twentieth-Century Architecture*. Cambridge: MIT Press, 1995.

Friedman, D. S. Introduction to *The Salk Institute*, by Ezra Stoller. Building Blocks. New York: Princeton Architectural Press, 1999.

Gast, Klaus-Peter. *Louis I. Kahn: das Gesamtwerk/Complete Works*. Stuttgart: Deutsche Verlags-Anstalt, 2001.

Giurgola, Romaldo, and Jaimini Mehta. *Louis I. Kahn Architect*. Zurich: Verlag für Architektur, 1975.

Goldhagen, Sarah Williams. *Louis Kahn's Situated Modernism*. New Haven: Yale University Press, 2001.

Green, Wilder. "Louis I. Kahn, Architect: Alfred Newton Richards Medical Research Building, University of Pennsylvania." Museum of Modern Art Bulletin, 1961.

"Home in a Barrel Vault." *Time*, 23 February 1968, 67.

"How'm I Doing, Corbusier?" *Pennsylvania Gazette*, December 1972, 18–26.

Howe, George, Oscar Stonorov, and Louis I. Kahn. "Standards Versus Essential Space: Comments on Unit Plans for War Housing." *Architectural Forum* 76, no. 5 (May 1942): 307–11.

Huff, William. "Kahn and Yale." *Journal of Architectural Education* 35, no. 3 (Spring 1982): 22–31.

Hughes, Robert. "Building with Spent Light." *Time*, 15 January 1973, 60–65.

Jenkins, David, ed. *Norman Foster: Works 1*. New York: Prestel Verlag, 2002.

Joedicke, Jurgen. *Shell Architecture*. New York: Reinhold, 1963.

Johnson, Nell E. *Light Is the Theme: Louis I. Kahn and the Kimbell Art Museum*. Fort Worth: Kimbell Art Foundation, 1975.

Jordy, William. "Criticism: Medical Research Building for Pennsylvania University [*sic*], Philadelphia." *Architectural Review*, February 1961, 98–106.

————. *The Impact of Modernism in the Mid-Twentieth Century*. Vol. 5 of *American Buildings and Their Architects*. New York: Oxford University Press, 1976.

————. "The Span of Kahn." *Architectural Review* 155, no. 928 (June 1974): 318–42.

Kahn, Louis I. "1973: Brooklyn, New York." *Perspecta: The Yale Architectural Journal* 19 (1982): 89–100.

————. "Form and Design." *Architectural Design*, April 1961, 145–54.

————. "Monumentality." In *New Architecture and City Planning: A Symposium*, edited by Paul Zucker. New York: Philosophical Library, 1944.

————. "Not for the Faint-Hearted." *American Institute of Architects Journal*, September 1971, 25–31.

————. "On Philosophical Horizons." *American Institute of Architects Journal*, June 1960, 49.

————. "On the Responsibility of the Architect." *Perspecta: The Yale Architectural Journal* 2 (1953): 10–27.

————. "Order in Architecture." *Perspecta: The Yale Architectural Journal* 4 (1957): 58–65.

————. "The Philosophical Creative Approach." *PCI Journal*, September 1961, 75–79.

————. "Spaces, Order and Architecture." *Royal Architectural Institute of Canada Journal*, October 1957, 375–77.

————. "A Statement." *Arts and Architecture*, February 1961, 14–15, 28–30.

"Kahn-Noguchi Playground Proposed for New York." *Progressive Architecture*, March 1964, 67.

"Kahn's Kimbell: A Building in Praise of Nature and Light." *Interiors*, March 1973, 68–79.

"Kahn's Museum: An Interview with Richard F. Brown." *Art in America* 60, no. 5 (September–October 1972): 44–48.

"Kimbell Art Museum." *Architectural Record*, November 1972, 43.

Komendant, August. *Contemporary Concrete Structures.* New York: McGraw-Hill, 1972.

————. "Komendant on Concrete." *Progressive Architecture*, October 1966, 208–14.

————. *My 18 Years with Architect Louis I. Kahn.* Englewood, N.J.: Aloray Press, 1975.

————. *Prestressed Concrete Structures.* New York: McGraw-Hill, 1952.

"Laboratory for Life Science Designed to Defy Time." *Engineering News-Record*, 27 January 1966, 78–80, 83–84.

"Labs Slab." *Architectural Review*, March 1968, 173–74.

Latour, Alessandra, ed. *Louis I. Kahn: l'uomo, il maestro*. Rome: Edizioni Kappa, 1986.

————. *Louis I. Kahn: Writings, Lectures, Interviews*. New York: Rizzoli, 1991.

Leidigh, Thomas J. "From Architect's Conception to Concrete Reality." *PCI Journal*, September 1961, 80–85.

Lobell, John. *Between Silence and Light: Spirit in the Architecture of Louis I. Kahn*. Boulder, Colo.: Shambala, 1979.

"Logic and Art in Precast Concrete: Medical Research Laboratory, University of Pennsylvania." *Architectural Record*, September 1959, 232–38.

Loud, Patricia Cummings. *The Art Museums of Louis I. Kahn*. Durham, N.C.: Duke University Press, 1989.

————. *In Pursuit of Quality: The Kimbell Art Museum*. Fort Worth: Kimbell Art Museum, 1987.

Louis I. Kahn Archive. Personal Drawings: The Completely Illustrated Catalogue of the Drawings in the Louis I. Kahn Collection, Buildings and Projects. New York: Garland Architectural Archives, 1988.

"Louis I. Kahn." Special issue, *Architecture + Urbanism*, 1975, 327.

"Louis I. Kahn." Special issue, *Architecture + Urbanism*, 1983, 240.

"Louis I. Kahn: 1901/1974." *Rassegna* 7, no. 21/1 (March 1985): 4–88.

Louis I. Kahn Collection. The University of Pennsylvania and Pennsylvania Historical and Museum Commission, Philadelphia.

"Louis I. Kahn: Silence and Light." *Architecture + Urbanism*, January 1973, 5–222.

Margolius, Ivan. *Architects + Engineers = Structures*. New York: John Wiley & Sons, 2002.

McCoy, Esther. "Dr. Salk Talks about His Institute." *Architectural Forum*, December 1967, 27–35.

McQuade, Walter. "Architect Louis Kahn and His Strong-Boned Structures." *Architectural Forum*, October 1957, 134–43.

————. "Wind Bracing Comes Out from Behind the Curtain." *Fortune*, May 1965, 145.

Meyers, Marshall. "Masters of Light: Louis Kahn." *American Institute of Architects Journal*, September 1979, 60–62.

"The Mind of Louis Kahn." *Architectural Forum*, July–August 1972, 42–89.

"Modern Space Framed with Traditional Artistry." *Architectural Forum*, September 1950, 100–105.

"The Museum Explosion." *Newsweek*, 17 September 1973, 88–89.

"New Buildings for 194X." *Architectural Forum* 78, no. 5 (May 1943): 69.

Newman, Oscar. *New Frontiers in Architecture: CIAM in Otterlo, 1959*. New York: Universe, 1961.

"The New Treasure Houses of Texas." *Fortune*, May 1974, 207–13.

"P/A Views." *Progressive Architecture*, May 1954, 15–16, 22, 24.

Peter, John. "Architect Kahn and Scientist Salk Create a Landmark for Medical Research." *Look*, 10 January 1967, 52–53.

Piano, Renzo. "Structure, Production, Environment." *Zodiac*, 1974, 126–47.

Pinnell, Patrick. *Yale University*. Campus Guides. New York: Princeton Architectural Press, 1999.

Plagens, Peter. "Louis Kahn's New Museum in Fort Worth." *Artforum*, February 1968, 18–23.

Powell, Kenneth. *Richard Rogers: Complete Works*. Vol. 1, *1961–88*. London: Phaidon, 1999.

"Procession of Massive Forms." *Architectural Forum*, May 1965, 36–45.

"Progress Report: Weiss House." *Progressive Architecture*, August 1950, 13–18.

Pushkarev, Boris. "Yale University Art Gallery and Design Center." *Perspecta: The Yale Architectural Journal* 3 (1955): 355–61.

[Read, Vernon]. "Building Engineering: Tetrahedral Floor System." *Architectural Forum* 97, no. 3 (November 1952): 148–49.

Ronner, Heinz, Sharad Jhaveri, and Alessandro Vasella. *Louis I. Kahn: Complete Works, 1935–1974*. Boulder, Colo.: Westview Press, 1977.

Rose, Barbara. "New Texas Boom." *Vogue*, 15 October 1972, 118–21, 130.

Rowe, Colin. "Neoclassicism and Modern Architecture." *Oppositions*, September 1973, 2–27.

Salvadori, Mario, and Robert Heller. *Structure in Architecture: The Building of Buildings*. 1963. Reprint, Englewood Cliffs, N.J.: Prentice-Hall, 1975.

Sanderson, George. "Extension: University Art Gallery and Design Center." *Progressive Architecture*, May 1954, 88–101, 130–31.

Scully, Vincent. *American Architecture and Urbanism*. 1969. Revised edition, New York: Henry Holt, 1988.

———. "Archetype and Order in Recent American Architecture." *Art in America* 42, no. 4 (December 1954): 250–61.

————. "Architecture and Man at Yale." *Saturday Review*, 23 May 1964, 26–29.

————. "Light, Form and Power: New Work of Louis Kahn." *Architectural Forum*, August–September 1964, 162–70.

————. *Louis I. Kahn*. Makers of Contemporary Architecture. New York: George Braziller, 1962.

————. "The Precisionist Strain in American Architecture." *Art in America* 48, no. 3 (1960): 46–53.

————. "Recent Works by Louis Kahn." *Zodiac*, 1967, 58–117.

Sheppard, Richard. "After a Six-Year Honeymoon, the Kimbell Art Museum." *ARTnews*, October 1972, 22–31.

————. "U.S. Wartime Housing." *Architectural Review*, August 1944, 29–58.

Simon, Maron J., ed. *Your Solar House*. New York: Simon and Schuster, 1947.

Smith, C. Ray. "The Great Museum Debate." *Progressive Architecture*, December 1969, 76–85.

Smythe, J. B. "Concrete Results." *PCI Journal*, September 1961, 86–91.

Solomon, Susan G. "Beginnings." *Progressive Architecture*, December 1984, 68–73.

"Spatial Triangulation: City Hall, Philadelphia, PA." *Progressive Architecture*, June 1954, 102–103.

Steele, James. *Architecture in Detail: Salk Institute, Louis I. Kahn*. London: Phaidon, 1993.

Stern, Robert A. M. *George Howe: Toward a Modern American Architecture*. New Haven: Yale University Press, 1975.

————. "The Impact of Yale." In *Norman Foster: Works 1*, edited by David Jenkins. New York: Prestel Verlag, 2002.

————. *New Directions in American Architecture*. Revised edition, New York: George Braziller, 1969.

————. "Yale 1950–1965." *Oppositions*, October 1974, 35–62.

Temko, Allan. "Evaluation: Louis Kahn's Salk Institute after a Dozen Years." *American Institute of Architects Journal*, March 1977, 42–49.

"Ten Buildings that Point to the Future." *Fortune*, December 1965, 174–79.

Thomas, George E., et al. *University of Pennsylvania*. Campus Guides. New York: Princeton Architectural Press, 2002.

Thompson, D'Arcy. *On Growth and Form*. Cambridge: Cambridge University Press, 1961. Revised edition, Mineola, N.Y.: Dover, 1992.

"Three Shoe Stores." *Architectural Forum*, December 1949, 92–97.

Torroja, Eduardo. *The Structures of Eduardo Torroja: An Autobiography of Engineering Accomplishment.* New York: F. W. Dodge, 1958.

Twombly, Robert. *Louis Kahn: Essential Texts.* New York: W. W. Norton & Company, 2003.

Tyng, Anne Griswold. "Kahntext." *Architectural Forum*, January–February 1973, 9.

Tyng, Anne Griswold, ed. *Louis Kahn to Anne Tyng: The Rome Letters, 1953–54.* New York: Rizzoli, 1997.

Tyng, Alexandra. *Beginnings: Louis I. Kahn's Philosophy of Architecture.* New York: John Wiley & Sons, 1984.

Venturi, Robert. *Complexity and Contradiction in Architecture.* 1966. Reprint, New York: The Museum of Modern Art, 1977.

Wittkower, Rudolf. *Architectural Principles in the Age of Humanism.* New York: W. W. Norton & Company, 1971.

Wurman, Richard Saul. *What Will Be Has Always Been: The Words of Louis I. Kahn.* New York: AccessPress/Rizzoli, 1986.

ILLUSTRATION CREDITS

Chapter 1
Architectural Archives, University of Pennsylvania, Philadelphia (photographs by
    George Pohl): 2, 41
Architectural Forum (May 1943): 28 (top)
Architectural Record (June 1926): 20
Author: 31
Keith De Lellis Gallery, Ebstel Collection, New York: 39
Louis I. Kahn Collection, University of Pennsylvania and the Pennsylvania Historical
    and Museum Collection, Philadelphia: 26 (both), 28 (bottom), 32, 34, 38

Chapter 2
Author: 63 (after drawings in the Kahn Collection), 74 (left)
Keith De Lellis Gallery, Ebstel Collection, New York: 77, 81
Louis I. Kahn Collection, University of Pennsylvania and the Pennsylvania Historical
    and Museum Collection, Philadelphia: 61, 62, 72 (both), 73, 80, 85
Manuscripts and Archives Department, Yale University Library, New Haven, Conn.: 49,
    50, 74 (right), 75, 76 (photograph by Lionel Freedman)
Yale University Art Gallery, New Haven, Conn.: 54, 55, 56, 58, 59

Chapter 3
Architectural Archives, University of Pennsylvania, Philadelphia (photographs by
    Marshall Meyers): 114 (both), 115
Author: 94, 102, 110 (after drawings in the Kahn Collection)
Keith De Lellis Gallery, Ebstel Collection, New York: 95, 107, 108
Louis I. Kahn Collection, University of Pennsylvania and the Pennsylvania Historical
    and Museum Collection, Philadelphia: 98, 99, 100, 101, 104, 105, 116, 117
    (photograph by Joseph W. Molitor), 118 (photograph by Malcolm Smith), 119
    (photograph by Joseph W. Molitor), 122 (photograph by Robert Lautman)
Kimbell Art Museum, Forth Worth, Texas (photograph by Bob Wharton): 97
Kevin Scott (both after drawings in the Kahn Collection): 112, 113

Chapter 4
Author: 148, 158, 159, 160
Author (after drawings in the Kahn Collection): 139, 146, 147, 151 (both)
Louis I. Kahn Collection, University of Pennsylvania and the Pennsylvania Historical
    and Museum Collection, Philadelphia: 135, 138, 142, 144, 145, 152, 153, 156
    (photograph by Dick Whittington), 157 (photograph by Dick Whittington), 161
    (both), 163, 164
San Diego Historical Society (*San Diego Union*, 25 May 1960): 134

Jeffrey Stafford: 140
Time magazine (© 1954 Time Inc.): 131

Chapter 5
Fred Angerer, *Surface Structures in Building: Structure and Form* (London: Alec
    Tiranti, 1961): 193
Architectural Archives, University of Pennsylvania, Philadelphia: 184, 188
    (Marshall Meyers Collection), 189, 190, 210 (right, Marshall Meyers
    Collection)
Author: 196 (after drawings in the Kahn Collection), 210 (left), 211 (both), 212
    (after drawings in the Architectural Archives of The University of Texas at
    Austin), 214, 217, 218, 220
Chris Beorkrem: 219
Fort-Worth Telegram Photograph Collection, The University of Texas at Arlington
    Libraries: 202
Kimbell Art Museum, Forth Worth, Texas (photographs by Bob Wharton): 179, 181,
    185, 205, 206 (both), 207, 208, 209
M. García Moya (reproduced from Eduardo Torroja, *The Structures of Eduardo
    Torroja: An Autobiography of Engineering Accomplishment* [New York: F. W.
    Dodge, 1958]): 191, 192

Chapter 6
arcaid.co.uk: 235 (bottom, photograph by Joe Cornish), 236 (middle and bottom,
    both photographs by Richard Bryant), 237 (middle, photograph by Richard Bryant)
Architectural Archives of the University of Pennsylvania, Philadelphia: 262
Author: 229 (model by Sara Esser)
Foster and Partners, London: 234, 235 (top and middle), 237 (top, photograph by Ken
    Kirkwood; and bottom), 238 (top)
Louis I. Kahn Collection, University of Pennsylvania and the Pennsylvania Historical
    and Museum Collection, Philadelphia: 228, 232
Renzo Piano Building Workshop, Genoa, Italy: 233 (both), 238 (bottom)
Richard Rogers Partnership, London: 236 (top)

Opposite: Architectural Archives, University of Pennsylvania, Philadelphia
    (photograph by George Pohl)